TATARSTAN: A 'CAN-DO' CULTURE

TATARSTAN: A 'CAN-DO' CULTURE

President Mintimer Shaimiev
and the Power of Common Sense

Ravil Bukharaev

GLOBAL
ORIENTAL

TATARSTAN: A 'CAN-DO' CULTURE
PRESIDENT MINTIMER SHAIMIEV AND THE POWER OF COMMON SENSE

By Ravil Bukharaev

First published 2007 by
GLOBAL ORIENTAL LTD
PO Box 219
Folkestone
Kent CT20 2WP
UK

www.globaloriental.co.uk

© Ravil Bukharaev 2007

All rights reserved. No part of this publication may be reproduced or transmitted in any form or by any electronic, mechanical, or other means, now known or hereafter invented, including photocopying and recording, or in any information storage or retrieval system, without prior permission in writing from the publishers, except for the use of short extracts in criticism.

British Library Cataloguing in Publication Data
A CIP catalogue entry for this book is available from the British Library

ISBN 978-1-905246-45-8 [English Edition]
       978-1-905246-46-5 [Russian Edition]

Set in Stone Serif 10 on 11.5pt by Mark Heslington, Scarborough, N. Yorkshire
Printed and bound in England by Cromwell Press, Trowbridge, Wilts.

CONTENTS

PLATE SECTION FACING PAGE 102

Preface	*vii*
List of Illustrations	*ix*
Introduction: The Moment of Truth	1
Chapter 1: Blessed is the Motion of Life (*Harakatta barakat*)	17
Chapter 2: The Word Unuttered	36
Chapter 3: End of Symmetry	54
Chapter 4: Kazan Gateway	71
Chapter 5: 'Village Culture'	89
Chapter 6: 'We Need Millions of Proprietors'	109
Chapter 7: Mother Tongue	132
Chapter 8: Tatarstan in the Global World	152
Chapter 9: The National Idea	171
Index	*204*

PREFACE

In 1994, the term 'Tatarstan model' came into use to describe the path which one of Russia's constituent republics had adopted during the unprecedented conditions of its transformation from a Soviet-period pseudo-autonomous entity into a democratic market-economy state. Since then, this particular model of development has often attracted the attention of both domestic Russian and international observers. My earlier book on the subject was published in 1999, immediately following the colossal financial crisis, which had all but permanently crippled Russia as an independent economic and political entity.

Russia's remarkable renaissance, despite the catastrophic ordeal of the 1990s, has undoubtedly taken the outside world by surprise. But those who know their history will remember that Russia is a very fast learner indeed. For example, Russia entered the nineteenth century knowing nothing of professional music and literature and yet, by the middle of the century she already had produced Tchaikovsky, Musorgsky, Pushkin, Tolstoy and Dostoevsky to her credit. And for those who prefer sports to history, there is a fine example of Russians emerging amongst the world's top professional tennis-players, despite the fact that tennis only became a popular sport in Russia as recently as ten years ago.

Alas, history is a less popular subject these days, and so are the lessons of history. Despite all the previous sympathy engendered by her twentieth-century plight, Russia's re-emergence as a world power is today viewed in the West with increasing suspicion and prejudice which, sadly, is based on centuries-old bias (as this book tries to explain) rather than on any objective evaluation of Russia's own particular pathway to achieving a democratic market economy. Focusing as it does on one of the most interesting and unusual regional examples of the Russian market transfiguration, this book also argues that whilst there may be no third way between democracy and tyranny, also in economic terms, there may be and, indeed, are different forms of successful transition not necessarily foreseen or properly understood by Western observers.

Tatarstan: A 'Can-do Culture' is a continuation of my research into the particular characteristics of the 'Tatarstan model' at this new stage of its development, when the Russian Federation has seemingly overcome the greatest burdens placed on her by the collapse of the USSR and has started to undo the immense mistakes made at the beginning of her market transition. It looks at the major regional developments of 2000–2006 and tries to explain the apparent success of Tatarstan's economic and political revival firmly based on her enduring ethnic and religious multiculturalism.

I would like to thank the many people in Tatarstan and Great Britain who helped with my research and made publication of this book possible. I owe special thanks, however, to the President of Tatarstan Mintimer S. Shaimiev who made time for several long interviews exploring his vision of the present and the future of his 'can-do' country.

RAVIL BUKHARAEV
London, August 2006

LIST OF ILLUSTRATIONS

Photographs by Mikhail Kozlovsky and others

See Plate Section facing page 102

1. President Mintimer Shaimiev.
2. Tatarstan leads many Russian regions in sustained agricultural development
3. Volga ethnicities flourish in Tatarstan's multi-ethnic culture
4. New Year celebrations
5. With Chulpan Khamatova
6. At the opening of a new seafood restaurant in Kazan
7. At the newly refurbished Kazan railway station
8. 'Tug of War' at the Sabantui festival
9. The revered sixteenth-century icon of 'Our Lady of Kazan' is returned
10. With the Moscow and all-Russia Orthodox Patriarch Alexis II, et al
11. The Kul Sharif Mosque
12. With former Russian Prime-Minister Victor Chernomyrdin, et al
13. With Tatarstan's Prime-Minister Rustam Minnikhanov
14. Kazan's 'Pyramid'
15. At the opening of the Hermitage Rooms in the Kazan Kremlin
16. With Alvaro Gil-Robles, et al
17. With newly-wed wife Sakina
18. A life-long passion for horses
19. At the official opening of the St Petersburg Street
20. At the parental house in the village of Anyak
21. At his father's grave
22. With the leaders of the Commonwealth of Independent States (CIS)
23. With the presidents of the CIS countries
24. With President Vladimir Putin
25. Suyumbika Tower, Kazan.
26. Spasskaya tower, Kazan
27. Aerial view of the Kazan Kremlin
28. With the leaders of the 'United Russia' political party
29. With the Culture Minister of Azerbaijan Polad Byul-Byul Ogly, et al
30. Traditional Tatar wrestling
31. Feodor Chaliapin monument

32. Planting trees in the new Millennium Park
33. With former Mayor of Kazan, et al
34. With Iranian Ambassador to Russia Golam-Reza Ansari
35. A pause for thought
36. Tatar tea-ceremony
37. Motherland Memorial, Kazan Victory Park
38. With Boris Yeltsin
39. With Mikhail Gorbachev, et al
40. At a new medical facility
41. With the President of Kazakhstan Nursultan Nazarbaev
42. Kazan students
43. Playing chess with children
44. The future of Tatarstan sports
45. Some of Tatarstan's 100+ ethnicities
46. Tatar beauties
47. Delight in self-sufficient farming
48. With the Director General of the Tatneft Oil Company Shafagat Takhautdinov.
49. With writer Chinghiz Aitmatov
50. With Tatar tennis player Marat Safin
51. With American Ambassador William J. Burns
52. Time for reflection
53. Kazan's ancient market square
54. The Millennium Bridge
55. The face of the future.

INTRODUCTION

THE MOMENT OF TRUTH

If the Confederacy fails, there should be written on its tombstone: *Died of a Theory*.

Jefferson Davis (1808–1889)[1]

Sancta simplicitas! The present-day Judases no longer know what they betray, any more than they know what they like: what they know is only the preface written by another hand, the lecture given by a parson or professor, the interpretation of the well-known critic.

Walter Kaufmann[2]

On 16 October 2003, at Utah University's Hinckley Institute of Politics, during the annual Middle East and Central Asia Politics, Economics and Society Conference in Salt Lake City, I gave a lecture on my homeland, the Republic of Tatarstan. There, just like a week earlier during my dinner-speech at the Milwaukee Country Club, I started by explaining where the republic is to be found on a map of the world and why, of all things, it should be a topic of interest not just to American scholarly and business circles, but to the wider American public as well.

'Tatarstan', I said, 'is one of the most economically and politically advanced constituent regions of the Russian Federation and, in more ways than one, a unique showcase for a sustainable and successful transition from the Soviet socialist system to a market economy.' It is, of course, a major source of oil in the European part of Russia, but its assets also include a developed petrochemical industry, as well as other significant enterprises, including military and civil aircraft, as well as heavy truck-building plants.

It is also a country with deep Islamic roots, in which, approximately, one half of the population is Orthodox Russian and the other half Muslim Tatar. Although, after decades of atheism, the religious divide is somewhat misleading, the Kazan Tatars, as they are called after their capital city on the Volga River, are a separate ethnicity compared to the Slav Russians. Despite their name, bringing forth nomad allusions, the Kazan Tatars are a nation of a thousand-year-old urban civilization, bound together by their language, religion, history and traditional culture. The republic is located, in spite of her rather exotic name, not in Central Asia, but in the very heartland of Russia, just over five hundred miles to the east of Moscow between the Volga River and the Ural Mountains.

Why this most distinctively ethnic, let alone Muslim, republic should lie in the middle of European Russia is a fascinating story of national resilience. But for all her genuine historical grievances and all occasional nationalistic talk of the 'Muscovite occupation lasting for more than four centuries', Tatarstan has avoided any inter-ethnic strife in the ideological void and social upheaval following the collapse of the USSR. At the same time, she persistently, yet intelligently and peacefully, defended her proclaimed and officially assumed right to follow a path of market transition which was strikingly different from the rest of Russia.

The result of these endeavours, which bore fruit in the mid-1990s, was little short of a miracle. Since then, the completion of the huge renewal programme in agriculture, which made Tatarstan self-sufficient in all basic foodstuffs before the financial crisis of 1998, the high rate of the well-paced privatization and the sustained investment in industrial and urban reconstruction predictably brought the republic under the spotlight of attention from Russia as well as a number of foreign observers.

Everything that was achieved was against all the odds with a backdrop of a shaky political and economic situation in the rest of Russia, with which Tatarstan managed to conclude a separate bilateral treaty, having flatly refused to sign the inadequate federal treaty of 1992. This apparent stubbornness, initially not unlike that of the ill-fated Chechnya, did not, however, bring the republic into military collision with Moscow, but rather opened the gateway for the development of an unheard-of democratic federalism within Russia.

I went on to say: 'In the present climate of "globalization and its discontents", such rare political and economic success of this peculiar market transition invites many questions as to its underlying causes. It, also, calls for the scrutiny of the political philosophy of Tatarstan's leadership, starting with her President Mintimer Shaimiev.'

The lecture, which was simultaneously broadcast by Utah University's radio channel because of the inquisitive American interest regarding all Islamic matters, was well received. There were many follow-up questions, to which I tried to provide honest answers to the best of my knowledge and ability. But I recall this particular event not because it is yet another opportunity to reduce the deficiency of practical knowledge about the realities of today's Russia and its constituent regions, which purpose, of course, is the reason for the present book.

I recall the event mainly because a member of the audience, a young woman, approached me after the lecture and said: 'Throughout your speech, I tried to figure out, what was so different about your presentation. I now realize what it was. The thing is – you are sincere in what you are saying.'

It was an eye-opener, the examination of which could probably set the overall context for this book.

Indeed, in the world of post-modern political and economic science, when the main emphasis is placed on, however illusory, 'objective and value-free knowledge', such matters as 'one's sincerity', or vague concepts like 'the pursuit of happiness', should apparently have neither place, nor application. In this context, and especially as far as the countries in transition are concerned, the same is meant to be true with regard to concepts such as 'goodwill', 'good faith' or the very notion of the 'countries with leaders dedicated to the well-being of their people'.[3] The perception is that, in the widest possible variety of developing countries, the self-serving interests of 'the elites' and the alleged corruption of the leadership are the only constants that always need to be addressed.

These are the presumptions of many studies, including PhDs, reinforced by studies of the post-Soviet transition in Russia.

It is believed that any research in the field of political science claiming to be properly founded on Western-style scholarly objectiveness is always true to its purpose, if only because it completely avoids 'values' in preference to 'facts'. And yet, however 'free, objective and unbiased' one's academic study may appear to be, PhDs are seldom completed without taking into account a certain set of beliefs, which often enough chime with the scholarly works of one's head of department or academic supervisor. Similarly, facts are often taken at their face value, without even looking into their possible rationales, which could otherwise present them in a different and probably much more meaningful light.

Theoretically, the 'pure' post-modernist approach to history and the socio-economic sciences should reject any positivism in the cognitive process and, with it, the entire idea of the continuity of history along with its division into certain imminent evolutionary phases. It is presumed that such methodology of deconstruction and refutation concerning the existence of universal and objective truth, along with any 'goals of social evolution', will enable us to see the world as it is, and, for whatever selfish reasons, not as it was portrayed for many preceding centuries. But the problem with any 'revolutionary' philosophy of this kind always means, that, by implication, in rejecting one universal truth, it promotes the idea that 'anything is permissible', and in such a situation it is inevitable that 'the truth of the strong' will always dominate. The notion that post-modernism, among other things, rejects the idea of the 'superiority of the Western world', is therefore particularly cunning as, in fact, it is nothing more than yet another product of the Western world in unfair competition with the traditional beliefs, values and life philosophies of non-Western societies. For all the theoretical eloquence of post-modernist thinkers, the reality of post-modernism, supported by the Western power of publicity and advertisement, dismisses 'truth' while promoting 'interest', because, in the absence of 'universal truth', there are only interests left at play, and most powerful ones at that. Thus, the Bohemian, all-embracing and 'liberating' post-modernism leaves the door wide open to the very thing it supposedly rejects, namely, to the positivist promotion of Western-style liberal market democracy as the one and only valid model of social and economic development.

In this real post-modernist world, we should, among other things, just forego historical notions like 'politics is not exact science', even if the latter epitomizes the experience of those who applied *Realpolitik* as successfully as Otto von Bismarck[4] himself. Any set of definitions of 'exact' political or economic science should be, or so we are told, universally applicable to all societies of the world, irrespective of their belonging either to the 'developed', or 'developing' nations. Thus, despite the fact that political and economic scientism has most spectacularly failed with regard to the 'only true' Marxist teachings, some of today's scholars of politics and economics endeavour to articulate yet another universal approach to the mind-boggling variety of societies. Or, at least, to those of them which belong to the developing world, as if the developed world is 'scientifically fine' for all time to come.

Here, coincidentally, one recalls a famous opening statement by the philosopher Søren Kierkegaard in his book *The Present Age*, where he defines the Western society of his time in these words: 'A revolutionary age is an age of action; ours is the age of advertisement and publicity. Nothing ever happens but there is immediate publicity everywhere. In the present age a rebellion is, of all things, the most unthinkable.'[5] This was, of course, written in 1846, just before a wave of revolutions swept across Europe. Present-day scholars may argue that the Paris Commune in France, ever ready to erupt, and the Hungarian revolution in the Austrian Empire were just aberrations of Kierkegaard's axiom. However, his belief is not unlike the modern notion that the social evolution of the Western-type societies has reached its climax and is ready to be exported all over the world.

The mantras of this approach are, of course, *liberal democracy* and *globalization*, as if these terms were self-explanatory. But, for all the immense academic and practical work already invested into the process of 'value-free' understanding of these concepts, we still do not possess any exact scholarly definition for either of them. What I am driving at here is that instead of 'value-free' definitions we still widely use elegant maxims like 'government of the people, by the people and for the people', choosing to overlook the fact that the concept of 'the people' is heavily value-laden in itself.

But, for all the efforts of introducing a universal pattern of Western liberal market democracy to the 'developing societies' in the East and South, it seems that the only 'scholarly' definition of democracy available is still its interpretation by antonym: democracy is, perhaps, not tyranny. But then, was it not one of the fathers of American democracy who said: 'despotism, or unlimited sovereignty, or absolute power, is the same in a majority of a popular assembly, an aristocratic council, an oligarchical junto, and a single emperor'?[6] Today, those who think that this notion sounds like a joke, might as well note another American catch-phrase, typical of our own age, when political theories are still practised at all costs: 'It became necessary to destroy the town to save it.'[7]

For all the controversies, which occasionally envelop cold-blooded scientism in social and economic studies, the irrelevance of normative concepts and ethical values to any scholarly political research is still, in practice, a sacred axiom not to be questioned. Questioning it in the real world is not dissimilar to disputing the merits of modern art in front of some hardened intellectuals, for whom the artistic worth of a discarded garden shed receiving the Turner Prize is as indubitable, as any other taboo in their illusory realm of 'no taboos'.

It is useless to try and persuade such cosmopolitan intelligentsia that, historically, art sprung from a spiritual urge to share one's, often sadly unappreciated and thus lonely, love. The purpose of art was to light up the human heart and soul with the beauty the artist saw and felt in the world. The genuine artist's vision of beauty is often strange, but then it always had some criteria, by which a real talent could be distinguished from a third-rate charlatan. What is called modern art has done away with all criteria to the joy of those who use it to only promote their own, often rather ordinary personalities through the shock of the casually thought-out and thus often dull and boring so-called 'ingenuity'.

Using a metaphor, it would seem self-evident that sex, however ingenious, cannot substitute true love for those who are genuinely longing for it. But even the concept of love, being a normative and, for some, an archaic religious concept, is being heartily disputed by those who may have never experienced that very feeling with the unmistakable difference: it always calls on the person for some kind of altruistic sacrifice, and not just for another kind of intellectual or carnal pleasure.

But here again, the prophetic vision of S. Kierkegaard comes to mind, for it is he who said:

> The fewer ideas there are at any time, the more indolent and exhausted by bursts of enthusiasm will it be; nevertheless, if we imagine the Press growing weaker and weaker because no events or ideas catch hold of the age, the more easily will the process of levelling become a harmful pleasure, a form of sensual intoxication which flames up for a moment, simply making the evil worse and the conditions of salvation more difficult and the probability of decline more certain. Although the demoralization brought about by autocracy and the decay of revolutionary periods has often been described, the decay of age without passion is something just as harmful, though, on account of its ambiguity, it is less obvious.[8]

Who is there to exclaim, 'The king is naked', as that little child from the famous Hans Christian Andersen fairy tale? Well, almost anyone who even in this 'age without passion' is still capable of thinking for oneself and still appreciates one's common sense. It is always one's common sense that gets one through real life, and never a theory. It is another matter, however, that such childlike revelations may prove in this age to be very costly indeed.

Yet, even those honestly believing in modern art and/or the universalism of the Western-style market democracy can surely agree that 'all political concepts, descriptive as well as normative, need to be understood in the light of the ideological perspectives of those who use them'.[9] For all the wealth of books on political studies, which one can browse and buy in Western bookshops, one major best-seller reprinted over and over again is always there. That is, of course, *The Prince* by Niccolo Machiavelli, first published in 1513. It is a rude worldview, no doubt, but still the best political reading for those who will do anything to achieve their goals at someone else's expense.

In today's world, the interests of the leader are not that paramount any more and the public good is on everyone's tongue. But then again, 'In politics, individuals who seek to promote only the public good are led by an invisible hand to promote special interests that it was not part of their intention to promote.'[10]

Political science is, therefore, not a 'pure', but, rather, an applied science: for all its theorizing, it always tries to develop workable instruments of practical policies. And here one may artlessly ask, what are all its theories for, if in scholarly pursuits and not-so-harmless practical applications it is often inclined to lose sight of the only goal, which historically brought it into existence? This ideal goal, from the times of Aristotle and Cicero, was basically one and the same: 'the good of the people', even if the ways, in which this good is being achieved today, might sometimes drastically differ from those recommended by academics.

Of course, any proper science, through its natural growth and expansion, tends to overlook an earlier set goal in pursuit of the never-ending auxiliary questions, which inevitably arise in the course of study. These questions, in themselves, are very important, but their importance is rather related to the substantiation of science, or a theory, itself, and not to those initial aims and objectives, which once set the whole engine of research in motion. Established political theories, of course, have their own validity and, therefore, can be useful as tools of research with a certain degree of approximation.

Yet, in matters concerning not just the issues of governance and its underlying causes, but actual human lives in their struggle for economic and spiritual survival, simple common sense dictates, at the very least, a variety of approaches.

Having been educated at the Departments of Mathematics of both the Kazan and Moscow State Universities, I believe I am still mathematician enough to distinguish between 'apparent' and 'objective' truths. I also believe that political and even economic science cannot be equated to exact sciences if only because their practical experiments fail much more often than not, and, in these failures, usually cause enormous pain and suffering to the very objects of their experimentation.

The true results of experiments with human societies and their time-tested taboos can only be verified over time – meaning much longer than a few decades, or even a single century.

The highly controversial twentieth century, when a huge diversity of political and economic theories were developed on both sides of the Great Divide of the Cold War in competition with each other, is too close to us in terms of history for us to be able to draw any definite conclusions. Its lessons are still being learned. Many lessons of the Russian transition are especially instructive, or, rather, tragic, and not only because of the dire statistics for her general population: 'In 1989, only 2 percent of those living in Russia were in poverty. In 1998, that number had soared to 23.8 percent using the $2 a day as standard. More than 40 percent of the country had less than $4 a day, according to a survey conducted by the World Bank.'[11]

The Russian statistics have been steadily improving since 1998, when Russia chose to discard the 'shock therapy' prescriptions of market fundamentalism then preached at the IMF and the World Bank, and since then strongly criticized even by such erstwhile propagandists as Jeffrey Sachs. It is he who, in 1995, summed up the 'shock therapy' treatment of Russia in these words:

> When we got down to reforms, we felt like doctors invited to the patient's bedside. But when we put the patient on the operating table and cut him open, we suddenly discovered that he had a completely different anatomical structure and inner organs, which we did not study in our medical college.

But even after such treatment, the Russian economy (having at its disposal, after all, about 38% of all the world's natural resources and a most educated, if not properly motivated, labour force) in 1998–2005 continually improved in the market, not least because of the boost from burgeoning oil prices.

But what about 'the public good'?

The Second World War cost Russia (USSR) more than twenty million lives of its citizens. The 'shock therapy', its material and, what's more, spiritual devastation, has already cost Russia – in peace time! – some six million lives, so much so that the country is threatened by depopulation: Russia's death rate is 1.6 times higher than in the developed countries. According to the 2005 annual survey by the World Bank, Russian men live on average sixteen years less than men in Western countries, and fourteen years less than Russian women. If the present tendency persists, the average life expectancy for Russian men will soon drop to fifty-three years of healthy life. In 1975, Russia occupied 35th place in the world for life expectancy. Today, Russia occupies 142nd place on that list.

Due to the low birth rate, which over the last fifteen years has dropped by nearly 30%, the country loses 700,000 lives annually – by 2025, its population may decrease by another eighteen million and, by 2050, may constitute only a half of what is it now. By 2070, the country occupying 13% of the earth's landmass may have just 1% of world population.

Is it surprising then that, in his 2006 annual address, Russian President Vladimir V. Putin stressed the 'conservation of the nation' (using A. Solzhenitsyn's words) as the most important priority for the Russian state today and for years to come. One may doubt the outcome of the proposed measures, but one is also encouraged, for a change, to truly believe in Russia's future when such sober and common-sense words are spoken:

> If the state is genuinely interested in increasing the birth rate, it must support women who decide to have a second child. The state should provide such women with an initial maternity grant that will improve their social status and avoid future problems. Mothers could use this grant in various ways: put it towards improving their housing situation, for example, by partially financing house purchase, getting a mortgage or other loan scheme once the child is three years old, or using it for the child's education, or, if they wish, adding it the personal portion of their own old-age pension. Experts say that the amounts of these state supports should be at least 250,000 roubles, and that this should, of course, be indexed to annual inflation.[12]

Is there any other country on earth prepared to support the birth of a second child with over £5000 (sterling), taking inflation into account? One wonders why it has taken so long for this kind of support to be made available to the Russian people.

□

I know the pain of an inexplicable loss only too well: my sincerity in speaking to American audiences in October 2003 should be judged against the sudden demise of my only son in Moscow just a month earlier. My son Vassily was a healthy young man of twenty-nine who died of a sudden heart attack – at home, in broad daylight. Like many other people in Russia, he was used to thinking for himself and could not bring himself to straightforwardly worship the Golden Calf of the 'shock therapy' era of the nascent Russian capitalism with its sole emphasis on human greed as the driving force of life. The everyday abasement of the normative concepts, or else, spiritual values, in which he was brought up, finally overtook him.

Many people in Russia died not because they were 'less enterprising'. They perished because they felt, and indeed were, unwanted and not called for in the process, when the fate of the largest country on earth was decided by a group of cronies far removed from any notion of national interest. 'The people' were thus completely forgotten in this process of supposedly 'making life better'. The sudden abundance of consumer goods and the unbridled propaganda of sex for sale, all that 'fun of life' was not enough to fill the spiritual void of any person used to soul-searching in the Leo Tolstoy and Dostoevsky tradition. They felt estranged and betrayed by their country, when she saw nothing for them in the misty illusions of her 'shock therapy' madness. They lost the sense of destination and, with it, the will to struggle and live.

Maybe, this is indeed something 'uniquely Russian', but it does not diminish the scope of this man-made human suffering. Sir Isaiah Berlin, one of the last true philosophers of the twentieth century, who really knew Russia, had once said: 'The fundamental sense of freedom is freedom from chains, from imprisonment, from enslavement by others. The rest is extension of this sense, or else metaphor.'[13] His first two conditions may have been generally fulfilled in Russia, although some people would argue with that. But the feeling of enslavement and major deceit is still there, and not because of the perceived capitalist exploitation and bafflement at one's inability to influence things of vital public and stately importance. It is the feeling of being enslaved by that rough and utterly cynical materialism, which took the majority of the Russian people completely unawares.

Neglect of values caused the death of millions, and that is a fact. Were, then, these norms and values less important in the Russian market transition, than other 'scientific facts' relating to it?

Of course, Russia believed in myths and miracles throughout her history and more than once believed in them against all odds and all common sense. At least twice its destiny was saved by a miracle of the weather. It was during the Napoleonic War and, later, in November 1941, when German tanks and soldiers were stopped on the very threshold of Moscow – not only by the audacity and courage of Soviet soldiers, but also by an unusually cold and freezing winter.

This national belief in miracles, as it happens, seems to have swayed the Russian 'shock therapy' reformers as well, despite all their schooling from the sober IMF and the World Bank. These Russian 'Chicago boys', probably, in all truth believed in the miraculous healing powers of the completely unregulated market for the ailing Soviet socialist-style economy of 1990. But this academically designed, yet entirely unrealistic miracle could not and therefore did not materialize. What is worse, the economy contracted catastrophically. As Joseph E. Stiglitz has stated: 'The devastation – the loss in GDP – was greater than Russia suffered in World War II. In the period 1940–1946 the Soviet Union industrial production fell 24%. In the period 1990–1998, Russian industrial production fell 42.9% – almost equal to the fall in GDP (45%).'[15] Inflation went up 1000%, the population's life-savings were immediately devoured by it, and the Russian people, for whose good all of it was supposedly done, yet again found themselves totally destitute and on the bitter end of someone's experimentation based on a 'solid' theory.

Even for such a gullible Russia, her painful transition to market capitalism of sorts was devoid of any general political motivation, except the, soon divested, myth that the one-time painful injection of a liberal market medicine would be an instantaneous panacea for all the ills and wants of Russian society. 'An unregulated market will work wonders all by itself', was the order of the day. The hard truth of the matter would be that building, from scratch, a functioning market economy and working democracy would take considerable time, effort, a fair bit of boring bureaucracy and consistent, thoughtful, scrupulous legislative and executive work anticipating the possible pitfalls of this mammoth, totally unprecedented task. In short, it would need 'pacing' and not the 'rush-rush' dismantling of economic and civic institutions in the mad hope that democratic and market structures would grow on these 'brown sites' all by themselves.

But this knowledge came much later and at a huge price. In the early days of transition, it was not considered relevant or appropriate to discuss with the masses who once again would have to be called on to suffer for a distant 'bright future'. In the process, which was called 'democratization', despite the state withholding crucial information from the public domain, it was a no vote-winner for the 'party of power', which would more accurately be called the 'party of insiders'. And so, the crony government of the Yeltsin era never believed its own people and chose instead to deceive it time and again, talking about an economic miracle waiting just around the corner and making all the right noises about a growing democracy, which was so reassuring for its Western sponsors.

But was this suffering really necessary on such a monstrous scale? Could the people be re-assured and gradually involved in the process, if they were made to realize their own and, indeed, the national interests in the success of this grand project of market and democratic transition?

There was only one Russian region, the Republic of Tatarstan, which did not believe in miracles and strongly, albeit peacefully, protested against being carried along the path of self-destruction by the liberal market euphoria of the 1990s. The historic pragmatism of the people and their leader, President Mintimer Shaimiev, deeply rooted in centuries of the bitter experience of national survival, led the republic along the path of self-reliance – in word and deed. And, despite the fact that all Tatarstan's achievements regarding the economy, practical federalism and inter-ethnic co-existence were dictated by common sense, or, as President Shaimiev prefers to say, 'by life itself', the model of Tatarstan's transition did indeed resemble a miracle come true.

Of course, this was noticed not only in Moscow and the republic itself. A host of articles and research papers were written in the foreign press on the Tatarstan model, with mostly a positive evaluation of the republic and the practical policies of her leadership. The Tatarstan model has also merited several monographs ranging, in English, from the thoroughly researched, if already outdated, book *The Economic Development of Tatarstan* by Leo McCann[16] to the somewhat opinionated study of *Islam in post-Soviet Russia* edited by Hilary Pilkington and Galina Yemelianova.[17] Based on the scrutiny of political and economic events before 2003, these books could not, however, take into account the quintessential developments of 2005, the analysis of which is important to the proper understanding of Tatarstan's path of transition in its all-Russia perspective.

In August 2005, the celebration of the millennium of the foundation of the city of Kazan crowned Tatarstan's most triumphant five-year economic and social development programme thus far. While visiting Kazan, the Chairman of the Russian Audit Chamber, S. Stepashin, referred to it as 'the most successful, the most efficient implementation of a specially designated federal programme since the collapse of the Soviet Union'. In such an atmosphere, when the Russian government is still very apprehensive about using even a small part of its huge petrodollar stabilization fund for regionally and nationally important projects, ever fearful that it will be squandered and go to waste, the above-cited words are especially notable. The said federal programme, however, was solely based on Tatarstan's own proposals and her on-going economic and social projects. Under this federal programme Tatarstan received some 250 billion roubles ($8.9 billion) in capital investment for its social and economic infrastructure. Yet, the republic actually paid more in taxes to the federal centre in the same period. Looking back, one can assume that if the fiscal status quo between Moscow and Kazan did not change in 1999, the republic would have been able to fulfil all realistic objectives on her own.

As history would have it, the Russian Federation was in the twenty-first century once again blessed with a major miracle, which saved it from suicidal self-destruction. The sky-high oil prices and steady growth of other tax revenues made all the difference, but only after Moscow had abandoned the 'shock therapy' medication in the wake of the 1998 financial crisis. All but bankrupt and totally disillusioned, Russia adopted a much more gradual approach to her market transition, carefully evaluating all special circumstances and conditions, in which she was destined to perform this epochal task.

In my own book on the Tatarstan model written in the heat of the 1998 crisis,[18] I compared the common-sense policies of the 'soft landing' adopted by the Tatarstan leadership as early as 1990 to the realities of the all-Russian 'shock therapy' methods and their consequences. I also argued that it was the underlying idea of democratic federalism born out of Tatarstan's claim to shared sovereignty with Russia, that eventually made the pacing of reforms not only possible, but also fruitful.

At the end of another of my books published in Russian in 2000,[19] I made a hopeful prediction or, rather, an educated guess, that under the then newly elected President Vladimir Putin all of Russia would eventually follow the general patterns of Tatarstan's reform route. This hope has since been fulfilled, although not fully, because Russia, as opposed to Tatarstan, in the very beginning of her market metamorphosis has made some crucial mistakes, which continue to prove very difficult to undo.

However, now in the third millennium, Tatarstan's particular experience has offered yet new political and economic lessons, instructive not just for Russia and the CIS states, but also for many other countries undergoing their own transition to market democracy. This book, therefore, is focused on a close evaluation of these lessons in the context of the Russian and, indeed, world journey to the new, still largely unknown and unpredictable order of things.

Today's consensus is that neo-liberal market theory has won the day, and it indeed seems to be the case, at least to its hardened proponents. But if the twentieth century has taught us anything, the principal lesson to be learned is surely from studying (or experiencing) the consequences of the worldwide misuse of political power. The twentieth century has, if anything, proved that raw power, be it the power of an ideology or of an immense quantity of liquid money smashing through national barriers, cannot, by itself, transform societies into something historically durable by speeding up the natural pace of things. Driven by the unstoppable inertia of its own unchallenged might, raw power always tends to bring about rapid change which very often is against common sense and human dignity.

'You cannot humiliate people into being happy' – as I once suggested with regard to the present war in Iraq. If applied to the decades of Communist rule in the USSR, the remark may be equally valid. This alone shows that basic biblical tendencies still persist in the world, despite all the talk of the age of globalization supposedly opening a completely new page in human history, especially if this history has finally and, for some, most conveniently ended. Those who, in the words of the Communist *L'Internationale* hymn, are now building another 'new world of their own', seem to have honestly believed in Francis Fukuyama's famous comment: 'What we may be witnessing is not just the end of the Cold War but the end of history as such: that is, the end point of man's ideological evolution and the universalism of Western liberal democracy.'[20]

And yet, in this approach to the main issues of this book apparently dealing with only one federal republic of the Russian Federation, I choose to be a historian rather than a political scientist. For all my sincerity as a creative author and poet, I do not choose to be a 'village fool', all the more so against the notion of the Global Village. It would be overly naïve on my part to argue against the evident and the inevitable, as far as the global changes are concerned, but I still insist on my human right to question certain ideas of today against the realities of their political and economic applications.

One cannot simply calculate the future on the basis of a theory or a prejudice. One cannot bring this future any closer by being indifferent or arrogant towards it.

In this book, therefore, I will try to argue, albeit on a scale much smaller than any grand designs of the ongoing global *perestroika*, that the country, which has no destination of its own, has no destiny. If, in doing so, I will have to turn to human virtues and common-sense values so hateful to the prevailing postmodernist, end-of-history outlook, I will be able to excuse myself simply on the basis of my own 'field' experience acquired during over half a century of my own life and the power of judgement based on this experience. After all, during those years I have not just personally lived through all the Russian political and economic realities which are only academically known to the vast majority of Western political scholars. I have also tried, to the best of my human and academic integrity, to set down as objectively as I can this short, but immensely condensed fraction of modern history.

But from where, one might ask, do I find the audacity to believe that history is still there? One answer is that globalization, whatever term may turn out to connote its reality, never does away with the principal causes of the world's social diversity.

It cannot change these causes whilst being itself governed by them.

Indeed, if we simply look at its basic tenet, it maintains that it is the 'free global flow of information', which will transform our world and eliminate a host of 'backward' outlooks and traditions hindering the progress of the New World Order. There would be no argument against this, but for the meaning of the very word 'free'.

Apparently, that principal postulate of neo-liberal capitalism, 'there is no such thing as a free lunch', should preclude any flow of valuable information *gratis* and, indeed, it is the case. 'Capital must be propelled by self-interest; it cannot be enticed by benevolence'[21] – it is only one of the many variations of the same irrevocable postulate. In today's world, information is power, and any information that is worth something has to be paid for. Therefore, developing countries, and their citizens, will imminently have to find the means for purchasing much-needed information before entering the brave new world of 'prosperity for all'. But from where will the money come to do that on a scale required for the metamorphosis of becoming 'more like the developed countries'? Will the people who are able to buy the crucial information (the *elite* in the parlance of modern political science) share it 'for free' with their less fortunate compatriots? This notion is much more relevant to an imagined Communist-style comradeship, than to the neo-liberal agenda of globalization.

The sad conclusion from this observation is that the 'free flow of information' may turn out to be yet another myth for gullible humanity. Any information, which is today flowing free around the world, is either the good old, and previously available knowledge, or, much more often, pure advertising and propaganda, which, of course, are always paid for – in kind.

Where there is advertising and propaganda, there is always a vested interest. Although this is but a brief analysis, it is clear that by doing away with normative and ethical values, there are not just academic and philosophical, but also tangible materialistic rewards, when a concept such as 'sincerity' is promoted another one called 'hypocrisy' disappears. The unfortunate thing is, however, that, in my own experience of conversing with Western colleagues, the term 'hypocrisy' can be very rarely applied to actual attitudes towards countries in transition. Despite the use of the term 'hypocrisy' by such 'value-free' critics of certain global economic practices, as Joseph E. Stiglitz,[22] the proponents of neo-liberal and neo-conservative theories and practices are, in fact, stringent believers in their own infallibility and, strictly speaking, cannot be labelled as hypocrites.

How a single set of political and economic views 'from above' can dominate the future global liberal democracy, is a totally different question. Suffice it to say here that one does not need to believe in global conspiracy theories, if only because the tyranny of self-righteousness is not a recent phenomenon, and history abounds with examples of this kind.

With the arrival of the Age of the Internet, many things may change and, indeed, are changing in the world, except for that fundamental pillar of economics that you shall always pay a price for anything you obtain, whether you need it or not. And, in the process of economic and political transition, which is the main feature of large parts of the world today, this price is sometimes very high indeed.

That having been said, however, it is not my intention to diminish the importance of internet communications as an ever-growing field for discussion, as it is only honest discussion that can bring us all back from the edge of the precipice of global misunderstanding of each other's values.

'History is past politics, and politics is present history.'[23] Of course, the politics of current affairs can be seen only as a draft of history. So many things come and go, so many talk-shops open and close; so many political programmes fail at their first contact with reality. But what makes politics history, as practical experience shows, always seems to be somehow connected with the driving ideas of the national past, offering a historical continuity manifestly or latently shaped into the body of national politics.

Remaining fair to my modest knowledge and experience, I will confine the scope of this suggestion only to the countries of the former USSR and the regions of the Russian Federation. And yet, their present-day transition to a kind of democracy and market economy offers a fertile ground for deliberating on seemingly inexhaustible potential of national ideologies even in the present climate of post-modern disinterest towards nation-states as such.

Looking at the available lessons of the post-USSR transition, one cannot fail to notice that any success in this transition, if judged by 'the good of the people', always seems to possess some peculiar features of the national character. Very rarely, if at all, does it come from universal 'laissez-faire' schemes and slogans.

☐

One can also note that in recent years, once Russia began to assert her national interests both at home and abroad, though most warily and guardedly, there has been an ever-growing outcry about her alleged deviation from the prescribed path of economic and democratic reforms; and by domestic interests I do not mean the somewhat controversial policies towards the freedom of the press or the treatment of the oligarchs, but just this slow movement of the state turning its face towards long-neglected social and infrastructural issues. Remarkably, the chorus of disapproval is at its loudest on the part of the very same members of the Russian public who, by the virtue of being closest to the media, term themselves as the only true Russian intelligentsia, despite the fact that these folk were, in the early 1990s the first to quickly betray the values of human compassion towards 'the people' instilled into the fabric of Russian life by Gogol, Tolstoy, Dostoevsky, Chekhov and Solzhenitsyn. For all the reservations as to the source of the following quotation, the situation today in certain parts of the Russian population does merit a very similar observation: 'A spirit of national masochism prevails, encouraged by an effete corps of impudent snobs who characterize themselves as intellectuals.'[24]

And yet, for all the benevolent eloquence of the globalization gurus, for any transitional, or, indeed, developed economy there is still no instrument as powerful as a clearly defined and rightly understood national interest. This national interest may be woven into the interests of the groupings which are larger than a nation-state, but the national interest it is, if it indeed cares for the tangible good of the nation itself.

For national interests, however, one needs a nation, and not a mere ethnic group, which has no memory of statehood, while its political leadership has little, or no experience of state bureaucracy and impartial responsibility for all its members. Instead of political responsibility, a most rigid nationalism is still being practised in some states and ethnic regions, which got their first bloody taste of the 'free-for-all' freedom after the sudden collapse of the USSR. But nationalism, having been so successful in destroying the former order of things, proved absolutely helpless in building the new order. If politics, as it is said, is indeed a 'systematic organization of hatreds',[25] then nationalist states have already failed in their transition, because instead of organizing hatreds, they are just fuelling them.

The example of the Chechen Republic in Russia and some of the all-but-failed states in the Commonwealth of Independent States of the former USSR (CIS) seem to confirm this sombre observation. Indeed, without some kind of dull continuity in a historical sense, and even the duller work of regulating the changing political and economic networks in society, nothing can be achieved by slogans and outside help alone.

Somebody has said that a nation is a mass of people 'sticking together because they know that they have done great things together'. The new Russia has long struggled to define her national idea, without which it is impossible to comprehend true national interests. This struggle of self-definition is far from over for Russia. Indeed, with so many ethnic minorities calling the Russian Federation their home, one is seemingly lost in defining a single course to satisfy this multitude of ethnic and regional interests.

But for Tatarstan, with all its most acute national self-awareness, this has never presented a problem. The Tatars know only too well that the state edifice of Russia historically rested on two main nation-building corner-stones – the Slav Russians and the Turk Tatars. It is not at all coincidental that it is Tatarstan and her leadership that have shown the path, which, while respecting national traditions and values, can reliably lead to the establishment of a federal Russia equally good to her own people and her far-away and close-by neighbours, even if Russia has always been and will always be different from the Western expectations of her.

All things considered, in my thirty years of research on Tatarstan and her culture I have finally realized that I am not just a chronicler, but also an eyewitness and, in a way, the by-product of a phoenix-like resurrection of this nation, which for centuries has been precluded from following its true calling by the obstacles of history and persistent bias as to its name – the *Tatar*stan. I have also understood that the main assets of any economy are not its natural resources or industrial and financial capacity, but the people when they are naturally motivated to make it all work. It was with this frame of mind that I had the temerity to write this book, trying to explain the phenomenon of the nation still capable of using its thousand-year-old historical memory in the new age, where the memory of the past has again become a most rare and therefore most precious commodity.

The experience of Tatarstan is, of course, only one local example of a rapid market metamorphosis, but it also confirms that sometimes it is very important and maybe even crucial to listen to one's common sense, however value-laden it might at first appear. It is all the more important to understand Tatarstan's approach given the outcomes from the most recent decades of our own 'age without passion' neo-liberal, as well as 'neo-conservative' methodology of 'one-size-fits-all' approach, which had so often, and at times tragically, failed with regard to political and economic issues all over the world. In so saying, I do not mean to wage a kind of Don Quixote war on post-modernist idleness towards those 'backward' cultural and moral values, which, they say, had outlived their practical usefulness. It is clear, however, that this book will be, at best, of limited appeal to the practising advocates of the global procrustean strategies and to the political positivists insisting on probing the realm of social life by universal methods similar to those of the natural sciences, be they Marxist or neo-liberal (neo-conservative) in their convictions. But then, my credo is not so far removed from the present-day beliefs of those world economists who have recovered their sight following their bitter experiences of trying to solve economic problems by making developing countries suffer:

> All of these problems are solvable, but they are not being solved in many places. Instead of hearing more lectures from the IMF about cutting budgets, poor countries need larger budgets to pay for the required investments – roads, power supplies, ports, schools, and health clinics – to jump-start economic growth. The IMF should spend less time telling the poorest of the poor to cut their spending, and more time telling rich countries to give more money to help the poor to meet their investment needs. (...) None of this makes sense for global security, or even for the financial interests of donor countries. The failures of economic development in the Andes, Central Asia, and Africa contribute to global instability, local insurrections and violence, drug trafficking, and bases for terrorism. Military approaches alone will not work, because the root of the problem is the vulnerability of the poor, hungry people to the prophets of hate.[26]

The fact that Russia still budgets on the basis of oil being US $27 a barrel and uses her multi-billion stabilization fund to pay off her foreign debt, at the same time trying to maintain fiscal discipline at home, is a common-sense policy, which definitely serves her national interests. She has also started, albeit rather cautiously, to explore the possibilities for centrally financing some vitally-needed national infrastructural projects, which will further help her economic security by creating work opportunities nationwide.

So, will the all-Russia market metamorphosis at last work for the good of all her peoples? Immense, seemingly insurmountable tasks still lie ahead.

But I, for one, remember that during the August 2005 celebrations of Kazan's millennium the President of Tatarstan, Mintimer Shaimiev, understandably proud of his republic's achievements, came up with a slogan, which he, in his pragmatism, does very rarely, if indeed at all. In a speech to members of the International Congress of Tatars and other guests of the jubilee, he said – in his Tatar mother tongue: 'After we have successfully done what we planned to do up to now, let us go forth with the motto of "Buldyrabyz!" – "We can!"'

Such confidence in one's own people, expressed after a millennium of so much unpropitious history and in the wake of the last fifteen years of everyday struggle against overwhelming economic and political odds, is surely worth writing about – hence this book.

NOTES

1. American statesman, President of the Confederate states (1801–1805).
2. Walter Kaufmann.
3. J. E. Stiglitz, *Globalization and its Discontents*, W. W. Norton and Company, New York, London, 2003, p. 39.
4. Chancellor of the new German Empire (1815–1898), who also famously said 'The secret of politics? Make a good treaty with Russia!'
5. Søren Kierkegaard, *The Present Age*, translated by Alexander Dru, ibid., p. 35.
6. John Adams (1735–1826), second president of the USA, from his letter to Thomas Jefferson, 13 November 1815.
7. Comment by a US Army major during the war in Vietnam, *New York Times*, 8 February 1968.
8. Søren Kierkegaard, ibid., p. 64.
9. Andrew Heywood, *Key Concepts in Politics*, Palgrave Macmillan, 2000.
10. Milton Friedman, American economist, 'Bright Promises, Dismal Performance: An Economist's Protest', 1983.
11. J. E. Stiglitz, *Globalization and its Discontents*, W. W. Norton and Company, New York, London, 2003, p.153.
12. President V. Putin, Annual Address to the federal Assembly, 10 May 2006.
13. Isaiah Berlin, introduction to 'Four Essays on Liberty'.
14. Peter Berger, political scientist, *Oxford Dictionary of Political Quotations*, Oxford University Press, 2005.
15. Joseph E. Stiglitz, ibid., p. 143.
16. L. McCann, *Economic Development in Tatarstan. Global Markets and a Russian Region*, RoutledgeCurzon, Taylor & Francis Group, London, 2005.
17. *Islam in Post-Soviet Russia. Public and Private Faces*, edited by Hilary Pilkington and Galina Yemelianova, RoutledgeCurzon, Taylor & Francis Group, London & New York, 2003.
18. Ravil Bukharaev, *The Model of Tatarstan under President Mintimer Shaimiev*, Curzon Press Ltd, London and St. Martin's Press, NY, 1999.
19. Ravil Bukharaev, 'President Mintimer Shaimiev and the Model of Tatarstan (Президент Минтимер Шаймиев и модель Татарстана)', in Russian, Blitz, St Petersburg, 2000.
20. *The Independent*, 20 September 1989.
21. Walter Bagehot (1826–77), English economist, from his 'Economic Studies', 1880.
22. See, J. E. Stiglitz, *Globalization and its Discontents*, W. W. Norton and Company, New York, London, 2003.
23. E. A. Freeman (1832–92), English historian, from *Methods of Historical Study*, 1886.
24. Spiro T. Agnew (1918–96), Vice-President of the USA 1968–73, in his speech in San Diego in September 1970.
25. Henry Brooks Adams (1838–1918), from *The Education of Henry Adams*, 1907.
26. Jeffrey D. Sachs, 'Making Globalization Work for All', Project Syndicate, www.project-syndicate.org.

CHAPTER 1

BLESSED IS THE MOTION OF LIFE
(*Harakatta barakat*)

The power, indeed, of every individual is small, and the consequence of his endeavours imperceptible, in a general prospect of the world. Providence has given no man ability to do much that something might be left for every man to do. The business of life is carried on by a general co-operation; in which the part of any single man can be no more distinguished, than the effect of a particular drop when the meadows are floated by a summer shower: yet every drop increases the inundation, and every hand adds to the happiness or misery of mankind.

Samuel Johnson (1709–84)[1]

There is no history of mankind; there are only many histories of all kinds of aspects of human life. And one of these is the history of political power. This is elevated into the history of the world.

Karl Popper (1902–95)[2]

Every historical nation contains within itself creative forces, which keep it in existence and fuel its optimism for the future. To understand these forces, make use of them and give them direction, even in the most demanding circumstances, is the task of an able leader. It is indeed, if the nation is lucky enough to have one at a time in history when the nation confronts a major crossroads. The ancient Tatar proverb says, 'harakatta barakat', which means, 'blessed is the motion of life'. This folk wisdom rightly applies to every man and woman in their daily life, but it is always the leader who is called to feel and sense the hidden purposeful motion, which carries along his entire nation to its historical destination, and, sometimes, even against the general flow of events. Moreover, you need to understand that this motion is the motion of growth, not unlike that of the mythical Tree of Life, deeply rooted in the earthly soil and reaching the heavenly heights with is mighty branches. The fact, that this symbol was universally present not only in the ancient Turco-Ugric, but also Celtic mythology, encourages one to hope that mankind today has inherently much more in common than it transpires from the utterly materialistic neo-liberal concepts of 'one-size-fits-all' philosophy.

The Tatarstan model is now more than twenty years old. One hopes that, however brief a period in terms of history, it is still long enough to evaluate the soundness of the direction taken by the republic facing the dawn of the all-Russia transition to the as yet unknown, but, expectantly, better future. Tatarstan's drive forward is a spectacular one; indeed, from the outset and in every sphere it has always had a clear vision of its purpose and destination. But if we were to say that those were, and are, the generalized and therefore less defined goals of a market economy and liberal democracy, we would be only partly right, because we would again mistake the means for the aim.

There is, however, one word, which sums up the purpose driving Tatarstan along its unique path. The word historically is 'statehood'. The drive for statehood equivalent to the creative potential of the nation is the key to the secret and the enigma of Tatarstan's success, achieved against all possible odds during an unprecedented transition from being a barely known Soviet region with historically arrested cultural development to becoming a main showcase of an all-Russia transformation into a democratic and federalist market economy state.

Moreover, the same belief might be helpful in defining not only Tatarstan's fundamental aim, but also the most essential characteristic of her long-serving leader Mintimer Shaimiev. Apart from his many personal qualities, it is the sheer extent of his achievements that is so impressive, ensuring that his epithet will be defined as that of a visionary statesman with an instinctive vision of where his country should be heading in the context of a rapidly changing world, linked to his conviction about his country's historical destiny.

Of course, Tatarstan is only equal to Ireland and Austria in its geographical size. But the achievements of a politician, let alone a leader of a large nation, are to be judged against the realities of his own country at a given time. In this light, the story of Tatarstan might be worthy of the annals of Russian history, as well as world history itself. To be a regional leader in Russia, with her long traditions of centralized rule, could never be an easy task. But to become a statesman capable of influencing the historical path of Russia from the seemingly powerless periphery is a truly remarkable and, from certain points of view, one might even be tempted to add, mysterious, accomplishment.

With some countries in transition, hindered by lack of debate of a more tangible nature, it is mainly the national past that is used for justification of political actions. We can find many examples throughout the world, when historical myths are readily employed, to justify demands for greater autonomy, or even political sovereignty. More often than not such insistence on 'historical rights' leads to bloodshed and only further entangles the already complex situation it was supposed to resolve.

In the case of Tatarstan, however, for all the covert richness and controversy of her own past, history was never utilized for political clarification of the republic's demands, at least on a decision-making governmental and presidential level. But it would be entirely wrong here not to seek to encompass the republic's great history as a legitimate tool in explaining her path of transition, which, at a first glance, seems completely unique – so much so, that some observers have described Tatarstan's recent socio-economic history and the policies promoted by Mintimer Shaimiev as 'phenomenal'.

Indeed, however intently we look at the Tatarstan model, we clearly see that in all its many facets it offers valuable lessons to other Russian regions and countries in transition. Whether it concerns the republic's inter-ethnic civic accord, her diplomatic foresight in relations with the Moscow federal centre or her policies of paced privatization and sustained economic reform based not just on her naturally exhaustible oil wealth, but much more on the technical innovations of the modern age, these lessons beg questions as to how all of this became possible under the extraordinary circumstances brought about by the sudden and almost total change of the state's foundations which was of truly gigantic proportions?

To answer these questions in a meaningful way, we could use a variety of approaches, including the advice of the British nineteenth-century prime minister Benjamin Disraeli who famously said, 'Read no history: nothing but biography, for that is life without theory.' Indeed, arguably the biographical scrutiny of the life and policies of President Mintimer Shaimiev could be an entirely valid approach for assessing the uniqueness of the Tatarstan model. And yet, to gain most from a biography, one needs more or less a clear understanding of the historical setting. Disraeli's advice can only be sparingly applied by a Western reader in understanding Russian, let alone Tatar history of the Soviet period, because even that, despite its apparent closeness to us in terms of time, still remains a mystery shrouded in many 'self-evident' clichés.

This may sound a little disturbing for Western and 'new' Russian scholars; but for those who are aware of the fact that almost all Soviet studies in the USA were once largely based on the so-called Smolensk archive – the files and records of the Smolensk district taken to the USA after the Second World War and only recently, in 2005, returned to Russia – this statement must contain some food for thought. The deductions, which were made about the top to bottom 'totalitarian' workings of Soviet power on the basis of this comparatively small provincial archive were consecutively applied to the entire state machine of the USSR, which was, of course, much more intricate and sophisticated than is widely assumed today. Yet, even the conclusions based on the Smolensk archive research sometimes mutually excluded each other in evaluating the extent to which the central Soviet power regulated all provincial affairs. Russia, let alone the USSR, being so vast and diverse in her regional faces, could not, of course, be ruled as an authoritarian state per se; the role of regional structures was, as we will see later, rather important in deciding day-to-day economic and social matters. But the Soviet period, with all its difficulties, is not the only background, against which the Tatarstan model and the policies of her leader could be fairly judged.

In Russian folklore, there is a magnificent tale of a city called Kitezh, which, as legend has it, had submerged into a lake to save itself from a devastating foreign invasion. This clandestine and magical city might also be a metaphor for the Tatar civilization, so rich and instructive and at the same time so little known to the wider world that even a glimpse at its centuries-long trials and accomplishments might bring veritable discoveries and thought-provoking revelations 'to those who tend to think', as the Holy Quran, the book that had shaped and safeguarded the Tatar national identity, often states. Therefore, this journey will regularly refer back to Tatar history, since, without doing so, it would become just another narrative in the current discourse on the Russian transition.

□

History may be very useful in a pragmatic sense. For instance, at the beginning of the 1990s, Tatarstan scholars, in cooperation with their colleagues from Moscow and St Petersburg, as well as Hungary, Sweden, Norway, Finland, Germany, Austria, France, the Czech Republic, Turkey, Egypt and other countries embarked upon new research based on thirty-two archaeological excavations at the Kazan Kremlin, as well as on archival searches in sixty-two archives and libraries, including forty-six libraries and archives in Europe, Asia and North Africa. During the latter search, the scholars discovered ten previously unknown manuscripts relevant to Kazan's past and found fifty-six previously unknown maps, on which, under various names, an urban settlement in the location of the present-day city of Kazan is shown.

Yet, the archaeological digs in the ancient Kazan Kremlin, which were prohibited in the Soviet period because the Kremlin was an 'officially restricted' and therefore a 'no-go' area for scholars, proved especially fruitful. Archaeologists made more than two thousand finds, but the discovery, in 1997, on the territory of the Kazan Kremlin of two historical coins was by far the most important single piece of evidence as to the existence of a military and customs post on the Kremlin hill already in existence by the end of the tenth century AD.

One of these coins is a half of an Arab Dirham, which in itself once again proves the fact of the circulation of such coins to the north from the Volga Bulgaria up to Scandinavia, and in this light it is not something unusual. Another coin found in 1997, the Czech Denarium of Great Bohemia of the early Middle Ages, is much more interesting. This coin bears the name of Saint King Vaclav, or Winceslas (907–929), the first Christian King of Bohemia.[3] On top of this sensational find, the thousand-year antiquity of the city was also confirmed by other archaeological evidence: spherical beads of black glass with dark blue, 'cornflower-blue' eyes, which had already become old-fashioned by the beginning of the eleventh century, and other ornaments of the tenth century; and also by a most rare gold-plated bronze strap on a belt, the kinds of which are only encountered in Hungarian monuments of the time of the 'Conquest of the Homeland'. Similar straps were in use in Hungary up to middle of the tenth century. Many other finds have also been unearthed in this most ancient cultural layer of the Kazan Kremlin. As a result, all attributes of an urban settlement – the ramparts, wooden palings, stone fortress wall, evidence of urban crafts and manufactures and attributes of international trade have been unearthed in the Kremlin. In 1998, on the basis of the archaeological materials obtained, under the auspices of the Institute of History of the Academy of Sciences of Tatarstan, Kazan University and the Society of Orientalists of the Russian Academy of Science, the seminar on 'The Sources for the Study of the History of the Ulus Dzuchi, or the Golden Horde' and the symposium of 'Historical Geography, Trade Routes and Cities of the Middle Volga region in the ninth to the twelfth centuries' were held in Kazan. Finally, in 1999, the international conference 'Medieval Kazan: Foundation and Development' took place in the capital of Tatarstan. There and then, more than 150 researchers from sixteen countries adopted a resolution, in which it was agreed that the complex analysis of the available materials provided the basis to date the foundation of Kazan at the end of the tenth to the beginning of the eleventh century. As a result, the Presidium of the Russian Academy of Sciences unanimously accepted the date of the foundation of Kazan as AD 1005 and thus the pathway for celebrating the Kazan millennium on an all-Russia and world level became feasible.

□

It is no coincidence that I choose to describe these scholarly investigations in some detail. Being typical of how things are done in Tatarstan, it demonstrates the attention to detail and depth, which are characteristic of the firm ground on which Tatarstan's achievements are built, be it in the field of historical research, or, as we shall see, in the political, social and economic fields. The outcome of the international scholarly team-work described above, was that in August 2005, the capital of the Republic of Tatarstan, Kazan, celebrated its millennium anniversary, – which was an event of not just huge cultural and political significance, but also of profound historical import as well.

For the first time in centuries the fact of the existence of a thousand-year-old urban civilization of Kazan Tatars was clearly articulated for the entire world and, notably, Russia herself, thus dispelling that prevailing, if sometimes honest, prejudice that Tatars in Russia were nothing other than 'barbarians' – nomad invaders with no civilization of their own.

In August 2005, among other guests and workers of the Kazan millennium, I was asked how I perceived this event. I answered that, for me, there was only one event in the history of the Tatars comparable with the Kazan millennium in its import for the future, and that was the event at the other end of the millennium – the official acceptance of Islam by the state of Volga Bulgaria in AD 922. Then, as now, such a claim demands that it be substantiated, which duly follows.

HISTORICAL OVERVIEW – THE STORY OF TATAR STATEHOOD

Important though the foundation of Kazan later proved to be, the Kazan Tatar urban civilization actually took root a century earlier with the acceptance of Islam as the state religion of Volga Bulgaria – a Turkic polity, which in the tenth century developed in the Volga-Kama basin. There are numerous works about Volga Bolgars,[4] who the modern Kazan Tatars have every right to count among their direct ancestors. For example, Gustav Burbiel in his research devoted to Kazan Tatar history states that the beginnings of Bulgar-Tatar history can be traced to the seventh century, when nomad Bolgar tribes first moved north towards the confluence of the Volga and Kama rivers:

> Today's Kazan (or Volga) Tatars are descendants of the Volga-Kama Bolgars, the Qypchaq Turks from Central Asia, who came to the Volga-Ural region in the thirteenth century, and the Turkicized Finnish tribes. The Turkic-speaking Bolgars

appeared in the region in the seventh century. By the ninth century they formed a state which expanded gradually to include those Bashkirs living west of the Urals. They accepted Islam in AD 922. The Bolgar state eroded during the early 1200s when Mongol-Tatars under Batu invaded the area and established the Golden Horde. The Mongols, a small minority in the conquering force, were quickly assimilated by the Turkic majority, and the Bolgars and Qypchaq Turks became ethnically dominant elements in the Golden Horde. During the second half of the fourteenth and into the fifteenth centuries the Bolgars moved further north and west: merging with the Turks and Finns, they became known as 'New Bolgars' and, finally, 'Kazan Tatars'.[5]

The classical Russian historians shared this opinion. N. Karamzin called the Volga Bolgars 'a trading and industrial people' who had good trade and cultural relations with northern Russia, Persia and other countries of the Muslim world. S. Solovyev, in turn, wrote:

> In times long ago, Asia, and that is to say Muslim Asia, had established its foothold here, not in the context of some nomad hordes, but in the context of a settled civilization. Long ago the Bolgars – a trading and industrial nation – had established themselves on these lands; at a time when the Russian Slavs had not yet begun to build Christian churches on the Oka river, and had not yet occupied these places in the name of European civilization, the Bolgars already listened to the Quran on the banks of the Volga and Kama rivers ...

Tenth to Twelfth Centuries

The acceptance of Islam, which at this time still was the main driving force of world civilization, gave a huge boost to Volga Bulgaria and in a matter of decades turned it from a semi-nomad polity into one of the largest and most unified and economically viable states of Eurasia. The rapid and dynamic growth of Bolgar towns in the second half of the tenth century is a most interesting phenomenon, one of many in Tatar history. Even the rather scrupulous and cautious *Encyclopedia of Islam* terms the soaring urbanization of Volga Bulgaria in the tenth century 'a huge progress', and, indeed, by the end of the tenth and the beginning of the eleventh centuries Volga Bulgaria already had up to 150 urban settlements, and with the addition of the increasingly Islamicized Burtas lands down the Volga this number reached 200.

In AD 922, when a union of Bolgar tribes accepted Islam, as recorded by the Arab man of letters Ibn Fadlan, Bolgars were still at the first stages of transition to urban life. Their marketplace of Bolgar-on-the-Volga at the Volga-Kama interflux was a rather motley settlement of people of many tongues and cultures. The Bolgar Tsar and aristocracy still preferred to live in spacious tents, and only occasionally do we hear about the construction of mosques, trading warehouses and living quarters. But why did Bolgar urban culture begin to develop so dynamically?

It happened mainly because in the second half of the tenth century the Bolgars had already become masters of the Great Volga waterway throughout its entire extent from the mouth of the Kama down to the Caspian Sea. In 960, Bolgars ceased to pay tribute to the Empire of Khazars, which hitherto dominated much of Eurasia. With the fall of the Judaic Khazar Empire, the Volga River became free for trade with Muslim countries – initially with the princedoms and emirates of Iran, Khwarezm and the Bukharan lands of the Samanids, through which the route to China, Afghanistan and India then passed. The national economy of Volga Bulgaria started to gravitate towards profitable trade and craftsmanship, whereas all existing geographical, political and religious advantages of its location at the end of the tenth century came together, contributing to both the economic and spiritual prosperity of the state. As always happens in such instances, the Bolgar rulers began to accumulate additional wealth, which made urban construction possible. These cities, as we see from Arab accounts, were open to anyone, regardless of his belief or ethnic origin. In this respect, the Tatar scholar Mirkasym Usmanov rightly termed the Bolgar civilization as an 'open society', which preceded the Western idea of the same notion by some 900 years.

With all its economic might derived from prosperous and free-flowing trade, Volga Bulgaria never presented any imminent danger to its immediate neighbours. In 985, Volga Bulgaria and the Kievan Rus' concluded their first 'eternal' peace treaty. After that both states enjoyed a 150-year-long period of peaceful relations, allowing both countries to develop not only their economy and culture, but also to establish dynastic links with the entire known world. In 1006, a new trade treaty, which allowed Bolgar merchants a free enterprise in towns of the Kievan Rus', was concluded. As early as 1006, Bolgar and Russian merchants also conducted mutual wholesale trade in towns along the Volga River.

The entire energy of Volga Bulgaria was apparently directed towards its internal development, and even the most biased historical sources do not find any excuse to blame Volga Bolgars for excessive bellicosity. The oldest Russian historian V. Tatischev noted:

> Although Bolgars on occasions fought with Russians, they apparently were not zealous in this warfare, and did not aspire to appropriate the property of others, but rather to protect their own. (...) Of earthly fruits, they had everything in abundance, so much so, that they time and again provided Russia with cereals in the days of famine, and always demonstrated their industriousness in trade and crafts.

The inherent creativity of Islamic thought and the flourishing culture of Islam influenced the history of Volga Bulgaria in a most productive way. The city of Bilyar, the capital city of Volga Bulgaria, which Russians called 'The Great City', was a great city indeed. The citadel alone, located at its centre, occupied an area of 500,000 square metres, but the 'inner town' of Bilyar occupied, in all, an area of two million square metres, which exceeded the area of all other Bolgar towns and far exceeded the area of Paris, or London, at that time. Comparative archaeological researches show, that, in all of Europe, there was no city equal to the capital of the Volga Bolgars,[6] except Cordoba and Constantinople. Within the city there were streets and squares with public water reservoirs. The houses of inner Bilyar, with their central heating systems, were constructed of wood, brick and white stone, and in its architecture apparently there were various mixed styles imported from other countries, and local building styles called for by the climatic and cultural specifics of the lands of northern Islam. Volga Bolgars, just like their progeny, Kazan Tatars, were not dogmatic and willingly used any practical knowledge, wherever it came from, thus following the early example of the Muslims of the Arab Caliphate. But they pioneered many things as well. Volga Bolgars were the first in all of Eastern Europe to smelt pig-iron and mint their own silver coins, and excelled in chemical and other knowledge required in ceramics and jewelry. Fine leather in Iran is even now called 'bulgari', and the tradition of leather-making and leather application, like many other Volga Bolgar traditions, lives on in today's Tatarstan. Volga Bulgaria also did extremely well in agriculture, being known as 'the granary' of the Volga region.

The first centuries of coexistence of the Muslim and Orthodox Russian states on the Volga presented a 'golden age' in their mutual relations. But eventual political collision between the two neighbours as to who would command control over the Volga market was historically inevitable. The ensuing conflicts of Volga Bulgaria with north-east Russia carried not only the character of trade wars, but also a political character, as Volga Bolgars were obliged to stand for the peoples, which then lived under their protectorate. It is thought, therefore, that the capture of Murom by Volga Bolgars in 1088 was dictated both by the need to protect their economic interests against the arbitrariness of the Novgorod intruders (ushkuiniks), and as a duty to defend the tribes of Muroma and Metschera, in whose lands these Novgorod robbers held sway. In respect of this, N. Karamzin writes:

> Devoid of military spirit, loving trade, agriculture and, in case of a poor harvest feeding the eastern part of Russia, they (Bolgars) wanted, probably, to repay the inhabitants of the Murom area for some offence or injustice: at least, this war had no further repercussions, and the city taken by them was under their authority for only a brief period.[7]

In any case, the disputes of Vladimir-Suzdal Russia with Volga Bolgars became aggravated only towards the end of the twelfth century, starting from the times of Andrey Bogolyubsky, who in every way tried to force open for himself the trade route along the Volga and appropriate the market, which since earliest times was in Bolgar hands. In 1183 and 1186, new campaigns to Volga Bulgaria were undertaken by another son of Yury Dolgorukyi – prince Vsevolod, The Big Nest. In 1220, Svyatoslav, the brother of the grand duke Yury Vsevolodovich, had taken the Bolgar city of Oshel. As F. Huzin writes:

> Some modern Russian researchers see the purpose of the 1220 campaign in Svyatoslav Vsevolovich's aspiration to renew trade treaties with Bolgars concluded in previous times. Trade, certainly, was the guarantor of all friendly and the reason for all hostile relations, between the two neighbours. However, there hardly is any basis for blaming Bolgars for the infringement of the existing trade relations, which were threatened, ostensibly, by enormous losses and a crisis of financial operations not only in Vladimir and Suzdal, but also in Kiev, Novgorod, Galich, Riga and Smolensk. We can convincingly judge that Bolgars are not to blame not only by the absence of big resistance from the Bolgar side, but also by their enviable persistence in attempts to conclude peace with Svyatoslav.

Indeed, the good neighbourly intentions of the Bolgars during the eleventh and twelfth centuries are proved by the fact that, in lean years, they supplied Russian cities with wheat. This, for example, took place in 1024: 'all people went by the Volga to Bolgar-on-the-Volga, and brought back wheat, and thus returned to life'. V. Tatischev also wrote that during the terrible three-year-long famine in the land of Suzdal, 'Bolgars brought cereals up the Volga and Oka in all Russian towns, and sold them, and, by that, offered a great help. The Bolgar Prince had sent, as a gift to the Grand Duke Yury, thirty boats with cereals, which the Grand Duke had accepted with gratitude, and, in turn, had sent to him cloth, brocade with gold and silver, fish bones and other beautiful things.'

However, the strained relations between Bolgar and Russian cities were brought to a permanent halt in 1236 by the Mongol invasion, which forever altered the geopolitical map of Eurasia. We may note that Volga Bolgars who in 1223 successfully fought back the Mongols at the Yaiyk river, had in 1229 in good time advised their Russian neighbours about the approaching disaster. But, in 1236, the great Volga Bulgaria city of Bilyar was razed to the ground by the Mongol invaders. The commercial state of Volga Bolgars had fallen, as in many other countries, in its struggle against a professional army of the notorious 'Tartars' of Russian annals and West-European chronicles. This marked the end of the first, completely independent stage of Volga Bulgaria history. It became an integral part of a new empire – that of the Golden Horde.

Thirteenth to Fifteenth Centuries
If the laws of geopolitics are to be believed, it is worth noting that the territory of Eurasia was historically prone to producing empires, as if the geopolitical lines of energy always induced gravitation towards unity on these vast expanses. Starting as a pagan nomad polity ruled by primitive power, with its gradual conversion to Islam the Golden Horde became a prosperous state built on the rule of law. It seems obvious that the Volga Bolgars, as the most educated and enterprising part of its population, played an important role in such a transformation.

In the Middle Ages, Volga Bulgaria was absorbed into the political, economic and cultural orbit of the Turkic Muslim state culture of the Golden Horde. It is important, however, that as both ancient Russia and Volga Bulgaria similarly belonged to the Golden Horde, ostensibly their historical relationships were never based on 'eternal opposition'. On the contrary, these relationships were defined through the centuries by an ongoing economic, cultural and spiritual exchange, which, having entered the flesh and blood of both nations, became the basis and the fundament of the Russian multinational state.

The fact of history is that the empire of the Golden Horde has contributed to the development of modern Russia much more than was once believed, even if the first decades after the Mongol invasion were very hard for both Russia and Volga Bulgaria. Whatever reputation the Golden Horde may hold with present-day Russians, facts and figures tell us that those 'Tartars' were not the principal cause of disruption in Russia during the thirteenth and fourteenth centuries. According to Solovyev, for the entire period of the existence of the Golden Horde, 'The round number of enemy invasions is 133; from this number, 48 count as Tatar devastations, including all information about the tyrannies of Baskaks (governors) in various towns; having applied to the number of devastations from external enemies the number of devastations from internecine wars, we get 232, hence, almost a devastation a year'. As we see, of the general number of invasions only forty-eight count as part of the Golden Horde, eighty-five – on the part of other external invasions, whereas the number of internecine wars during these years totals ninety-nine. For all that, the punitive invasions of the Golden Horde were sometimes more destructive than intrusions from Livonia and Sweden.

The image of the Golden Horde as the main 'dark force' of Russian history was in fact only introduced to historical science by the first Russian classical historian, Nikolai Karamzin. Be that as it may, Karamzin himself did justice to the facts of history: 'It is not Tatars who had taught our ancestors to constrain female freedom and keep man in a servile estate, to trade in people, to take lawful bribes in courts (which some people call the Asian tradition): we saw all that, among the Russians, long before that. The Tatars never interfered in our civic judicial proceedings.'

The domination of the Golden Horde, whatever it was in reality, did not violently change either Russian laws, or Russian culture. Russian princedoms indeed paid the Golden Horde tribute, although it would be more accurate to call it a tax. This tax was set at 10% and, from the end of the thirteenth century, was collected by the Russian princes themselves. Russian researcher S. Nefedov even considers that the Golden Horde tribute 'was insignificant in comparison with the subsequent epoch; in fact, after the reign of Ivan the Terrible taxes and duties took away about a third of a farmer's income . . . Abundance of land and grain, low taxes, peace and tranquility, communal self-management – such was the life of peasants in the fourteenth century. Perhaps it was the best time for peasants in Russia's entire history – the "golden age" of Russian peasantry.'

Those who even today repeat the thesis about the 'robber character' of the Golden Horde, do not take into account the very fact that the Golden Horde khans never hid their tribute in field chests, but spent it on the creation and maintenance of a ramified and extremely safe road system, on maintenance of state order and the protection of internal and international trade, including that of the Russians. The mere fact that, as a rule, a sustained civil peace reigned in the territories of the Golden Horde, speaks volumes. An impartial historical overview confirms that peasant rebellions and civil disturbances were much more often observed in those parts of Russia, where the stately 'eye' of the Golden Horde did not reach – principally in the Russian North.

Much is written about Mongol hostility towards urban life, which they indeed considered a breeding ground for decadence and troublesome customs. However, the fact is that the Mongols never 'razed cities to the ground': they only destroyed the military ramparts. Thus, the cities of the Golden Horde epoch, risen from ashes and built anew, were peaceful trade and craft cities, which did not require expensive fortifications, as the power of the Golden Horde's laws protected them from civil disorder and armed assaults. The urban prosperity of the Golden Horde cities was helped also by the fact that during the reign of Berke-khan from 1257 to 1266 the Golden Horde began to benefit from the much more advanced Muslim culture by establishing trade, and political and cultural connections with the Islamic states, first of all with the then most powerful and brilliant of them – Egypt of the Mamluks. This diplomatic breakthrough prompted constant cultural and economic exchange between the Golden Horde and Egypt, having opened, for the inhabitants of the Golden Horde, practically all of the Muslim world: trading and educational centres of

Tunis, Morocco and, certainly, Spain with its great cities of Cordoba, Seville and Granada.

The heir of Berke-khan, Mangu-Timur, continued to develop the international relations of the Golden Horde by granting decrees to Italian merchants and craftsmen for the Crimean and Azov trade. These decrees were later confirmed by the subsequent khans of the Golden Horde, including the powerful Uzbek-khan:

> From now on and henceforth the Venetian merchants coming to us by ship and making commercial transactions in the city of Azov and other cities, shall pay into our treasury the trading tax at a rate of three per cent; if sale and purchase is not made, nobody shall demand from them the trading tax. Also, as from olden times the trading tax from the trade in jewels, pearls, gold, silver, gold thread was not taken by us, it shall not be taken now either. Also, if any goods are sold by weight, the khan's customs officer and the (Venetian) consul each accordingly allocate one representative, both of whom shall stand together and watch after the accuracy of weighing and the payment, by the seller and the buyer, of the trading tax and weighting duty to the treasury under the law. Also, the parties making among themselves the purchase and sale shall give to the intermediary or accept from one another a deposit; such deposit shall be considered valid and shall enter into the cost of purchase. Also, if our person shall quarrel with the Venetian, and one shall make a complaint about another, our governor of the territory and, accordingly, the Venetian consul shall carefully investigate the conflict and shall determine the measure of the responsibility of everyone; and let the innocent not be seized instead of the guilty.

This document alone shows the immutability of the law, which one can hardly characterize as 'arbitrary violence'. Karamzin remarks: 'Merchants went from Khiva to Crimea without the slightest danger and, knowing that they would spend about three months on the road, did not take with them any edible supplies, as they found everything they needed in hostels: this proves, to what extent the Moguls liked and patronized trade.' The hostels mentioned by Karamzin were the road inns, so-called 'yams', which fulfilled the role of resting places, postal and guard stations. The Golden Horde authorities paid constant attention to the security of roads and travelling merchants, as trade played such a significant role in the economy of the Golden Horde:

> The Golden Horde prospered, both in an economic and cultural sense, in the first half of the fourteenth century under the successive reigns of Uzbek-khan and Janibek-khan. By the fourteenth century, densely-populated cities had blossomed on the banks of the Middle and Lower Volga. According to archaeological and historical research, trade and industrial cities of the Golden Horde totalled about a hundred, and the old and new capitals of Sarai-Batu and Sarai-Berke in the thirteenth and fourteenth centuries grew to rival the largest cities of Eastern Europe.[8]

The urban culture of the Golden Horde, however, went into terminal decline after the crushing defeat of the Golden Horde army by Timur (Tamerlane) in 1395. But the primary cause for the abandonment of the Golden Horde cities was the plague pandemic of the 1440s. Even though the impact of the Black Death on the culture and economy of Europe has generated many scholarly works, this terrible affliction is often simply ignored with regard to the Golden

Horde, although the devastation inflicted by the plague had most tragically affected the trade and crafts culture of its urban civilization. It is only in Tatarstan, in the historical and architectural reserve of 'Bolgar-on-the-Volga' that not just the ruins of remarkable monuments of Bolgar architecture of the Golden Horde epoch, but also entire buildings are still visible: the Small minaret, the Black chamber, the Khan's tomb, the foundation and walls of the Great cathedral mosque . . .

The legacy of the Golden Horde is further traced not only in the vocabulary of the Russian language and main principles of Russian military organization, but also in the business of government – starting from the idea of a state census to the concept of uniform and regular taxation. From the language of the Golden Horde, a whole set of words and terms passed into the Russian language. Many ancient samples of armoury and items of daily use in the Moscow Armoury Chamber and the Petersburg Hermitage carry 'the stamp' of the Golden Horde, down to the name 'Allah' engraved on Russian helmets and armour. However, by far the most important legacy of the Golden Horde, which provided for the development of Russian culture, was its universal religious tolerance. The Orthodox church was completely exempt by the Golden Horde not just from taxes, but from any intervention into the church's affairs. This protection of monasteries and clergy from all external troubles created conditions for the blossoming of the Russian Orthodox iconographic, decorative and literary culture. The Golden Horde *yarlyks* (state acts) protected sacredness and the inviolability of belief, mode of worship and laws of the Russian Church; inviolability of all persons of spiritual rank, and also all church people, i.e. the laymen under the church government and living on the church lands, and, finally, all church property; exempted all clergy, and also church people and church property from any sort of taxes, duties and payments to the khans; exempted clergy and church people from any responsibility in front of authorities and courts in all civic affairs, even for robbery and murder, and subordinated these people only to the church authorities and church courts. As the Metropolitan of Moscow and Kolomna Macarius Bulgakov wrote in his 'History of the Russian Church', the reverent attitude of Golden Horde khans towards the Christian Orthodox Church are to be accepted 'as plain truth, and not at all as some kind of false pretence'.

In the second half of the fourteenth century, after the death of khan Janibek in 1357, the state of the Golden Horde gradually lost its grip on power – a process accelerated, as noted above by the outbreak of the plague pandemic. The loss of central government was accompanied by the natural separatism of the Golden Horde uluses (principalities), which were already enjoying essential economic and political autonomy. Deprived of the protection of the Golden Horde, these principalities, including the Kazan princedom, were compelled to take care of their own defence by strengthening their fortifications. If until the first half of the fifteenth century the Kazan metropolis was the centre of the Kazan princedom that formed part of the Golden Horde, from the middle of the fifteenth century it emerged as an independent khanate ruling over all lands of former Volga Bulgaria. The latest and last stage of independent statehood of Kazan Tatars lasted until 1552, when it was finally subdued by the Muscovite forces of Ivan the Terrible.

Fifteenth and Sixteenth Centuries
With the establishment of the Kazan khanate in the mid-1400s Kazan became not only a trade, religious and cultural hub, but also the political capital of the entire Middle Volga region. In this sense it is possible to say that Kazan became the heiress to not only the cultural and economic legacy of Volga Bulgaria, but also to the stately rule of law of the Golden Horde era. Not all governors of the Kazan khanate period understood their responsibilities equally well, but those who did distinguished themselves by a genuine foresight. It is quite remarkable that, to a larger degree, we are able to say this about the female rulers of Kazan.[9] In response to those who still believe that Kazan for more than a hundred years of its existence, as the capital of the Kazan Khanate, was the embodiment of greedy and aggressive intentions towards Russia, the well-known historian of Kazan M. Khudyakov published the following figures in his 'Sketches on the History of the Kazan Khanate' published in 1923:

> Out of thirteen wars between Moscow and Kazan, in seven cases the initiative belonged to the Russians (in 1467, 1478, 1487, 1530, 1545, 1549, 1550) and in six cases to the Kazanians (in 1439, 1445, 1505, 1521, 1523, 1536). Thus, it is impossible to accuse the Kazan Khanate of harbouring aggressive plans against Russia. Russia was no less guilty than Kazan in starting the wars, which flared up in the Volga region.

The problem of the Moscow-Kazan political confrontation, which sometimes resulted in wars, was not because of any particular 'bellicosity' on the part of the Kazan khanate, the inhabitants of which were presumably preoccupied with agriculture, trade and crafts. The fact of the matter was that the developing economy and the advantageous location of Kazan on the influx of the Volga and Kazanka rivers quickly transformed Kazan into a strong geopolitical competitor of Moscow, which was also blossoming on the ruins of the Golden Horde. In a certain sense it is possible to say that Kazan and Moscow asserted their right to the outstanding legacy of the Golden Horde in equal measure. At the same time, Kazan's aristocracy had actively participated in the establishment of the unified Russian state.[10] The context of the entire history of Tatar-Russian relations in spite of all their complexity leads us to agree with the opinion of the French scholar Jean-Robert Raviot that: 'From the very beginning the Tatars participated in the creation of the Russian state. Today, they also represent much more an element of continuity, rather than any counteraction.'

In 1526, the Austrian ambassador S. Herberstein summed up his impressions of the Kazan khanate in these words:

> The word 'kazan', in Tatar, means 'the boiling cauldron'. These Tatars are more cultured than others, as they till their fields, and live in houses, and engage themselves in various trades, and rarely wage war ... The transportation along the rivers running from Muscovy into the Volga is convenient, and they cannot do without mutual trade.

The geopolitical rivalry of the two equally powerful and influential states, Moscow and Kazan, proceeded until 1552, when the armies of Ivan the Terrible after a long siege undermined the walls of the Kazan Kremlin and stormed the city. Final resistance to the onslaught came from the students of the madrasa at the Kul Sharif Mosque led by the imam of that ancient temple – the poet, scholar and diplomat Kul Sharif. The defenders of the mosque, as the conqueror of Kazan, Prince A. Kurbsky, later wrote in his Lithuanian exile: 'came towards us and fought with such conviction that not one of them survived this battle'. According to the anonymous author of 'The Kazan Chronicler', Ivan the Terrible could only enter Kazan after giving orders 'to clean the city, both the tsar's courtyard and all the streets and squares of the dead bodies, and to pull all dead citizens of Kazan out from the city, and to leave them far behind the city walls'. Only then: 'The tsar went to the imperial courtyard, and to entrance-halls and chambers, and into the golden-roofed palaces, and walked there, flaunting and rejoicing, because they were destroyed by the frequent bombardment and their beauty had disappeared. (...) The tsar also ordered damaged buildings to be razed to the ground and re-built to make the city even stronger.'

In place of the completely destroyed medieval Kul Sharif Mosque, the present-day Cathedral of the Annunciation was built in the Kazan Kremlin. Kazan became not only a Tatar, but also a Russian city. Russian annals speak about the goods and treasures taken by the victorious army in Kazan: 'a countless multitude of gold, silver, and pearls, and jewels, and smart gilded clothes, and perfect expensive veils, and both silver and gold vessels'. However, the biggest trophy of the capture of Kazan was the status of a tsar received by the Grand Duke of Moscow along with the city of Kazan, which the Muscovite sovereigns viewed as the heiress to the imperial cities of the Golden Horde. In this regard, in his book 'Sketches on The History of the Spread of Muslim Civilization' Tatar scholar S. Muhamedyarov writes:

> The golden crown with which the Russian tsars were crowned, was created in the beginning of the fourteenth century by Golden Horde masters and was initially a female headdress. (...) The cap of Monomakh, as against the so-called Kazan cap, was brought to Moscow after the capture of Kazan in 1552, and was probably a part of the inheritance of the Moscow prince Yury Danilovich from his wife Konchaka (in baptism, Agafya), the sister of khan Uzbek who ruled the Golden Horde in 1512–1542.

Russia's legacy, as well as that of Kazan, was also its ancient Bolgar-Tatar written culture, which during the following centuries had in many ways shown itself as the model of statehood, the economy, politics and language for the Russian state. Moreover, this Kazan bequest also included other cultures of the Volga region, as the subjugator of Kazan, A. Kurbsky, remarks: 'Besides the Tatars, in that tsardom there are five other tongues: Mordovian, Chuvash, Cheremis, Udmurt or Arsk, and the fifth is Bashkir.' Thus, the capture of Kazan turned Russia from a unitary into a multinational state, which was a transformation that has not only essentially altered her national image, but also made her the world power that she continues to be today. However, with the capture of Kazan the five-centuries-old statehood of Kazan Tatars came to an end only to be revived in the twentieth century.

□

The loss of statehood, tragic though it was, did not preclude the national development of the Kazan Tatars, although this part of the amazing story of Tatar national resilience belongs to a different chapter. Kazan Tatars have learnt the painful lessons of history by heart – the memory of sovereign statehood and the experience of national survival, which has with the passage of time turned into veritable political wisdom, is in their blood. In general, they know that the dramatic fall of Kazan in 1552 was precipitated by the growing discrepancy between the political depravity of the productive forces of the state and its outdated authoritarian system. Therefore, the compatibility of political power and the interests of the people expressed in the structure and *modus operandi* of the republic always was and is of paramount importance in the fundamental concept of the Tatarstan model.

Indeed, the Kazan Tatar statehood, especially at the beginning of the sixteenth century, was too often stifled by the military-aristocratic rule of the khans, under which her simple citizens – industrious peasants, handicraftsmen, scribes, and, first and foremost, her strong Tatar merchant class were refused any participation in state affairs. This lack of democracy, however limited, when it was historically called for, proved fatal. The very system of state rule inherited from the Golden Horde times, long gone by the sixteenth century, did not correspond either to economic realities, or to the long-term national interests of the Kazan khanate. The khans' disregard for traditions and the industrial legacy of the former Bolgar state and the all too frequent reliance on military solutions in 1552 brought the Kazan khanate to a national tragedy on a truly gigantic scale. Having said that, we should not underestimate either the forward pressure of the Russian state towards economic expansion and political domination of the lands of the former Golden Horde, neither should we forget all the historical excesses connected with it. At the same time, we must remember another legacy – those thousand-year-old traditions of the Volga Bulgaria which created, on the Volga, not only a still-living commercial, industrial and agrarian civilization, but also its art of peace and creative coexistence with different peoples.

It is precisely this art – the art of preservation, against all odds, of a multinational and multi-confessional balance – which constitutes the main legacy of Volga Bulgaria to Tatarstan, forever defining the human and political position of the Kazan Tatars as grateful descendants of the Volga Bolgars and other peoples of the Middle Volga region, continually enriched with further historical experience.

When President Shaimiev on behalf of the entire population of the republic argued about the right of Tatarstan to claim an enhanced status *vis-à-vis* the Russian Federation, he himself spoke as a representative of the nation, which managed to survive for over 400 years in the midst of Orthodox Russia without having lost her religion, language and culture, and, most importantly, her historical drive for self-determination. So, when we scrutinize the political efficacy of the Tatarstan model, we might as well assume that her present leader, President Mintimer Shaimiev, is not so much a 'phenomenon' of political shrewdness, but rather a classical embodiment of the historical wisdom of his nation, in the sense that his finer leadership qualities are reflecting those of his ancient and not-so-ancient predecessors. For all the outstanding political achievements, of which we have yet to tell, President Shaimiev is not a unique case in the history of Tatar politics, if only because he follows in the line of the prominent politicians of Kazan Tatar origin who have powerfully influenced not only Russian, but global political culture on the threshold of the nineteenth and twentieth centuries.

The rapid appearance of a mature Tatar political culture out of the centuries of seeming cultural and economic wilderness would be a worthy subject for a separate monograph. At the same time, the political platform upon which Kazan Tatar political culture evolved at the end of the nineteenth to the beginning of the twentieth century was never a purely nationalistic one. It was always much broader than that. It empowered itself, firstly with the belief in its Muslim cultural unity in the face of political, racial and religious discrimination in Russia; secondly, it empowered itself by calling for the 'establishment of a democratic regime in Russia'; and, thirdly, by demanding cultural autonomy and equal legal and civil rights for Muslim and Russian subjects of the Russian empire.

At the beginning of the twentieth century, two fundamental political visions took shape among Kazan (Volga) Tatars who then 'ideologically and numerically' dominated the quest of all Russian Muslims for political and cultural equality with the ethnic Russian peoples of the Russian empire. One of those encompassed a moderate liberal trend emphasizing the unity of all Muslim subjects of the Russian empire beyond ethnic and sectarian differences. The other was a fashionable leftist and Socialist tendency, which, although combative and uncompromising, never took deep root among Volga Tatar politicians. At the turn of the century, all Tatar leftists ended up bitterly disappointed in the Russian Social-Democratic-turned-Bolshevik movement. After the 1917 Revolution, most of them emigrated or fought against the Bolsheviks on the side of the White Army in the Civil War of 1918–24. But, even before the Bolshevik revolution, many Kazan Tatar and Bashkir intellectuals and political leaders emigrated to Turkey and played a significant role in devising the democratic and liberal philosophy of the country. The names of Musa Aq'eget, Yusuf Akchura, Sadri Maksudi, Zaki Validi Togan and other Tatar economists and cultural philosophers are still revered in Turkey as are those of the advisers to Ata Turk and great contributors to modern Turkish culture and political philosophy.

In Russia itself, amidst the chaos of the 1917 revolution, the main Tatar political activity brought about the creation of the so-called National Cultural Autonomy of the Tatars of the European part of Russia and Siberia, which subsequently prompted the declaration of the short-lived territorial state of Idel-Ural. This idea, which became the harbinger of the vision of future federalism in Russia, was, however, immediately high-jacked by the Russian and Tatar communists who created, instead, an autonomous Tatar-Bashkir Republic (23 March 1918) which was later divided into two federal entities, Bashkir and Tatar. Thus, on 27 May 1920, the Tatar Autonomous Soviet Socialist Republic was created. However, once the reliance of the Soviet state on Tatar and Bashkir military formations during the Civil War subsided, the autonomy of the Tatar and Bashkir republics was quickly curtailed, bringing the once powerful vision of the creators of the Idel-Ural state to a mere shadow of it.

Under the Communist regime, a political vision of autonomous ethnic development experienced a different metamorphosis and became transformed into the idea of National Communism, which declared that the impoverished and colonized nations of the Muslim world were 'proletarian' by definition and did not require, as far as their development was concerned, any enforcement of Socialist and, in particular, atheist values. In the view of the National Communists, an 'enlightened and rejuvenated' Islam already contained and upheld the Socialist values of social fairness in their entirety, and the only problem was to unite all oppressed Muslim nations under a slogan of freedom, religious reformation, enlightenment and brotherly solidarity in this pseudo-Socialist quest for the common good.

Indeed, the most prominent National Communist, Mirsayid Sultan-Galeev, is still called by many the father of the very idea of the Third World in suggesting a different path of development for non-European nations, which resulted in the eventual elaboration of the concept of the Third Way in global politics.[11] A Kazan Tatar, he was the highest-ranking Muslim official in the Communist Party from 1918 to 1923, after which he was arrested and purged 'for counter-revolutionary nationalist conspiracy against the power of the Soviets'. He was arrested again in 1924 and 1928, and finally executed by firing squad in 1938. And yet, his doctrine of Muslim National Communism, conceived between 1918 and 1923 and further elaborated between 1924 and 1929, 'remains even today a treasure-trove of prophetic ideas'.[12] Suffice it to say that as early as 1929, Sultan-Galeev already prophesized the eventual collapse of the USSR.

The political ghosts of Sultan-Galeev and other Tatar 'revolutionary romantics' have haunted the Soviet authorities ever since. No Tatar leader was ever again elevated to the highest ranks during the heyday years of Soviet power, even though some of them carried considerable political weight. The Tatar leaders like Fikret Tabeev who helped implement giant Soviet economic projects, such as the oil bonanza of the early 1970s and the construction of the KamAZ truck plant (the biggest in the world of its kind), were still too unpredictable to become Secretaries of the Central Committee, let alone members of the Politburo of the Soviet Communist Party. From their own point of view, the communist bosses of the USSR were right, because for all their fidelity to the Soviet course, the Tatar Communist leaders never completely forgot their national identity and the drive for broader development inherent in the true meaning of it.

Strange as it may seem today, but the question of elevating the status of the Tatar Autonomous Republic to that of the Union Republics of the USSR was first pushed onto the agenda as early as 1936 during the drafting of the 1937 Soviet Constitution and since then time and again it has re-surfaced in various guises, despite the obvious dangers of questioning the seemingly solid and unshakable structure of the USSR. It is long forgotten now that before the federal structure of the USSR was finalized in the 1937 constitution, the Ukraine and Azerbaijan also bore the status of mere autonomous republics of Russia on a par with the Tatar republic. But while they were elevated to Union status, requests of the Tatar republic were denied on the grounds that it had no external borders with foreign states. However, the official definition, if not the rights, of a state was given to Tatarstan even as an autonomous republic and thus the resemblance of its latent historical status already began to take shape in the first quarter of the twentieth century. The last quarter of that century was to see the proclamation of her sovereignty. The distant dream of such towering, if completely different, figures of Tatar political thought as Sadri Maksudi and Mirsayid Sultan-Galeev was fulfilled by the Soviet-period parliament of the republic and its then Chairman, Mintimer Shaimiev.

Has the legacy of Tatar political thought – so full of revolutionary romanticism and belief in national identity – ever transpired in the common-sense policies of President Mintimer Shaimiev? In recent years, so many words have been uttered and slogans pronounced about the power of one's mother tongue and ethnic culture, so many people have believed that the very idea of nationalism based on those factors can bring about national prosperity and serve as a panacea against all social ills . . . But whatever President Shaimiev appears to be as a politican, a day-dreamer he is not. If anything, he and the entire government of Tatarstan might base their sustained pragmatic vision on the following quotation from Mirsayid Sultan-Galeev's later writings, which, in its essence, corresponds to Mintimer Shaimiev's political credo:

> Culture is defined by economics, and any language is only a superstructure upon the basis of economics . . . 'National culture', as far as its necessity is concerned, can be further created and developed only upon the base of 'national' economics in the broad definition of the term . . . If you want to have 'national' culture, you must strive towards building a system of national economics, the condition of which will define the condition of your national culture with all its superstructures, regardless of the fact, in whatever state system, a bourgeois-capitalist, or a socialist one, your ethnicity is developing.[13]

The centuries-long idea of Tatar statehood, which re-surfaced even during the halcyon days of Soviet power, again articulated itself with the start of Gorbachev's *perestroika*. This time the leadership of Tatarstan resolved not to lose this great historical opportunity, because for the first time in Russia's history it could be done through democratic argument. It became possible, at the end of the 1980s, that the doors of democracy opened not just for individual citizens, but for all the nations which constituted the USSR.

NOTES

1. English writer, wit and journalist, 'Adventurer', No. 137, 26 February 1754.
2. Austrian philosopher, from *The Open Society and its Enemies*, 1945.
3. Present-day scientific consensus has it that this coin is an imitation of Bavarian-Swabian coins of the time of King Konrad I (911–918) and Prince Arnulf and, as such, could have been minted from AD 925 to 980.
4. On the links between Volga and Danube Bolgars see, for instance, Ravil Bukharaev, *Islam in Russia: the Four Seasons*, Curzon Press Ltd, London, and St. Martins Press, NY, 2000.
5. Gustav Burbiel, *The Tatars and the Tatar ASSR, Handbook of the Major Soviet Nationalities*, The Free Press, London, 1975, p. 392.
6. As Tatar historian F. Huzin calculated, 'no city in Western Europe could compare with Bilyar: the largest of them had an area of 200 to 500 hectares: Paris – 439 hectares (the beginning of fourteenth century), Bologna – 420 hectares (the beginning of fourteenth century), Milan – 234 hectares, Palermo, Naples, London – 200 hectares each.

Only Constantinople (1600 hectares), Baghdad (750 hectares, 4800 with suburbs), Merv (500 hectares, 1500 with suburbs), Samarkand (218 hectares, 1500 with suburbs) and some other cities surpassed Bilyar in respect of their territory and number of inhabitants.' See, R. Bukharaev, *Saga of Kazan*, Slavia, St Petersburg, 2005.

7. Even earlier, V. Tatischev wrote on the causes of disputes between Volga Bulgaria and Vladimir-Suzdal Russia in such words: 'Many Russians, having secretly come together on the Volga, plundered Bolgar merchants, and then devastated their Volga villages and towns, about which practices Bolgars twice sent to Vsevolod their requests to administer justice; but as the Russians involved were of Ryazan, Murom and of unknown cities, Vsevolod could not administer any justice, but sent a prohibition to all areas under his control that such robbers were to be caught and brought forth, but he never sent anyone to catch them on the Volga, upon which the embittered Bolgars, having collected a large army, came in boats up the river to the banks in the Byelorussian areas near the town of Murom, and from there up to Ryazan have made great ruin, and the armies sent against them could not defend anything against their multitude, and even, having themselves taken a lot of prisoners and cattle, turned back.'

8. 'Sarai-Berke with its 200,000 inhabitants was one of the largest cities of the contemporary world', states German scholar Klaus Heller.

9. The state system of the Kazan khanate was noted for sexual equality: this system, even in the most difficult years, allowed women to take part in the affairs of state, for example in the first half of the sixteenth century, when the Kazan princess royal Gauharshad and Tsarina Suyumbike ruled the khanate. But the essence of mutual Moscow-Kazan relations is even more brightly reflected in the life and destiny of another great woman of Kazan – Tsarina Nur-Sultan, the mother of the Kazan khans Abdul-Latif and Mohammed-Amin.

10. The Grand Duke Ivan Vasilyevich III, as both Contarini and Herberstein testify, highly valued the faithfulness of Kazan Tatar princes in his service: 'Ivan was in the habit of going round the different parts of his land possessions every year, and, in particular, of visiting one Tatar whom he kept in his service on the Tatar border for its safe-guarding'.

11. For more on National Communism see, for instance, A. Bennigsen and E. Wimbush, *Muslim Communism in the Soviet Union. A Revolutionary Strategy for the Colonial World*, Chicago-London, 1979.

12. Mir-Said Sultan-Galeev, *Articles*, Society for Central Asian Studies, Reprint Series 1, Oxford, 1984, p. 8.

13. Mirsayid Sultan-Galeev, 'Statements to the sitting of the Central Control Commission of the All-Russia Communist Party (of Bolsheviks), 27 February 1929, in the book Mirsayid Sultan-Galeev, 'Articles, Speeches, Documents', Kazan, 1992, p. 500.

CHAPTER 2

THE WORD UNUTTERED

'Asking much, you won't get little.'
Tatar proverb

History is seldom fair to its subjects. As we have seen, it was particularly unkind to Kazan Tatars, not least by labelling the indigenous nation 'the Tatars' with all the implications of bias and prejudice that follows from that. On many occasions, including recent years, the term 'Tartar' – drawn from history and carrying all the wrong connotations and implications – inevitably impacted on those evaluating the proposed steps to be taken by Tatarstan in the context of all the changes taking place in Russia as a whole. This is not the place to consider in detail how it came about that the Tatar name stuck to the progeny of the Volga Bolgars.[1] However, Russian historian and ethnographer N. Vorobyov, for instance, has stated:

> The name 'Tatar' (the official Russian term for the people of the Golden Horde), has been used by the Russians regarding the inhabitants of the Volga-Kama region only from the time, when after the foundation of the Kazan khanate and the glorious victories of this khanate over the Russians, the Kazan Tatars replaced, in Russian eyes, the genuine Tatars of the Golden Horde and the attitude taken by the Russians towards the Golden Horde had been applied to the Kazan khanate and its population. The Finnish tribes, who live there, do not call them 'Tatars', but 'Bolgars', as they always have done ... The Kazan Tatars themselves never (historically) used this name as a self-denomination.[2]

The controversy over the name Tatar may, of course, run deeper than that. However, as American scholar Uli Shamiloglu of the Department of Languages and Cultures of Asia at the University of Wisconsin, Madison argues:

> Following the conquest of the khanate of Kazan (1552) and the khanate of Astrakhan (1556), the name *Tatar* took on a new meaning: scholars in the service of the Russian Empire came to use this name indiscriminately for any of the non-Christian, non-Slavic peoples of the Russian Empire. In other words, probably all of the non-Christian, non-Slavic peoples of the Russian Empire in the Volga region, Siberia, the Caucasus, and Central Asia have been called *Tatar* in one Russian publication or another ... In this regard, the term 'Tatar' can be considered parallel to another European term, *Oriental*.[3]

What's in a name, one might ask, when we are talking of political, economic and social transition in the age of globalization? Even then, there are probably no other examples in the world, when the name of a nation would be known to all and sundry, but everything else in the common knowledge about this nation would be all but historical hearsay. The strangest thing of all, however, is that in Russia herself the common knowledge about Kazan Tatars is still rather patchy and based on proverbs rather than historical facts. From the beginning of 1990s and even after the signing of the Bilateral Treaty between the Republic of Tatarstan and the Russian Federation in February 1994, the republic and her leadership had to withstand daily media assaults not only on her policies, but also on her true intentions, which were all too often judged based on the endemic prejudices towards the Tatar people themselves. At that time, Kazan Tatars were then seen as an historical, 'naturally occurring' menace intent on undermining Russian statehood.

Has the situation changed fifteen years on? There are positive changes and these followed from an increasing recognition of the value of the Tatarstan model, including the ever-increasing stability in inter-ethnic relations in the republic despite all the predictions of failure by the Russian and foreign prophets of doom. And yet, the alarming fact is that at the beginning of 2006 the republic's parliament called on all-Russia authorities to pay much closer attention to the tendencies of xenophobia and chauvinism in Russia. As President Shaimiev has said, explaining to journalists the change to a parliamentary system:

> These questions must move to the forefront of the inner politics of the Russian state. . . . I constantly try through the media to bring to the attention of the Russian public the inadequate evaluations of the facts regarding our situation on the part of official departments, which time and again are made to sound like yet another act of extremism bordering on fascism.[4]

If the issues of xenophobia and chauvinism are still on the agenda after a decade-and-a-half of the democratization process, I am sure we can all imagine to what extent these issues marred the understanding of the Tatarstan model at the very outset.

When, on 30 August 1990, the Republic of Tatarstan on behalf of her entire multi-ethnic population proclaimed her Declaration of the State Sovereignty of the then Tatar Soviet Socialist Republic, Russian media, as well as political authorities in Moscow, only perceived it as a contrived separatist step aimed at undermining the integrity of the Russian federation and the then still exitant USSR. And it was not only the all-Russia media that had misgivings about Tatarstan. In their book *The Coming Russian Boom*[5] (which would have been much more prophetic if named 'the coming Russian doom' in light of the subsequent 1998 default) Richard Layard and John Parker also warned about the grave separatist threat coming from Tatarstan, which they mistakenly called 'the second largest of the Russian republics'.

When the republic declared its sovereignty in 1990, it was not the geographical size of Tatarstan that mattered. The essence of the Declaration went much deeper in all aspects – the historical aspect being less articulated, but no less emphatic. In actual fact, hardly anybody at the centre was interested in looking into the underlying causes of this Declaration or bothered to read and try and grasp the significance of the wording. It read:

> The Supreme Soviet of the Tatar Autonomous Soviet Social Republic,
> - being aware of its historical responsibility for the destiny of the multi-ethnic people of the republic;
> - bearing witness to the sovereign rights of all the peoples inhabiting the Russian Federation and USSR;
> - noting the disparity of the status of the Autonomous Republic to the objectives of further political, economic, social and spiritual development of her multi-ethnic people;
> - ensuring the inherent right of the Tatar nation and the entire people of the republic to self-determination;
> - aiming to create a democratic state based on the rule of law, proclaims the sovereignty of the republic and transforms her into the Tatar Soviet Socialist Republic – the Republic of Tatarstan.

The Declaration, which has served as the political basis for all of Tatarstan's subsequent actions and policies, was signed by the then Chairman of the Supreme Soviet of the Republic, Mintimer Shaimiev, who in June 1991 became the first President of the newly-proclaimed republic to lead her into stormy and largely unknown waters of the all-Russia political and economic tempest that was already raging. Again, were it not for the elucidating nature of Tatar history, the policies of this already historical figure – indeed flagship – of not only Tatarstan, but also the all-Russia politics and decision-making of the last decades would have been the poorer.

At the start of the 1990s the fear that communist ideology would return with a vengeance was so strong and overwhelming that it alone precipitated the rapid dismantling of not only communist state structures, but the Soviet economy and the Soviet state itself. In those days, as, in a much-diluted measure, today, one's communist past presented a label and a liability, which, as it were, 'spoke for themselves', always creating suspicions in one's actions and intentions. The President of Tatarstan also had to withstand those suspicions, especially at the beginning of Tatarstan's transition, when, in the heat of the all-Russia hyper-inflation of 1991 he came up with his famous motto of 'all reforms are worth nothing, if they make the people suffer'.

The political past of Mintimer Shaimiev was nothing unusual for a republican official of the Soviet era, even if his particular rise to power had much less to do with the nomenclature intrigues of the time, than with his economic expertise and practical experience. His career took off in 1969 when he became the Minister for Melioration and Water Resources of the TASSR, as the Republic of Tatarstan was then called. Yet, there were situations when his actions went counter to the 'general line' of the republican authorities. In his time as a minister, he made his ministry into one of the most successful in Russia and, at the same time, through his ministry, created a number of large enterprises producing fresh fruit and vegetables. These enterprises still function well in the republic, delivering their produce to republican customers and presenting an essential part of Tatarstan's agricultural system, which today helps to make the republic completely self-sufficient in basic foodstuffs. Yet, at the time,

Mintimer Shaimiev was accused of wasting government funds spent on the construction of comfortable accommodation for the workers of these enterprises, which the Minister himself initiated and supervised. Initiative is a punishable offence, as we used to say in Soviet days; nevertheless, the story sheds some light on Mintimer Shaimiev's beliefs and activities in those pre-liberation times.

Real leaders are created by the demands of the moment, and at the murky end of the 1980s no one could foresee that Mintimer Shaimiev would become the innovative and influential political figure that he is today. But then, for all his seemingly drastic political innovations in the field of Russian federalism and economic reforms, Mintimer Shaimiev maintained his mainstream vision of the future for his nation, which was always rooted in the continuity of Tatar history. Even his own biography reflects an ongoing desire for the return of the exiled Tatar culture from villages to cities, which will be considered in some detail later when scrutinizing the question of the 'elites of Tatarstan'.

Mintimer Shaimiev was born the ninth child of a traditional Tatar family on 20 January 1937 in the small village of Anyak in the remote Aktanysh region of Tatarstan, on the border with the neighbouring Republic of Bashkortostan. His four elder brothers died in their early childhood, so he was given a name 'Mintimer', which, in Tatar, means, 'I am made of iron'. The name, according to ancient Tatar tradition, was meant to safeguard him from all the trials of life, of which there would indeed be many. Later, he graduated from the Kazan Institute of Agriculture and worked as an engineer and then as a director of an organization supplying logistical assistance to local collective farms. For all its excesses, the Soviet system did take notice of people's professional abilities, especially so during the 1960s, in the days of the short-lived attempt at the first Soviet *perestroika*, which Soviet dissidents named 'the time of the thaw' following the end of the icy Stalinist years. It was then that the first cautious attempts to introduce market forces into the Soviet economy were made, which, as French scholar Jean-Robert Raviot first noted, had some positive economic effect, but, crucially, they caused a change of mentality and stimulated the organizational skills of Tatarstan government officials, whereby they had to unite to work together because of their collective responsibility to implement reforms foisted upon them by the Moscow centre. The so-called 'Liberman reform' of creating *sovnarkhozes* (joint enterprises of the state and the people) introduced into the Soviet economy some elements of market accounting, which were further spread by the then Soviet Prime Minister L. Kosygin into the agricultural sector. This resulted in the enhancing of the private sector; however, the communist ideology was soon back in control again and cut off the process of cautious decentralization of Soviet economy, as well as the welcome liberalization in the sphere of politics and culture. It was a drastic blunder, which, despite the huge oil revenues resulting from the world oil crisis of the 1970s, meant that at the end of the decade the Soviet state economy had ground to a virtual standstill.

Nevertheless, the innovative economic thinking of the 1960s made a lasting impact on the philosophical outlook of the first Tatar president. In 1983, he briefly became the Vice-Premier and, in 1985, the Prime Minister of the republic. It was, however, not the best of times to become Prime Minister, as

Soviet power was already nearing its end with all the overwhelming economic and political implications of its progressive collapse.

The first political implication of the Gorbachev *perestroika* soon proved to be the weakening of the Communist Party hold on power throughout the USSR. At the end of the 1980s, the communist power structure was outwardly still intact, but, in essence, state officials on every level already sensed that the ideological levers of power were giving way to economic ones, and so, when on 23 September 1989 Mintimer Shaimiev was elected the First Secretary of the Tatar Republican Committee of the Communist Party of the Soviet Union, it was already being acknowleged that this post no longer held the real power once vested in it. The most outspoken opposition newspaper of today's Tatarstan, 'The Evening Kazan', published an interesting article, from which it becomes clear that the election of Mintimer Shaimiev to the then highest office in the republic, far from being assured, in actual fact, might have been an incidental occurrence.[6]

The previous First Secretary of the Tatar Republican committee of CPDU, Gumer Usmanov, was then suddenly promoted to the post of the full Secretary for Ethnicity Affairs of the Central Committee in Moscow – as he says, against his will, but on the insistence of Mikhail Gorbachev. This once powerful position proved futile, because the top structures of the Communist Party were then disintegrating at great speed, and the only memorable thing Usmanov managed to do in Moscow was to argue about the necessity of raising the status of his republic to that of a union republic on the basis of her economic strength. He, as did Mintimer Shaimiev's government later, presented his case in the light of sociological studies, which then showed that 67% of Tatarstan's population were in favour of raising the republic's status to union level 'as the way out of the deformation of the Leninist nationalities policy'.

Meanwhile, the Soviet Union itself was already shaken by the events taking place in Nagorny Karabakh, which soon got out of hand and plunged two Soviet Union Republics, Armenia and Azerbaijan, into a bloody conflict, which still remains unresolved.

On 22 September 1989, at the plenary session of the Tatar Republican Committee, the two candidates for the then main post in the republic, namely, Rinat Galeev and Mintimer Shaimiev, failed to achieve a decisive majority and offered to withdraw their candidatures. Usmanov did not allow that and the sitting continued the next day. On 23 September, however, Mintimer Shaimiev gained an absolute majority, and the newspaper guessed that overnight Rinat Galeev, the then secretary of the Almetyevsk city committee of CPSU, persuaded the members of the plenary session not to support his candidature, as he already had his eyes on the post of the director of the Tatar Oil Company Tatneft, which, under the circumstances, was a much more promising option. Galeev realized, the newspaper argues, that increasingly real power was being vested into the running of the economy, and no longer in ideology. Thus, Mintimer Shaimiev became the leader of Tatarstan in the most difficult of times and it was up to him to prove that his election was not just an incidental occurrence.

In this world of fleeting TV and press reports, which are almost invariably sceptical about Russia and Russian politicians, Tatarstan is also often painted with serial journalistic disbelief regarding local leadership without even an attempt to research the reasons and causes of local developments. One wonders, in the words of the British journalist Mary Dejevsky, at 'how the countries that used to be bundled together as "the West" – and now usually meaning the USA and its protégés – have applied a glaring double standard in their condemnation of Russia'.[7] For all the years that people like me have spent trying to put Russian, let alone Tatarstan developments into a wider context, which are so often lacking in Western media reports, the overall superior attitude towards anything from that part of the world underwent precious little change. Even the most respected journalists, including, alas, those bound by the BBC's charter of objectivity, sometimes cannot bring themselves to report Russia and Tatarstan in the broader context of historical continuity, without which any reports of so-called 'facts' are, at best, a collection of half-truths. As one of my British friends says, the lack of context and historical scrutiny is an incurable decease of even the best Western journalists.

Any two half-truths, of course, never make one whole truth. One wonders, once again, how can it be forgotten that readers, radio listeners, or TV viewers for that matter, cannot construct a balanced picture on the basis of such ephemeral assessments and, therefore, are led to think that all developments in Russia, even positive ones, are only driven by self-promotion and the greed of the 'local elites'. We will look at the concept of 'the elites' as the operational instrument of choice in modern political studies later, but to illustrate the previous thought, it is enough to look at one report by the BBC's diplomatic correspondent Bridget Kendall, when, covering the opening of an indoor aqua park in Kazan in 2003:

> Suddenly, around the corner, we sensed the approach of the Tatar leader, President Mintimer Shaimiev. He moved forward with the quiet, regal manner of a leader who has no need to raise his voice to command attention. And behind him came the inevitable retinue of grey-suited official courtiers ... Tatarstan is a state within a state, a republic inside the Russian Federation. But it is also a signatory to a unique treaty which in 1994 gave the Tatars equal sovereignty alongside Russia and considerable control over their own laws and – crucially – tax income from their oil fields ... This, after all, is one of the perennial paradoxes about Russia. It is true that everything ultimately depends on the federal authorities in Moscow. But on the ground, it often seems that it is the local mayor or governor – or in Tatarstan's case, president – who is the feudal overlord, holding court and dispensing favours, too far away ever to be really under Moscow's thumb, however tightly the Kremlin tries to keep a grip on what is happening ... As the former local Communist party chief and an experienced political survivor, President Shaimiev knows the wisdom of keeping the broad mass of the population happy.[8]

What kind of picture does the broader Western audience get from such depiction full of allusions to the medieval past, and half-truths like the notion that it is only the Tatars of multinational Tatarstan, or even the local Tatar 'feudal lords', who got all the cream of 'equal sovereignty' with Russia? Is it not playing on the prevalent allusions of Tatars being a medieval tribe remaining faithful to its feudal traditions? I may myself be open to some criticism for being emotional in describing the Tatarstan model, but at least those emotions spring out of my own past and experience, and not from the inherent and unrelenting disbelief in all things Russian, or, in our case, Tatar.

However, the difficulty of arguing with such judgemental statements in describing the event, otherwise quite positive in delivering 'the good of the people', is that they cannot be rebuffed in a similarly superficial manner. As far as 'Tatar ethnic sovereignty' is concerned, President Mintimer Shaimiev stated:

> On the first day of declaring our statehood we announced that our sovereignty, by its nature, is not an ethnic one. No one could reproach us for deficiency of respect towards the interests of different nations and human dignity then, nor can it be done today. Such respect naturally flows out of our ethical principles.

But to judge the validity of this statement on the basis of the realities on the ground in Tatarstan, one needs to take a much closer look at Tatarstan's real achievements in both inter-ethnic and federal relations.

To explain fully what is wrong with certain journalistic reports, one would need a reader who still has time to think and does not presume that history has exhausted its lessons for modern humankind. Having previously read about the ghost city of Kitezh, one may assume that such miracles exist only in fairy-tales, and not in our supposedly clear-headed world of today. There are, however, numerous discoveries waiting in the still existing 'no-go' areas of research, be it in the field of archaeology or, indeed, social and economic philosophy. It is only a question of applying some imagination and faith, and the results may prove unexpectedly gratifying.

In the wider historical setting, it is indeed easier to see that President Mintimer Shaimiev's practical policies invariably reveal those quintessential characteristics of the Tatar nation as a whole, without which the Tatarstan model would be neither complete, nor particularly special. At the same time, it is difficult to argue that President Shaimiev's personal approach to politics and his deep economic and political insight, as well as his perception of the engine of continuity of Tatar statehood, proved vitally important for multi-ethnic Tatarstan at the troubled end of the twentieth century.

The years of Gorbachev's *perestroika* are already shrouded in the mists of legends and truisms, and very little is known about how the controversial policies of the time affected the Russian regions and their populations. When the majority of Russian and former USSR people speak about the collapse of the USSR as a colossal tragedy, thus sending shivers to those quarters in the West that still perceive the USSR only as 'the evil empire', they do not mean the crash of the rude might of the former Soviet state, but the vast sufferings and loss of human unity brought about by the fall of the USSR. When history does finally reveal the true nature of this enormous political cataclysm, it will probably bring to light the real cause of this well-intentioned disaster: the complete lack of sustained political will required for reform on such a monumental scale. The Soviet *perestroika* was the time of many dreams and good intentions, yet the naivety of such dreams and the gullibility of the dreamers seem all but surreal today. But then again, the process of reform that was put in motion was rather logical in its development, which was dictated by the long-time inequalities in the political standing of various republics and autonomous regions of the USSR. There was always a cause for conflict, and during the *perestroika* years this latent conflict increasingly came into the open. During the Carnegie Forum entitled 'Prevention of Deadly Conflicts: Strategy and Institutions' on 15 August 1996 in Moscow, President Shaimiev explained:

The main reason for conflict was the incompleteness and imperfection of the Union itself and of the state structure of the USSR. In such a huge empire, for such a disciplined state, to put it mildly, where everything was centralized, not one Union republic or autonomous republic, let alone the *oblasts* and *krais*, had any real rights. Everything was done strictly according to orders from the centre and through strict central planning, right down to the production of needles and threads. When *perestroika* began in 1985, everyone, and first of all the republics, began to speak about their rights. This should have been expected. Why? The international community had always spoken of human rights and of the rights of peoples for self-determination. These ideas fell on ripe soil. When the opportunity for realizing these rights opened up, all the ideas that had received lip service but not been realized in the USSR came to the surface . . . It was impossible to ignore these considerations. When the population rose up, it demanded autonomy. Those who are in power, when they are real politicians, cannot fail to take into account popular demands in a republic or region. The main thing is to know how to evaluate the processes occurring throughout the Soviet space and to understand what processes have begun in Russia itself.

When we try to make sense of Tatarstan's Declaration of Sovereignty today, we must never forget that this declaration was made not in the context of the Russian Federation, but in the context of the entire USSR. This declaration, for all its political novelty, did not emerge out of the blue for Tatarstan; quite simply, it was a logical step in the direction already anticipated by the republic in 1937 and 1967.

It was fundamentally a question of raising the republic's status based on her real economic weight within the USSR. Indeed, as the former Tatarstan leader Gumer Usmanov argued from the podium of the September 1988 plenary session of the CPSU's Central Committee, Tatarstan's annual turnover with its oil and industrial output was three times that of the Soviet Baltic states put together. With regard to the prevailing political and economic inequalities, the TASSR had a significant list of demands. According to Uli Shamiloglu:

> Each of these demands was a direct result of the reduced status of Tatars and the Tatar ASSR. Even though Tatars were the sixth or seventh largest nationality within the USSR, Tatars only had the status of an autonomous republic. In their eyes, the Tatars had more of a right to union republic status than many of the other fifteen union republics based on the criteria of their long history as a consolidated ethnic group with its own state tradition going back over a thousand years. The decline of the Tatar language and culture, especially in Kazan, was another emotional issue. It was my own experience in Kazan in 1989 that few young Tatars of my own age who had grown up in Kazan could speak Tatar as well as I, and there was often social pressure against speaking Tatar in public. [. . . goes on to say that, at the time] the budgetary allotments per capita for the socio-economic needs of Estonia was 1308 Rubles and for the RSFSR it was more than 800 roubles; yet the Tatar ASSR was allotted only 212 roubles, even though the economic production of the KamAZ industrial complex alone was as great as that of the Estonian SSR. As a result of its status, the Tatar ASSR was subsidizing other regions of the USSR.

This economic discrimination became the main argument for raising the status of the republic within the USSR, and was reinforced during the heated discussions of the so-called Novo-Ogarevo process of preparing a new union treaty in the period 1989–91. Mintimer Shaimiev who in 1990 left the post of the Republican First Secretary to concentrate on his other post as Chairman of the Republican Supreme Soviet, led the Tatar negotiating team throughout this process. The colossal preparatory work for arguing Tatarstan's cause was then undertaken, including an assessment of the republic's industrial capacity, which later helped Tatarstan to argue her case in the context of the new Russian Federation, with which Tatarstan had earlier aspired to equal status in the renewed Soviet Union.

The new union treaty, although dutifully prepared, was, of course, not signed because of the August 1991 coup and the ensuing disintegration of the USSR. However, believing in the strength and fairness of her case together with the lack of political will on the part of Mikhail Gorbachev and his allies in Moscow, Tatarstan decided to take the political initiative. To be fair, it was the Russian Federation itself that had started 'the parade of sovereignties', which led to subsequent events concerning Russian federalism. On 12 June 1990, the Russian Federation proclaimed her state sovereignty in the still existing USSR, thereby closing down the entire process of the joint re-thinking of the union treaty. In August 1990, the Chairman of the Russian Federation Boris Yeltsin (keen to break free from the patronage of the first and last President of the USSR Mikhail Gorbachev) visited Kazan, where he coined the famous phrase oft repeated since then: 'The Tatar Republic is free to take as much sovereignty as she can possibly swallow.' Yeltsin assured the Tatar leadership that the Russian government would not object to Tatarstan's aspiration's for sovereignty, provided that the republic clearly stated which powers she would delegate to Moscow and which she would keep to herself. Thus, the process of delimitation of federal powers was set in motion, even if only by the word of mouth. Nobody was expecting then that the reality of this process would demand so much political will and painful negotiations, the alternative being nothing less than the abyss of an all-out war. These were the grounds, upon which the republic declared her sovereignty on 30 August 1990 in the context of the still-existent USSR.

In November 1999, looking back at those incredible years and recalling his brief speech just after the declaration was adopted, President Mintimer Shaimiev wrote:

> I often ask myself: how did it happen that after almost ten years after the event, I still hold to every word I said then? The speech was so spontaneous, and I did not prepare myself for it beforehand. But then, looking back at my life, I realized – I was prepared. I knew the history of the Tatar people, its need for rights in the Russian Tsarist Empire and during the Soviet years, its colossal economic and spiritual potential, friendliness, industriousness, historical willingness to live in peace and friendship with others, its great aspiration for freedom.

This, in a nutshell, presented the core of the Tatarstan claim for sovereignty, which, with a different leadership, could have easily plunged the republic into military hostilities with the Moscow centre, just as it did with Chechnya whose claims at the beginning of 1990s were much less demanding than those of Tatarstan. Indeed, in spring 1992, Moscow and Kazan came dangerously close to such a scenario, especially as it was at the point when the economic and political uncertainties in Russia were reaching their climax.

The years 1990–91 were marked, as we said, by the wavering political will of the outgoing Soviet leadership and by the increasing force of the revolutionary democracy being demanded by the people. In Tatarstan, as in other ethnic republics of the USSR, this democracy of the streets was no less insistent than in Chechnya or Nagorny Karabakh. There was always the danger of being carried away by the loudest slogan of the moment. Invariably, with such spontaneous expressions of unruly democracy, the most populist leaders of the crowd are the most active ones. An insistent crowd is a particular phenomenon of chaotic democracy, because it is there to destroy the prevalent order of things with only a vague idea of how to build another order instead. The crowds of the late Soviet Union managed to destroy a lot, and the consequences of this headless destruction are still hampering development in such former USSR countries as Armenia and Azerbaijan, Georgia and Moldova and, of course, in the long-suffering Chechnya.

To remain clear-headed in such circumstances is not easy, but to choose seemingly tedious evolution over spectacular revolution is even more challenging. In fact, in this context, a new light can be shed on the old saying that 'the first requirement of a statesman is that he be dull',[9] even though President Shaimiev's policies could never be described as boring. For a country in transition, it is, indeed, rarely the case. In Tatarstan, as in all other parts of the former USSR, economic hardships and historical grievances became the engine of promoting popular demands. In the 'state within the state' situated in the middle of European Russia, where approximately half of the population is Tatar and the other half Russian, any major clash between two ethnicities and two versions of history would be disastrous and much more dangerous than the infamous war in Yugoslavia, because it would inevitably herald an all-Russia civil war. Just imagine such a war in a country full of nuclear weapons ...

Today, it is all but forgotten how close this doomsday scenario was to becoming a reality. The potential conflict was real and as such required urgent, but well thought-through measures for its resolution. Mintimer Shaimiev, as he later told his listeners at Harvard University on 6 October 1994, was fully aware of that:

> When it became possible to speak freely about everything, when the people had had the opportunity to recall their past and assess their present, profound changes occurred in the people's mentality. The people in Tatarstan began wondering, why do we have to live like that? We must be independent and have our own state. The process of *perestroika* of the people's minds was developing rather rapidly.[10]

Sometimes, one uttered word can change the course of history. In the case of Tatarstan, it is one *unuttered* word that changed it, not only saving the Tatarstan people from seemingly imminent bloodshed, but opening an unprecedented avenue for further political and economic development of the republic. When history judges President Shaimiev's legacy (who during the course of his leadership had to make the most fateful decisions concerning all the people of the entire Russian Federation and therefore probably to the world at large) this one unuttered word might well be seen to outweigh a lot of momentous speeches of many other Russian politicians of the time.

The word in question was 'independence'. Had he, in the fervour of debates and demonstrations, uttered it just once, it could well have become a slogan. And as night follows day, bloodshed would have followed starting with inter-ethnic clashes within the republic, where many ethnic Russian were rather apprehensive of the true intentions of the republic's leadership at the start of her political and market transition. One has to imagine, under what intense pressure the president then was from the nationalistic quarters of his own nation and what kind of atmosphere reigned in the entire USSR – fatally shaken by the demands for self-determination by its many nations. By this point in time, had President Shaimiev been less prudent and more selfish as a politician, Tatarstan and, maybe, the entire Russian Federation could be by now destroyed by an inter-ethnic civil war, which, in the case of Russia, would be much more bloody, lasting and devastating, than even the 2003 war in Iraq. All the prerequisites for such world-wide disaster were there, especially ethnic and religious rivalries, only to be aggravated by the presence of nuclear arms in Russia.

Looking at thousands-strong demonstrations in Tatarstan demanding national freedom at the beginning of 1990s, one could easily succumb to the prediction of an imminent clash not only between Russians and Tatars in Tatarstan itself, but between Kazan and Moscow, and yet, this never happened. One is bound to ask – why?

In an earlier book,[11] I described the field of all-Russia political and economic decisions of the time as 'the minefield of ideas'. There were many theories in circulation then, and many self-fulfilling prophesies which were invariably based on the assumption that the post-communist leadership of the Russian regions was only motivated by self-promotion, the selfish hold on power and insider greediness – often, it was suspected, encouraged by self-interested foreign counsellors. Spontaneous ideas of democracy, as it happens, were then being dressed in scholastic garments and decorated by scholarly terms and theories the Russian people in their fight for survival had neither the time, nor prior knowledge to properly understand. In many instances, these theories were lethal as far as the realities of life were concerned, which was more than proved by the subsequent bloody conflicts in the former USSR, the echo of which is still ringing in the air. The inter-ethnic conflict in Moldova, and the less visible, but persistent civic strain in such countries as Georgia and Latvia was ensured, first of all, by the officially proclaimed dominance of the 'indigenous' nation and by the diminution of the Russian language to a second-rate, unofficial status despite the presence of millions of Russian-speaking minorities in these newly independent states.

In those days, President Shaimiev was branded a former apparatchik who would never understand or welcome the intricacies of democratic theories of transition. Indeed, he never had a theory of his own – he just had no time to devise one. But what he always had is the understanding that common-sense democracy consists, first and foremost, of respecting the rights of others despite all the prejudices of history and all the difficult circumstances of everyday life. That is why the wording of the declaration of sovereignty was so vital, when it not only said that 'irrespective of ethnicity, social origin, faith, political convictions and other differences, Tatarstan shall guarantee all citizens of the republic equal rights and freedoms', but also at once dispelled all potential for inter-ethnic strife by a simple statement that 'Russian and Tatar shall be the state languages and shall be equal in Tatarstan, and the maintenance and development of the languages of other ethnicities shall also be ensured'.

This equal status of the Russian and Tatar languages was the key factor from the very beginning of transition that decided the inter-ethnic accord in the republic and gave lasting significance to the political credo of President Shaimiev, that is, 'Civic accord in the name of development'. In Tatarstan's case, this credo is indeed multi-faceted, for it contains not only a vision for the future, but also an unstoppable drive of the less known, but rather instructive Tatar political history of recent times.

On 17 March 1991, the population of the USSR was given the choice of deciding the fate of the country in a referendum, in which Armenia, Georgia, Moldova and the Baltic republics declined to participate. However, in the rest of the USSR 80% of the electorate took part in the referendum and 76.4% voted to keep the union. This democratic decision had no impact on the eventual fate of the USSR – but in December of that year it was dissolved by the leaders of Russia, Ukraine and Belarus acting, as they claimed, upon the will of their respective nations. In Russia, there was only one lasting result of the March 1991 plebiscite, and that was the establishment of the post of President of Russia, which was proposed as a separate question in the same referendum.

On 12 June 1991, Boris Yeltsin was elected the first President of Russia, but the population of Tatarstan never voted for him. Instead, on the same day they voted for their own president, because, as things then stood, Tatarstan claimed to be equal to Russia in the context of the USSR. This is a very important point and all subsequent events, including the behaviour of President Shaimiev during the August 1991 coup, must be seen in this light.

Under the circumstances, when the negotiating position of Tatarstan was under threat and, as President Shaimiev himself said, 'the republic could have been thrown back to the worst times of Stalinist "autonomy"', he could have done only what he had actually did do: wait and temporize. He never obeyed either the orders of the coup leaders, or the orders of Yeltsin; to him, he never deemed himself subordinate as president of a sovereign republic in the context of the USSR. The waiting game was the only common-sense policy Mintimer Shaimiev could adopt, but then, this policy was based on the will of the people who voted him in as their president on the mandate of Tatarstan's sovereignty. He could not risk outright confrontation – the stakes were too high. What the government of the republic could do under the circumstances was to maintain public and state order in the highly flammable situation, and this they did impeccably. The main reason why they managed to do that was the fact that in those fateful days Tatarstan already had in place elected power structures with the democratic right to govern, and whatever President Shaimiev was doing then was based on his awareness of this fact. For all the ideological turmoil that followed in the wake of the August 1991 coup, which brought about the collapse of the USSR, one lesson of this period is clear: it was democracy that saved Tatarstan and safeguarded her interests, as opposed to the fate of the USSR with its lame-duck President Gorbachev who was voted in not by popular plebiscite, but by the last Supreme Soviet of the Soviet Union. Consequently, President Gorbachev lacked the popular mandate, which helped President Yeltsin and President Shaimiev to exercise their political will in the most demanding circumstances of the momentous change not only of ideology, but of the very nature of the state itself.

And here President Shaimiev never spent his tenure politicking. The Tatarstan model, which surprised the world by its successes in 1994, was already taking shape in its political and economic aspects in the turgid ideological solution of the last years of the USSR, because President Shaimiev understood that it was the economy, and not political slogans, that would decide the future of Tatarstan. During his first hundred days in power as president, Tatarstan adopted twenty-four laws, including the Land Code and the law on land reform. The republic's constitution was amended in the process of drafting the new constitution and, crucially, the presidency became a coordinating and consolidating force in the relations between parliament and the republic's cabinet of ministers. The vertical structure of power, to which Russia had begun paying attention only with the arrival of President Putin in 2000, was developed in Tatarstan in the first years of its transition, because it was always clear what she wanted politically as well as economically.

The main characteristic of the Tatarstan model is that it is distinguished by the unity of its purpose. In the most turbulent of times, when Russia at large was still painfully so confused as regards which path of transition to take, it nevertheless grew and developed rather assertively, paying considerable attention to the legal foundations of her self-reliant development. In the new age, the main engine of her growth, the engine of historical continuity of Tatar statehood, was being transformed into a much wider vision of all-Tatarstan statehood on the basis that it is a multi-ethnic and multi-cultural democratic society which is where her future lies. From the very beginning, therefore, Tatarstan has maintained a clear vision of her nationhood, which Russia continues to search for, and that is: the creation of a society built on the consensus of the social, economic and, most importantly, ethnic interests of its members. Building and maintaining such an accord, in all its intricacies, was seen as serving the main national interest of Tatarstan, which did not want to run errands for anyone, but willingly participated in creating a just order in the community of nations of which it was part, be it a renewed USSR or, as the dream was then, the world community.

The end of the USSR in December 1991 came as a shock to many. For Tatarstan, it created a completely new situation, in which its earlier proclaimed sovereignty put her into direct collision with the Russian federal centre, not just in political terms, but also in an economic sense. When the Russian government liberalized prices in January 1992, promising stabilization in six to eight months, but in fact unleashing the beast of hyperinflation instead, President Shaimiev was one of those rare politicians who believed that the promised price stabilization would come 'not because there will be more goods on offer, but because the prices will become unaffordable for the majority of population'.[12] He firmly maintained that the uncontrolled growth of prices could only be stopped through an increase in production; but it was at the time, when all economic links in the former USSR were being severed and previously concluded contracts failed. The only thing President Shaimiev and his government could do was to soften the blow to Tatarstan's population by subsidizing the leap in prices from the republican budget and introduce special preferential coupons for republican customers so that subsidized goods would not flow out of the republic. But he did make the following statement: 'We should not imagine that Tatarstan will for long remain isolated from the wider market. We, too, will have to raise prices to the all-Russia level. But, importantly, it should not happen as abruptly as in the rest of Russia. As regards the raising of prices, we will not run in front of the steam engine.' In containing the growth of prices, the main emphasis was put on subsidizing rural producers, who were left in the cold in the rest of Russia, as agriculture was declared by the market reformers to be 'the black hole' of the Russian economy. As a result, at the end of September 1992, a basket of the nineteen principal foodstuffs in Tatarstan cost 1280 roubles, whereas the all-Russia average was 1903 roubles. This was the beginning of Tatarstan's 'soft entrance' to the market economy, but, to achieve that, President Shaimiev had to withstand a storm of accusations about being 'the enemy of the market' and 'Communist apparatchik', and in the Russian and foreign media Tatarstan was called nothing else but 'the island of communism in the sea of market economy'. However, when Tatarstan's farmers grew a rather good harvest in the tumultuous year of 1992, the Russian government chose to introduce measures similar to those introduced by Tatarstan a year earlier.

In 1992–93, the food situation in Tatarstan was kept stable, which cannot be said about her relations with the Russian federal centre. Tatarstan insisted on her sovereignty, but now this sovereignty was seen as a limited sovereignty in the context of the Russian Federation. For Moscow, this was one novelty too far. Tatarstan was blamed squarely for separatism, and even some of the foreign media maintained that Tatarstan's demands were unattainable. Again, in a simplification of events so characteristic for foreign observers, the stance Tatarstan took was seen as only confrontation of the local 'communist' elite with the darlings of the West – President Boris Yeltsin and his 'Chicago boys'. Despite the fact that President Shaimiev always said that he was against the disintegration of Russia, his words were never believed, particularly when the political situation on the ground developed rather alarmingly for the Russian presidency.

The power of the people had already shown itself in Tatarstan in 1991 when huge demonstrations in the oil capital of Tatarstan, the town of Almetyevsk, resulted in clashes with the police on 21 April. Before that, on 7 and 14 April, several thousand people in Kazan demonstrated for the full sovereignty of the republic. Another clash with the police occurred on 15 October 1991, the day of the fall of Kazan in 1552, when the radical nationalist wing of the Tatar popular movement demanded complete independence from Moscow and tried to storm the building of the republican parliament. The nationalist movement headed by the radical 'Ittifak' party presented such a strong separatist force that President Shaimiev and his government at the time found themselves 'between a rock and a hard place' in their dealings with the radical opposition and the Moscow authorities.

The Tatar radical opposition had evolved out of historical grievances and using economic hardships to promote their idea of 'Tatarstan as the new Kuwait' challenged President Shaimiev throughout 1990–92 with the full vigour of a confident political force. The Tatar popular movement started at the end of the 1980s as TOTS (Tatar Public Centre), which, in its search for the best accommodation of Tatar national interests within the USSR came up with a project of the

'Volga-Urals Constitution' envisioning the creation of a special inter-regional formation consisting of republics and regions between the Volga and the Urals. But, In March 1990, a radical nationalist group, the Ittifak (Alliance) National Party, was established and began to challenge TOTS for the leadership of the nationalist movement. Ittifak was insisting on immediate independence and openly articulated a programme of 'Tatarstan for the Tatars'. It insisted that Tatar be made the republic's sole state language and that Russians be denied citizenship, and it articulated Tatar territorial claims on Bashkiria and Perm and Ul'ianovsk oblasts.[13] In February 1991, Ittifak organized a Tatar convention (Kurultai), in which many Tatars from all over the USSR took part. This convention proclaimed the full state independence of Tatarstan, made the Tatar tongue into the only state language of the republic and elected seventy-five members of the newly formed national assembly (Milli Mejlis). During their second session at the end of March 1991, this national assembly declared itself the only legislative body 'of all Tatars' and proclaimed its right to veto any republican laws and decrees, which would, in their view, contradict the spirit of the Declaration of State Sovereignty of Tatarstan'. Essentially, the radical opposition formed parallel structures of power within the republic, emboldened by the popular quest for national renaissance which was so strong and so chaotic in those dramatic days.

Yet, despite occasional conflicts with the police, the Tatar radical opposition was always dealt with in a democratic way, with public support, as expected, gradually shrinking with the growing awareness of the futility and impossibility of their extreme demands. As Edward W. Walker further explains:

> As it turned out, the 15 October 1991 incident would prove to be the only significant 'ethnic violence' the republic experienced during its sovereignty drive from August 1990 through February 1994. Rather then attempting to exploit the situation for political gain by siding with the Tatar nationalists, Shaimiev continued to attempt to ameliorate tensions within the republic. He condemned the violence and issued a decree banning paramilitary groups. At the same time, he indicated that the concerns of the demonstrators, if not their methods, were justified.[14]

Instead of coming down heavily on the self-proclaimed National Assembly, President Shaimiev chose to recognize it, but only as another public organization in Tatarstan's then nascent civic society. Radical nationalist activities, however, played their political role in as much as they always presented, for the Moscow centre, the threat of extremism getting out of hand and gaining power in Tatarstan. Such a threat was recognized as a very realistic one given the popular nationalist movements running amok in Chechnya and other parts of the former USSR. In these circumstances, the President of Tatarstan had to use all his powers of persuasion and all his formidable political will to, on the one hand, satisfy the Tatar ethnic frustration aggravated by the economic difficulties of the Russian 'shock therapy' and, on the other, to persuade Moscow of the validity of the Tatar popular demands. The process of taming the radical nationalistic opposition resulted in the fact that 'the Tatar President demonstrated himself to be the only possible partner in negotiations with Moscow, because he gradually guaranteed within the republic the lack of relevant competition to that effect'.[15]

This did not mean that President Shaimiev did not have to deal with a veritable storm of criticism from all quarters. The Russian media, in their belief that Tatarstan was on the way out of the Russian Federation, was calling the president names and provoking him in public by questioning, for example, 'whether he was mixing up melioration with the role of the presidency'. President Shaimiev's answer was very quiet, but it is still echoing after all those years. 'No', he said, 'And why? Because I have a good grasp of both.'

The closed cauldron of Kazan was boiling so dangerously and the Moscow stance on Tatar sovereignty was so negative that the only way of letting off steam was to hold a referendum, the wording of which became another matter of contention. Radical parliamentary factions demanded a direct vote on independence, whereas pro-Russia factions of the Tatarstan Parliament opposed any referendum at all. The latter were supported by the entire might of the Moscow centre, which went to great lengths in order to undermine the plebiscite in Tatarstan. The Russian constitutional court declared the referendum illegal, truckloads of anti-referendum booklets were secretly brought into the republic and the directors of federal enterprises on Tatarstan's territory were commanded to order their staff to vote against the sovereignty of Tatarstan. The all-Russia procurator's office ordered the closing of all voting stations. Vice-President of Russia Aleksandr Rutskoi urged President Yeltsin to declare a state of emergency and to blockade Tatarstan, as he, like many other Russian politicians, believed that a 'yes' vote on the referendum would mean the disintegration of Russia. Vice-Premier Sergei Shakhrai called the Tatarstan referendum a *coup d'état*. In such circumstances, the wording of the plebiscite was indeed crucial. Eventually, it read: 'Do you agree that Tatarstan is a sovereign state and a subject of international law that is building relations with Russia and other republics and states on the basis of equal treaties?'

In the words of Edward W. Walker:

> Although the question was ambiguous, it tersely captured Tatarstan's position at the time. As a sovereign state and a subject of international law, the republic had the right to enter into a bilateral, state-to-state treaty with the Russian government, or any other government, in which it would voluntarily delegate some of its sovereign powers. The most provocative part of the claim, and the one that Moscow would consistently reject, was that the republic was a 'subject of international law'. Taken literally, this would have meant that Tatarstan was an independent state. Claims to 'statehood' and 'sovereignty', in contrast, were more acceptable – each had an ambiguous meaning inherited from the Soviet period, and ambiguity provided room for compromise. At the same time, the referendum's wording allayed the fears of Russians and Tatar moderates. It did not suggest, for example, that Tatars were demanding 'self-determination', which would have implied that Russians were either second class citizens or aliens in the republic. Nor did it indicate that the republic would press for full independence and international recognition. Indeed, the ambiguous wording of the referendum seems to have enhanced its popularity – polls indicated that a significant majority of Tatarstan's electorate favoured increased autonomy and 'sovereignty' but that an even greater majority opposed secession.[16]

As President Shaimiev later put it in his own words:

We were pressed to ask directly, 'are you for or against secession from Russia'? I was categorically against such an approach. Firstly, we did not want and do not want to split with Russia. This question never was on the agenda – then why ask it? A referendum is not the best way to satisfy one's curiosity. Secondly, during the period of the troubles we went through, no one could guarantee the outcome of the voting. Imagine that due to some unforeseen and incidental reasons the mood of the people would shift, and we would have a majority for the secession from Russia? What would the fans of impeccable formulations say then? With hindsight, I can reveal that while reading the Russian press of late it seems to me that a certain force tried to push us out of Russia.[17]

Edward W. Walker again:

On the eve of the Tatarstan referendum, President Yeltsin went on all-Russia television to dissuade the people of Tatarstan from voting. He repeated the general fears of the Moscow centre that the 'yes' vote would shake the very foundations of the Russian Federation and create chaos and bloodshed. After his televised speech, President Shaimiev also went on republican television and reiterated his position that Tatarstan is not voting for secession, but for the recognition of her increased political and economic rights *vis-à-vis* Russia. He urged the Tatarstan electorate, evenly split between Russians and Tatars, to vote 'yes'.

This was the most dangerous moment in the entire history of the Republic of Tatarstan. As Edward W. Walker recalls:

Most ominously, rumours began to circulate of Russian troop manoeuvres in Cheliabinsk. The Russian Interior Ministry informed Tatarstan's officials that all heavy weapons in the possession of the local militia were being removed from the republic, a move that Kazan interpreted as preparation for armed intervention.

And yet, the referendum did take place on 21 March 1992. In all, 82% of those eligible to vote took part, and 61.4% confirmed that 'Tatarstan shall be a sovereign state, the subject of international law, building her relations with the Russian Federation on the basis of a power-sharing treaty.' This was a triumphant affirmation of President Shaimiev's vision, because it once and for all allayed suspicions that Tatarstan was an 'island of national communism', where decisions are taken only from above. The March referendum gave the Tatarstan model genuine democratic credentials, which are valid even today.

On the basis of the referendum, Tatarstan proceeded to insist on the power-sharing treaty with Russia and refused, along with the Chechen republic, to sign up to the Federal Treaty on 31 March 1992. Answering the question, why Tatarstan declined the Federal Treaty, President Shaimiev responded by saying:

Tatarstan, like some other republics was not satisfied with a number of the treaty's statutes. We come out in favour of a new contractual relationship with Russia . . . If the Federal Treaty worked, I would to some extent understand Moscow's hostility towards Tatarstan's policies. But it does not work. I constantly hear about that in the sessions of the Council of the Heads of Republics. There is no mechanism to make it work. And, crucially, I have an impression that nobody wants it to work. Under such circumstances, by following her policies Tatarstan does a favour not only to herself, but to Russia as a whole. Reformation of the Russian state structure will help to create the much more democratic Russian Federation.

Indeed, the further steps Tatarstan took were entirely about common sense and consistency. Even in the heat of the 1992 debates, Tatarstan had signed her first economic treaty with Russia, which was followed by a whole range of similar agreements in the economic sphere. Politically, things did not go all that smoothly, although the first major negotiations on the power-sharing treaty between Tatarstan and the Russian Federation took place in Moscow on 30 March–2 April 1992. It took some two years before the Treaty of Mutual Delegation of State Powers was signed. But Tatarstan did not waste time waiting for this treaty. She considered herself a state, and therefore built her legislative and economic base accordingly. On 6 November 1992, the Tatarstan Parliament adopted and enacted her new constitution, which confirmed the status of the republic as the state associated with the Russian Federation on the basis of a bilateral treaty and the all-democratic proclamation of the Declaration of Sovereignty of 1990. Tatarstan's was the first new constitution enacted in the entire former USSR and the first law in the Russian Federation legally confirming the right to land ownership.

The latter was the first answer to the continuing accusations of Tatarstan being 'the island of communism'. All the other steps in the social market perspective only proved that the Tatarstan model is a sustainable model of transition, which has the sense of where it is and what it wants for the future.[18]

NOTES

1. See, for instance, R. Bukharaev, *Islam in Russia: the Four Seasons*, Curzon Press Ltd, London and St. Martin's Press, New York, 2000.
2. N. Vorobyov, 'The Kazan Tatars (Ethnographic Research of the Material Culture of the Pre-October Period)'.
3. Uli Schamiloglu, *Tatars: Past, Present, and Future*, keynote address presented at the conference: 'Tatars and Tatarstan', Marmara University, Istanbul, 27 February 2003.
4. M. Shaimiev, interview to Interfax news agency, 30 January 2006.
5. R. Layard and J. Parker, *The Coming Russian Boom*, The Free Press, Simon & Schuster, NY, 1996.
6. See, M. Yudkevich, 'The Night That Decided Shaimiev's Fate', 'Vechernyaya Kazan', No. 151 (3093), 23 September 2005.
7. Mary Dejevsky, 'Russia has good reason for what it is doing. Why do we have to keep demonizing it?', *The Independent*, 3 January 2006.
8. Bridget Kendall, 'Inside Putin's Russia', BBC World Service, 29 December 2003.
9. Dean Acheson, 1893–1971.
10. M. Shaimiev, Lecture at Harvard University, USA, 6 October 1994, in the book 'Sovereign Tatarstan', Moscow, Insan, 1997, p. 55.
11. R. Bukharaev, *The Model of Tatarstan under President Mintimer Shaimiev*, ibid.
12. 'We will not run in front of the steam engine', interview in the 'Kazanskie Vedomosti' newspaper on 16 January 1992.
13. Edward W. Walker, 'The Dog That didn't Bark: Tatarstan and Asymmetrical Federalism in Russia', UC Berkeley, 27 November 1996.
14. Ibid.
15. Jean-Robert Raviot, 'Types of Nationalism, Society and Politics in Tatarstan', http://miraska.narod.ru/tatars/.
16. Edward W. Walker, ibid.
17. Interview in 'Moskovskie Novosti (Moscow News)', March 1992.
18. More about Tatarstan being a model of Social Market Perspective see R. Bukharaev, *The Model of Tatarstan under President Mintimer Shaimiev*, ibid.

CHAPTER 3

END OF SYMMETRY

◻

> The final test of a leader is that he leaves behind him in other men the conviction and the will to carry on.
>
> Walter Lippman (1889–1974)

The days and months of 1992 to 1993 were indeed an extremely worrying time for the Russian Federation. It seemed that the entire world of the then Soviet way of life and its very existence imploded, destroying society's routine sense of equality and symmetry as well as the state structure itself. At the time, the predominant dreaded expectation was that the newly-formed Russian Federation would repeat the fate of the USSR and disintegrate, provoking all-out civil war in the process. A doomsday feeling of the End of History pervaded people's thinking. In Moscow itself, these years were marked by the stubborn and intransigent stand-off between the Russian Presidency of Boris Yeltsin and the Russian Parliament under the chairmanship of Ruslan Khazbulatov.

As often happens in contemporary history, those times are still close enough to be always mentioned, but already distant enough to become clouded in the myths and clichés of 'the uncompromising struggle between democracy and old order of things in Russia'. In fact, the 1992–93 period was marked by the all but total destruction of that idea of democracy, which came to the USSR with *perestroika* – the idea of democracy 'by the people'. Democracy became just a slogan in the Machiavellian power struggle aggravated by the murky process of 'insider' privatization, the beneficiaries of which were mostly interested in weakening the state and keeping the country in a constant state of flux and instability. In this political tug-of-war presented as the 'struggle for democracy' a vast number of the gravest of economic and political mistakes were made, which even today continue to prove most difficult to undo.

In the economic sphere, the liberalization of prices undertaken by the government of Egor Gaidar and the Russian 'young reformers' has unleashed hyperinflation, which in a matter of days devoured the life-savings of the Russian population. The 'voucher privatization', when seemingly every citizen of Russia was given privatization vouchers for his or her share in the country's wealth, turned out to be a monstrous scam, as no economic information whatsoever was made available to the masses, whereas the hyperinflation made the vouchers all but worthless. Many people just sold them below their nominal price, while others, like me, tried to invest them in the newly established financial vehicles, which proved to be short-lived and served only as an accumulator of funds for those who later used them to become the richest people in Russia and the entire world. I still have shares in some financial institutions, which have a funny name, to remind me of those days of colossal public deceit and contempt for the common man, by whose democratic choice it all was supposed to be happening. But, setting aside emotions and justifiable anger, we must look deeper into what was happening in Russia in those days. Only then can we fully appreciate the principles upon which the Tatarstan model rested then and which proceed through to the present day.

In 2001, the former Russian Prime Minister Victor Chernomyrdin who succeeded Egor Gaidar in December 1992, bitterly lamented:

> I had the task of creating a market economy. Was there anyone who knew what the word 'market' meant? Can the market function without private ownership? Look, what happened in 1992 ... The liberalization of the economy was undertaken, the prices were unleashed, and all of that was done without a single necessary law or decree. Therefore, we were forced to proceed with privatization quickly – in fact, forced to give away state property ... I cannot imagine what would happen if we had stopped then. Chaos would surely have ensued! In which case the people would definitely have risen to sweep away everybody in power ...[1]

Ruslan Khazbulatov, the then chairman of the Russian parliament, soon to be shelled by artillery, argued that V. Chernomyrdin was being hypocritical in his assessment, because some laws were in fact passed in parliament in an attempt to stop the chaotic stripping-off of the country's assets. But here lies the inherent problem with the all-Russian legislative process, which has completely undermined the entire process of Russian transition in its early years. The Russian parliament would hastily pass laws, which could not be enacted in practice, because they did not correspond to the realities of daily life, nor in economic or political terms either. Life in the country, increasingly devoid of institutions, was changing much faster than the legislative process, while at the same time the power struggle at the very top precluded the authorities from carefully watching and analysing, let alone managing the developments on the ground.

In the days when great quantities of new residential areas were being built throughout the USSR, there was a shrewd method of determining where the public footpaths and pavements would be built to service the new developments. First, the developers would see how the new residents of apartment blocks made their way from their homes to the amenities and bus stops. Always choosing the most convenient and shortest way to their destinations, the residents would walk their own paths, which would later be cemented over and made into proper walkways. If the paths were laid beforehand, people would still make their own shortcuts, even if it meant breaking through the fences and hedges of the public areas. This approach could be seen as one more significant difference between East and West, because, in the West, paths would be laid down first and the people would probably follow them, whereas the opposite is still the reality in Russia today, which needs to be reflected on.

The above observation offers a useful parable for the process of law-making in Tatarstan. Throughout the entire transition process, the Tatarstan laws were made according to common-sense practice on the ground, each practice being carefully analysed first through a small-scale experiment. Tatarstan always preferred laws that worked, seeing a law not as a declaration of intent and an end in itself, but rather as an instrument of the state for helping people to their chosen destination.

However, you cannot legislate for any developments on the ground, unless you first establish the main pillars of the country's judicial structure. For Tatarstan, these pillars were and are her constitution and the treaty, which maintain her identity with the Russian Federation and ensure her economic and political functioning within those parameters. As already noted, the Tatarstan constitution was enacted on 6 November 1992 and in doing so became the first post-Soviet constitution in the entire former USSR. This, however, does not mean that the Tatarstan constitution was prepared and passed in haste; indeed, its main provisions were devised and meticulously thought through during the preceding years of *perestroika* with a view to raising the status of the republic to that of a member of a Union of Republics. The emphasis in the constitution is not on who holds power (the bone of contention in the all-Russia constitutional process, which in September-October 1993 brought about the shelling and storming of the Russian parliament by forces loyal to President Yeltsin), but rather on the rights of Tatarstan herself *vis-à-vis* the Russian Federation. As a matter of political consistency, it was based on the articles of the Declaration of State Sovereignty of August 1990, which, most importantly, stated that: 'The land, its natural resources and other resources on the territory of the Tatar SSR are the exclusive property of the people of Tatarstan.' That being the case, the economic basis of the state of Tatarstan was constitutionally defined in the following articles of the constitution:

> ARTICLE 9. The land, mineral wealth, water, timber and other natural resources, the animal and vegetable kingdom, of the source state budget, assets of the national banks, cultural and historical values of the peoples of Tatarstan and other real estate ensuring the economic independence of the Republic, the preservation of material and spiritual culture shall be the property of the entire people.
>
> ARTICLE 10. The basis of the Republic of Tatarstan's economy shall constitute a social market economy, in which, in compliance with the law, the state shall allow the freedom of economic activities, the holding of various forms of property and equal conditions of legal protection. Economic relations between the citizen and the state, the consumer and the manufacturer, the employer and the employee shall be based on social partnership. In the interests of the society and within the limitations imposed by the law, the state shall oversee all economic activities.
>
> ARTICLE 11. The economic activities in the Republic of Tatarstan shall be conducted on the basis of private, state-owned (also, republic-owned, communal), municipal and public property. Private ownership may include land holding and other objects used in any legal sphere of activity allowed by the laws ...
>
> ARTICLE 12. Property shall be inviolable. Restriction of a property-owner's rights, acquired in a legal way, shall not be allowed ...
>
> ARTICLE 15. The economy of the Republic of Tatarstan shall operate on market economy principles ...

The 1992 constitution, which had to be amended after a decade of transition, was, nevertheless, revolutionary in the context of the complete uncertainty that obtained in Russia at that time. For all the accusations of Tatarstan being 'the island of communism', she was the first country in the former USSR to judicially adopt market principles, including the right of private ownership as such, and the right to own land, which was vigorously debated in Russia even five years later. This constitution established firm ground for market development in Tatarstan, which on each and every step was supported by additional, more precise laws governing the transitional process. This process had to transform Tatarstan from a Soviet republic, almost completely controlled by Moscow and owning all but nothing on its own territory, into a democratic state with a market economy owning its own assets and resources and having a solid legislative and economic basis upon which it could confidently face the challenges of her consistent, if totally unprecedented, evolution.

However, to adopt a constitution was not enough on its own. In 1992–93, after Tatarstan's refusal to sign the federal treaty on Moscow's terms, the fate of the republic hung in the balance and the overall situation in Russia was not at all conducive to sober negotiations concerning the future status of the republic. The Russian constitution of 1993 was a result of a power struggle, which resulted in civil bloodshed in October 1993, when the entire world media spoke of the 'rebel Russian parliament' opposing the true democratic course of President Yeltsin. Odd that in any democracy a term such as 'rebel parliament' should be coined, but I do not remember any Western journalist being interested enough to delve into the meaning of this self-contradictory term. The Yeltsin-era democracy was built on suppressing the will of the people as well as intimidation, thereby opening gates to the downright squandering of the country's wealth by the cronies of the victorious regime. The Russian constitution gave the President enormous personal powers over any democratic institutions and this was so-called democracy, for which many observers in the West expressed some nostalgia, and continue to do so up to the present time.

In this gory all-Russia battle for state property Tatarstan had almost no allies and more than enough enemies looking with envy at the republic's property, of which, thanks to President Shaimiev's policy of retaining Tatarstan's wealth in the hands of the citizens, they could get no share. Neither President Yeltsin and his administration, nor his adversaries in parliament would accept Tatarstan's right to pursue her chosen path. At the same time, another non-signatory to the federal treaty, the Republic of Chechnya, started to apply pressure on Russia demanding complete independence, which, as they thought, would come after a one-to-one summit meeting between President Dzhokhar Dudaev and President Yeltsin. In their revolutionary romanticism and euphoria, the Chechen authorities thought that such a summit meeting on the very top of Russian power structures would in itself be enough to resolve all issues between Russia and Chechnya. They never bothered to do their homework and overlooked a host of seemingly lesser matters, like the resolution of economic issues on every step of the hierarchical ladder leading to the top of the power struggle in Russia. They were bored with bureaucracy (not least the murky goings-on in the oil-producing Chechen economy) and presumed that it would be enough to declare independence and hold to such a declaration come what may in order to get what they wanted. The bragging and sometimes rather insulting rhetoric aimed at Russia and her president accompanied by all kinds of pressure and the outright refusal to obey any directive from Moscow brought about the war of 1994, the end of which may, finally, be in sight. In February of the same year, however, Tatarstan managed to conclude a ground-breaking bilateral treaty with the Russian Federation, although her demands sometimes exceeded those of Chechnya. How did this miracle happen?

Some will say that the Russian political turmoil of 1991–94 and the military conflict with Chechnya helped Tatarstan to achieve her goals through peaceful persuasion. There may well be some truth in that, as this was the reality of political life in Russia at the time, but the main reason is actually rather different. Those who know how the Russian state bureaucracy works will only grin at the suggestion that it can be persuaded by eloquent language, or logical argument. Bureaucracy is based on procuring a relevant signature on a relevant level in order to move ever upwards on the bureaucratic ladder of the state power structures. The main stratagem of this upwards-leading labyrinth is to always push things a level or two lower because of some minor inconsistency, even an imaginary one at that if need be. The strategy of the Tatarstan negotiating team in this context was always to scrupulously work out things on every bureaucratic level and obtain all necessary approvals before moving to a higher level. Thus, working upwards and presenting their case most comprehensively in every minor detail, they were able to make their way towards the eventual 'grand' meeting of the Tatarstan and Russia presidents. Presidential adviser, Raphael Khakimov, explains:

> Negotiations were held simultaneously on three levels: (1) the top level, where 'the political treaty' was being worked out; (2) the government level, which was concerned with working out the package of agreements determining the mechanisms for the realization of the 'big' treaty, and (3) the ministerial level, where specific issues of finance, the budget, the army, etc., were discussed. The tactics were to determine the basic principles of the bilateral relations as well as the mechanisms for the delimiting of powers. The shortcoming of the federal treaty [which Tatarstan refused to sign – R.B.] was not only its controversial character, but the lack of any mechanism for its implementation. Despite tremendous efforts on the part of the republics to bring it into force, it remained a mere declaration. The Tatarstan-Russia treaty, on the other hand, also involved a package of inter-governmental agreements on the most important aspects of Tatarstan life, which made it a practical document.[2]

There were, however, many open and hidden obstacles along the way, but it was the only way to proceed – ensuring every level of Russian bureaucracy could not find an excuse to halt the preparation for the Russia-Tatarstan bilateral treaty. It was a hard road to walk. As Edward W. Walker observed at the first inter-governmental meeting of Tatarstan and Russia at the end of March 1992:

> Initially, it appeared that agreement on a power-sharing treaty would be reached quickly. Serious differences were reportedly limited to Tatarstan's demand for a 'single channel' tax system whereby Kazan would collect all taxes on its territory and determine its own budget, with the amount to be turned over to Moscow agreed upon in advance. Differences proved significant enough, however, to prevent agreement. The negotiations concluded with a protocol that merely confirmed that the two sides would reconvene later that month, although the

protocol reiterated that both governments were committed to guaranteeing the 'rights and freedoms of individuals independent of national, confessional, or other differences'. Over the next two years, periodic negotiations between Kazan and Moscow would result in a series of inter-governmental agreements that resolved, at least temporarily, many of the most pressing conflicts between Moscow and Kazan. However, agreement on a treaty would not come until February 1994. Over this two-year period, Shaimiev faced a considerable political challenge. He had to secure his political standing in the republic by maintaining the support of both Tatarstan's electorate and its political and economic elite, which required a firm hand in negotiations with the Russian government. But he also had to avoid provoking Moscow's hardliners, many of whom continued to advocate the use of force to 'restore constitutional order' in Tatarstan. And to accomplish both these tasks, he had to preserve peace between Tatars and Russians within the republic.[3]

We can see that the process of preparation of the treaty bore all the hallmarks of the meticulousness and foresight so characteristic of Tatarstan and her leader, Mintimer Shaimiev. But it would be wrong to assume that it was his vision and will alone that led Tatarstan through the many thorny obstacles of the transition period, which were of both a political and economic nature. One of his main political qualities is unquestionably his organizational sense and respect for team-work, which has created in the republic a rank of politicians in their own right, thus restoring the tradition all but lost in the Soviet years. In the years leading up to the conclusion of the ground-breaking bilateral treaty a whole range of independent political thinkers grew up in Tatarstan unified by their common-sense approach regarding notions of their destiny, and this destiny was the restoration of Tatarstan's statehood in the context of a united Russia. The presidential team arguing for the greater autonomy of Tatarstan on all-Russia levels of power consisted of professional economists with the deep practical knowledge of the workings of the Russian economy in its regional and macro-economic aspects, but also of specialists in Russian and international law as well as culture and history, all seasoned in the many bigger and smaller political battles of that unforgettable period of Russian history. Among the members of the presidential working circle who greatly contributed to the new vision of Russia-Tatarstan relations were, first of all, the then Vice-President of Tatarstan, Doctor of International Law Vasily Likhachev, who later became the Chairman of the State Council of Tatarstan and the Vice-Chairman of the all-Russia Federation Council and Russian Plenipotentiary Ambassador to the European Union in Brussels, Dr Farit Mukhametshin, firstly the Chairman of the Tatarstan Supreme Soviet, and then the Prime Minister and Chairman of the State Council of Tatarstan, Dr Raphael Khakimov, the political adviser to the President and Director of the Tatarstan Institute of History, but also many others, of whose work R. Khakimov says:

> Conducting negotiations on three levels simultaneously made it possible to broaden the circle of the participants of the negotiation process. In Russia, there was considerable opposition to the 'separatist' deal with Tatarstan. From 1991, Moscow newspapers published articles denouncing the very fact of conducting such negotiations. That is why it was so important to have allies on all levels: in the circle of President Yeltsin's co-workers, in the government, in the parliament. Otherwise the great effort made by both sides on the summit level could be brought to naught

on the lower level – in the government and especially the ministries. Finally, the success of negotiations was assisted by the fact that Tatarstan delegation acted as one team, always composed of the same members. By contrast, in the course of three years, Russia changed all the members of its delegation.[4]

Eventually, a clear-cut political formula was reached that distinguished Tatarstan's approach to federal issues in Russia – an outcome was based on many internal discussions in the republic which were not always harmonious. There were crucial moments, when even those closest to the President publicly disagreed with him, but the reality always tended to demonstrate that President Shaimiev's judgement was the soundest one, because in all compromises and concessions he had to make he always saved the most valuable factor of all – the general momentum of the multi-faceted development of Tatarstan, even if, at times, it seemed well nigh impossible. In those days President Shaimiev earned the title of 'political pragmatist', but it was his common sense that led him to realize that it is in negotiations, however bitter, and not in declarative stand-off in the hope of gaining 'help from the international community' that the fate of the republic would be eventually decided. This wisdom of choosing development over confrontation will probably remain as the main legacy of Shaimiev's époque, especially now that its essence has already been installed into the political thinking of his preferred successors.

In addition to all the scrupulous behind-the-scenes work preparing the treaty, President Shaimiev still had to maintain his resolute political stance when it came to defending Tatarstan's right to choose on the all-Russia political scene. As we have already seen, time and again the power struggle in Moscow called for the participation of Tatarstan as a 'subservient' Russian region with regard to many aspects of the Moscow political machine, including the republic's participation in referendums and all-Russia parliamentary elections. In light of these issues, Tatarstan's stance was always that the republic cannot take part in such all-Russia enterprises before the question of her own status is successfully resolved. Despite all the considerable pressure and direct threats to her leadership, including the threat of applying forceful military measures, President Shaimiev stood his ground, consistently explaining his position based on the Declaration of State Sovereignty and the republican constitution, of which he was the guarantor in the eyes of Tatarstan's multi-ethnic population. He painstakingly rationalized his stance by maintaining that Tatarstan only exercises the democratic will of her people expressed in the famous referendum of March 1992. This level of popular democracy was the most important one in presenting Tatarstan's case at home and abroad. In his lecture at Harvard University on 6 October 1994 President Shaimiev once again underlined the main principle, upon which Tatarstan's political stance rested, by making the following statement:

> For three years we have conducted arduous negotiations with President Yeltsin concerning the character of mutual relations between Tatarstan and Russia. These were very hard days. But due credit must be given to President Yeltsin. Finally, on 15 February 1994, we have succeeded, after three years of negotiations, in signing the Treaty of the Mutual Delegation of Powers that corresponds to our Declaration of State Sovereignty. The treaty is, undoubtedly, a bilateral document. We made

mutual concessions. The principal thing is that we do not violate the territorial integrity of the Russian Federation. Finally, we came to a formula that Tatarstan is united with the Russian Federation on the basis of this treaty with the delimitation of powers between the bodies of the state power of the Republic of Tatarstan and the Russian Federation thereby recognizing both constitutions – the Russian and the Tatarstan one. Within the frames of clarification and implementation of this treaty we simultaneously signed fourteen inter-governmental agreements, involving issues of property ownership, military organization, banking, budgets, cadre training and so forth... And I regard this treaty as being beneficial for both Russia and Tatarstan. Those opposed to this treaty were many and they continue to accuse me. To a lesser decree they also blame President Yeltsin. Yet he, as a man of democratic principles, has shown courage in taking the responsibility. By now, the treaties with other republics are underway. That means that the true federation started forming itself from below, on a democratic basis. In my opinion, it is a great achievement, since Russia is a very peculiar country because of the nature of her national, ethnic and territorial composition.

The immense significance of what happened in Moscow on 15 February 1994 cannot be overestimated. For the first time in her centuries-long history, Russia recognized the rights of one of her judicially constituent regions to autonomous development in all spheres beyond federal prerogatives. For Tatarstan, it was a huge milestone in recognition of her centuries-long latent statehood and a legal precedent, upon which all future negotiations with the federal centre could be conducted. Like anything that is new and revolutionary, the treaty was not without its opponents, who for a decade afterwards insisted on its cancellation or, at least, its reformulation beyond recognition. The radical wing of Tatar nationalist oppositions maintained that President Shaimiev 'had sold out' to Moscow, sacrificing Tatarstan's claim for full sovereignty in order to secure his future in power. This was evidently not true, as throughout the fateful years the President enjoyed the healthy support of the Tatarstan electorate. For those who craved the spectacular, if unattainable, features of full independence, the treaty was a boring compromise. Yet, the essence of this treaty is so deep and profound that, after twelve years of its existence, it is well worth remembering as a celebration of Tatarstan's greatest political achievement of and leadership in a climate of extraordinary duress in the early years of the all-Russia transition; it was also a triumph of common sense over political irresponsibility.

This Treaty lasted until 2005, when the Russian parliament abolished all treaties with the constituent regions by passing, in June 2005, law No. 131 'On the general principles of the organization of the legislative, executive and representative powers of the subjects of the Russian Federation'. In fact, the original treaty was continuously under attack from the federal side, especially by those who always saw Russia as a unitary state and openly maintained that all of Russia's ethnic republics should be reduced to the status of federal 'districts'; however, this pressure greatly increased in 2000 with the election of the new Russian President Vladimir Putin, not least because the entire mechanism of internal treaties would be seen as one more unwelcome legacy of the Yeltsin era. But it will be appreciated why Tatarstan held this treaty so dear and did its utmost to ensure that all the key elements of the earlier treaty were incorporated into the new treaty which was up for signing in 2006. As one of the architects of the Tatarstan's political platform since 1985 Raphael Khakimov explained on the eve of the twenty-first century:

> The Tatarstan-Russia treaty is a means of settling the political conflict between Kazan and Moscow, which developed on the basis of two deeply rooted tendencies: the demand for the decentralization of power in the interests of the true federalization of Russia on one hand, and the striving to keep the maximum power in the hands of the central government, on the other. The latter tendency was the heritage of the old Soviet empire. Moscow was here guarded not by strategic, but by tactical considerations, hoping after some time to force Tatarstan and other republics to obey the commands of the 'centre'. Although the constitution of Russia stipulates the right to conclude treaties (Article 11, paragraph 3), it does not set out the principles or the scope of concordant relations. By contrast, for Tatarstan, the concordant character of relations with Moscow is a policy of principle reflected in many official documents. The treaty has historical significance, as it confirms Moscow's renunciation of the use of force. In legal terms, the treaty is to serve as a sort of buffer between the Russian and Tatarstan constitutions.[5]

The latter was always a matter for argument between Tatarstan and Russia. There were obvious differences in the Russian and Tatarstan constitutions, which did not correspond to each other in important matters, although Tatarstan always maintained that her constitution was, in fact, the more practical and workable one, especially that it was enacted earlier and with more economic foresight. On the basis of this constitution, necessary laws on private property and land ownership, as well as on safeguarding the rights and privileges of foreign investors were adopted in Tatarstan much earlier than in Russia at large. But the main point of contention was contained in Chapter III of Tatarstan's constitution, especially Articles 59 and 61, which proclaimed:

> Article 59. The Republic of Tatarstan shall independently determine its legal and statehood status, solve questions concerning its political, economic, social and cultural development. The laws of the Republic of Tatarstan shall enjoy supremacy over its entire territory, if they do not contradict international obligations of the Republic of Tatarstan.
>
> . . .
>
> Article 61. The Republic of Tatarstan shall be a Sovereign State, a subject of international law associated with the Russian federation – Russia according to the treaty of mutual delegation of authority and jurisdictional subjects.

In defending this constitutional statute, Tatarstan argued that the Russian constitution itself calls the federal republics 'states', and there is no state without some characteristics of sovereignty. The republic insisted and continues to do that it is sovereign in all issues of its own responsibility stipulated by the delimitation of powers between Russia and Tatarstan. Therefore, Tatarstan always spoke of her 'limited' or 'shared' sovereignty in the context of the Russian Federation. The federal centre, however, always maintained that it is the sole holder of state sovereignty and was supported by the all-Russia constitutional court in its arguments with Tatarstan. This question was not just a philosophical and linguistic one. Despite the colossal effort Tatarstan invested in demonstrating that the idea of shared sovereignty is successfully applied in many countries of the world, Moscow always feared that by allowing Tatarstan to hold to this idea it would be tantamount to undermining the Russian constitutional structure, thereby creating a loophole for potential separatism of the republic and asymmetry of federal relations with different regions of the Russian federation. In turn, Tatarstan argued that such asymmetry already exists in reality, especially in the field of economic relations, as some regions of the Federation are the donors to state coffers, others being the net receivers of governmental subsidies. In the words of Dr Vassily Likhachev:

> The grounds of new federalism should be established not on postulates of the models of the Soviet and post-Soviet period, which have outlived their usefulness, but on the basis of objectively existing social-economic factors and democratic mechanisms of governmental and judicial regulation of the relations of the regions. The new federalism is possible only through the balancing of interests, first of all economic interests, which determine the political priorities of the regions, constitute material fundament and the prime reason for the asymmetry of the future federation.[6]

In addition, R. Khakimov argues that:

> The asymmetry of relations between the Federal government and the subjects of the Federation is a fact that cannot be ignored or eliminated. Differences in the status of republics, '*oblast, krai* and autonomous *okrug*'[7] are obvious. The extent of powers devolved to Tatarstan and other republics are also different ... There are major disparities in the levels of economic development of various regions. Border regions have their own peculiarities. Subjects of Federation have their historical and regional traditions. Some cannot and will not accept greater responsibility for their regions. Finally, certain republics have claims rooted in their ethnic interests ... The policy of the central government with respect to its subjects should be flexible, taking into consideration the political realities. There are and there will be differences between the subjects of the Federation. This only reflects the natural variety of life. Unity and stability of the state are achieved not by making everyone fit some artificial standard, but by taking into account the peculiarities and requirements of each subject.[8]

This is an on-going argument, which is only natural, since it reaches to the very core of the new understanding regarding federal relations in Russia. These issues are seen to be controversial not only in post-Soviet Russia, but also in such politically stable countries as Spain and Canada. For all the apparent setbacks of this process, it still moves forward, and the role of President Shaimiev in this process cannot be overestimated. His credo in this respect never changed with changing circumstances:

> Russia cannot be seen as analogous to other states. She does not resemble any other country in its organization. Her colossal territory, geographical and climatic variations, her multi-ethnic composition inevitably transform her into an asymmetric federation. The sovereignty of Tatarstan was not some kind of political game. It is connected with deep historical processes, involving peoples' specific needs. These peoples remember their past, their desire for a decent life, in which there would be

no threat to their existence and would be a possibility of developing their culture. After all, it is elementary human rights we are speaking about here.[9]

When we talk of a transition lasting over a decade and a half, we may overlook the key feature of any transitional period, and that is the inevitability of constant change, which permeates the entire process. Such a process cannot flow without certain alterations, because it always has to balance the many interests and realities of political life. Some hold-ups, delays and impediments are inevitable, but as long as the momentum exists, there is a real hope that it will lead to satisfactory mutually agreed arrangements, which will benefit all sides and all participants of the transitional process.

In the history of Tatarstan, the period since 1990 will often be called 'the Shaimiev époque'. His presence in all decision-making processes in the republic, whether in the economic or political sphere, was and is indubitable, and many a time it is the weight of his authority and reputation that determined the outcome of the heated debates with the centre in Moscow. Clearly, his political skill and resolve have been tested not once, but twice with the succession of the Russian presidency from Boris Yeltsin to Vladimir Putin.

At the start of of Putin's presidency, it seemed that all the democratic achievements of Russian federalism would soon be undone. The campaign of 'strengthening of the vertical power' accompanied by renewed military activities in Chechnya and the division of the country into seven large federal districts overseen by presidential representatives, gave way to suggestions that, under Vladimir Putin, Russia will once again become a centralized state, in which all rights of the republics would be abolished. Alarmingly, the question 'Who are you, Mr Putin?' was being asked not just abroad, but in Russia itself. The year 2000, the first year of Putin's presidency, was the most crucial one with regard to determining the position of Tatarstan *vis-à-vis* the new political reality in Russia, and, at first, it seemed that a new confrontation between Moscow and Kazan was looming. Vladimir Putin's attitude towards Tatarstan at that time was indeed a far cry from his later comments, such as 'If the Tatars want to achieve something, they will no doubt achieve it', which he made while visiting the Tatarstan exhibition of innovative projects in the context of the X International Forum in St Petersburg in June 2006. A characteristic joke circulated in those tense times: 'President Putin opens the fridge and sees a jelly – green and trembling with fear. Do not be afraid, Putin says, I am only after the cheese.' To his credit, after personally visiting Tatarstan, the new Russian President saw for himself the economic and social achievements that Tatarstan had accomplished due to her unique position in the Russian federal system, of which more will be discussed later in this book. After meeting President Shaimiev in Kazan, President Putin came to his own conclusions and formed his own view regarding Tatarstan. But, as an old Russian proverb says, 'loved by the Tsar but not loved by his huntsman'. Given the considerable political forces at play within the presidential administration, the Russian government and legislature were only too glad to seize the opportunity to strip Tatarstan of her hard-won rights and force the republic into line with all the other Russian regions.

On 27 June 2000, the Constitutional Court of the Russian Federation decided that certain articles of the constitutions of six republics, including Tatarstan, did not correspond to the Russian constitution. As we have seen, there was nothing new in that, and President Shaimiev always made this point in his dealings with the Moscow centre. His argument, however, was that the discrepancies in the Tatarstan and Russian constitutions should be resolved by mutual concessions pointing out that, because of the flaws in the Russian constitution 'it could not serve as a universal standard within the federation'.[10] The question of bringing both constitutions into conformity was to be considered by both sides, he argued. Yet, the time to make any amendments to the Russian constitution had not yet come, as, for all its acknowledged imperfections, it was still considered rather dangerous to touch this 'sacred cow' of the Russian state. There may indeed be reasons for such fears, and the Tatarstan President, being the politician that he is, always saw the other side of the argument.

The nationalist opposition in Tatarstan was far less tolerant. On 29 July 2000, the Tatar Public Centre held its extraordinary plenum, where the decision of the Russian Constitutional Court was declared to constitute an aggression against Tatarstan's sovereignty and the rights of the ethnic republic of Russia. The plenum called for the restoration of Tatarstan's independence and the establishment of the Confederation of Ethnic Republics 'Idel-Ural'. It seemed that a fragile balance achieved during President Yeltsin's terms in office, had come to an abrupt end and Russia was about to plunge into another period of dangerous instability.

In this atmosphere, all eyes in Russia and abroad were turned towards Kazan, when the republic celebrated the tenth anniversary of the Declaration of State Sovereignty on 30 August 2000. This celebration was seen as a significant statement by Tatarstan in response to the central initiatives of President Putin. No wonder, then, that the members of the Russian Government and Presidential Administration, the heads of thirteen ethnic republics and deputies of the Russian parliament, as well as representatives of the European Union, and other parts of the world, came to take part in this event and listen to the speeches of the Plenary Sessions of Tatarstan's State Council.

I remember myself sitting there in the hall for guests and journalists listening to the direct broadcast of President Shaimiev's speech. Indeed, under the circumstances, it was not only a powerful, but a courageous speech, which might provoke second thoughts amongst those who consistently claimed that all of President Shaimiev's policies were directed towards strengthening his own grip on power. Considering that another presidential election in Tatarstan was just around the corner, and that no regional leader in Russia could hope to win without a tacit support from the centre, the stance taken by him was much more than a political gamble. The stakes were raised very high indeed and President Shaimiev was actually the only politician in Russia who dared openly speak about his Republic's disagreement with the new tendencies in the federal centre. Yet, in defending his country's right to differ, he also spoke for all ethnic regions of Russia.

Federalism is, firstly, a particular philosophy, the main feature of which is the ability to value uniqueness and variety giving bigger potential for development in any country. Secondly, federalism is nothing other than the territorial carcass of democracy, as it is based on respect and support of political, cultural and ethnic pluralism of society. If Russia has chosen democracy, she has chosen federalism. Therefore, any 'curtailment' of federalism in multi-ethnic Russia is fraught with the curtailment of democracy. Today, the whole of Europe relies on the principle of subsidiary relationships presupposing the maximum delegation of authority to lower levels of power. The powers that we have taken on ourselves are not a privilege, but a burden of responsibility, and the regions should be encouraged and not punished for it.

Again, President Shaimiev insisted that the most acceptable model of state organization for Russia is asymmetric federalism, taking into account historical, ethnic and geographical peculiarities of the regions.

I may excuse myself for feeling proud that day, a feeling shared by many people watching the proceedings in Kazan. The Tatar President demonstrated that the continuity of Tatarstan's progress towards democratic federalism would not be thwarted simply because of a change of power in the Moscow Kremlin. Against a storm of smears unleashed by the Russian press he stood firm in defending Tatarstan's right to determine her own future without infringing on the rights of other regions and the Russian state as such. In those uneasy days and months Tatarstan once again found itself the focus of accusations in political and even cultural separatism – the latter allegation coming from her attempts (once again since 1939) to introduce a modified Latin script for the Tatar language based on a modified Cyrillic script.

President Shaimiev's stance determined Tatarstan's position in the process of re-thinking both the constitutional and treaty relations between the republic and the Russian federation. But not only that. The Tatarstan President was also entrusted with elaborating the very concept of the new federal relationship between Moscow and the Russian regions and, to that effect, in December 2000, he presented this concept to the State Council of Russia. The key element of his presentation was to define exactly which spheres of responsibility applied to the federal centre and the regions, and to reduce as much as possible the areas of joint responsibility by delimiting powers within the federation. He again argued that asymmetry in federal relations was not just a whim of Tatarstan, but rather a necessity proceeding from the inherent differences among the people of the Federation. This, in turn, presupposed a contractual relationship between Moscow and those regions, which may choose to enter into bilateral treaties with the centre.

In the same vein, President Shaimiev spoke also at the III Worldwide Congress of Tatars in Kazan on 29 August 2002, underlining the need to safeguard and maintain the Tatar statehood:

> In the age of globalization Tatars should uphold their republic, their statehood and their constitution, as only in Tatarstan does there exist ample possibilities for developing our language and culture. If our statehood is maintained, only then will our people and our mother tongue survive.

Some people within Tatarstan and beyond the republic blamed Mintimer Shaimiev for giving away Tatarstan's sovereignty in a range of concessions to the federal centre. There was, however, a choice between keeping a semblance of sovereignty only in word at huge political and economic costs of confrontation, or safeguarding the spirit and economic essence of this sovereignty. In an atmosphere of steadily improving economic conditions, based on many links with other Russian regions and countries abroad, Tatarstan chose not to shake the boat and threaten Russia's growing political stability by refusing to engage in conciliatory procedures; instead, step by step, all the discrepancies with the Russian constitution were removed from the single legal entity of Russia. It was not an easy job, especially given Tatarstan's insistence on securing its unique legal status within the Russian federation and therefore she fought hard to retain the reference to her limited sovereignty in her amended constitution. Today, the main statutes of Tatarstan's constitution are as follows:

1. The Republic of Tatarstan is a democratic constitutional State associated with the Russian Federation by the Constitution of the Russian Federation, the Constitution of the Republic of Tatarstan and the Treaty between the Russian Federation and the Republic of Tatarstan 'On Delimitation of Jurisdictional Subjects and Mutual Delegation of Powers between the State Bodies of the Russian Federation and the State Bodies of the Republic of Tatarstan', and a subject of the Russian Federation. The sovereignty of the Republic of Tatarstan shall consist in full possession of the State authority (legislative, executive and judicial) beyond the competence of the Russian Federation and powers of the Russian Federation in the sphere of shared competence of the Russian Federation and the Republic of Tatarstan and shall be an inalienable qualitative status of the Republic of Tatarstan.
2. The Republic of Tatarstan and Tatarstan shall be equivalent names.
3. The status of the Republic of Tatarstan may not be altered without the mutual consent of the Republic of Tatarstan and the Russian Federation. The borders of the Republic of Tatarstan may not be altered without its consent.
4. Within its competence the Republic of Tatarstan shall independently participate in international and foreign economic relations.

Article 2
The individual, his rights and freedoms, shall be the highest values. The recognition, observance and protection of human and civil rights and freedoms shall be the obligation of the Republic of Tatarstan.

Article 3
1. The Sovereignty of the Republic of Tatarstan shall lie in its multinational people, which shall be the only source of power in the Republic of Tatarstan
2. The people shall exercise their power directly, through the state bodies and the bodies of the local self-government.
3. The supreme direct expression of the people's sovereignty shall be a referendum and free elections.
4. The Constitution of the Republic of Tatarstan and its amendments shall be adopted by the State Council of the Republic of Tatarstan or by referendum.
5. No one may usurp sovereign powers in the Republic of Tatarstan. The seizure of power or the usurpation of the State's competences shall be prosecuted by the federal law.

Article 4
1. Beyond the competence of the Russian Federation, shared competence of the Russian Federation and its subjects, the Republic of Tatarstan shall exercise its

own legal regulation, including adoption of statutes and other normative legal acts.
2. In case of contradiction between a federal law and a normative legal act of the Republic of Tatarstan issued on subjects belonging to the jurisdiction of the Republic of Tatarstan, the normative legal act of the Republic of Tatarstan shall prevail.

This amended version of the Constitution was signed in law by President Mintimer Shaimiev on 26 April 2002. Today, Tatarstan stands by it, even if certain circles of the federal power are still not happy with even the mentioning of the term 'sovereignty' in the constitution of Tatarstan. However, at this new crossroads of the history of the Tatar statehood, the political weight and will of the president of Tatarstan were crucial in seeing the task of preserving the spirit of the Declaration of State Sovereignty through all of the legal and political obstacles. The concessions made did not, in effect, touch the fundamentals of Tatarstan's unique position within the Russian Federation, and the main document of the republic is able to weather and accommodate any surprises of the all-Russia transition period. For instance, when, according to President Putin's decree that the election of regional governors would be replaced by a procedure for their appointment by the centre, subject to approval by the local parliaments, Tatarstan did not change its constitutional provision on the election of her president, but rather suspended the relevant article 91 and other respective articles, anticipating better times to come. Indeed, many constitutional lawyers, also in Moscow, recognize that the laws of Tatarstan are in many respects better crafted and much more workable than the relevant central laws – for example, the Tatarstan Land Code or the Law on Foreign Investment.[11] However, it has to be said that at the time of writing this book, the main political battle between Kazan and Moscow concerning the new bilateral treaty between Tatarstan and the Russian Federation was still to be resolved.

The first 'big' treaty of 1994 was effectively abolished by the June 2005 decree of the president of the Russian Federation and, strictly speaking, the judicial relationship between Tatarstan and Russia hung in a legal vacuum. However, Tatarstan, in the person of her president, persuaded President Putin of the necessity of having the treaty-based relations between Kazan and Moscow, although it was not at all easy at the beginning of President Putin's presidency. The tenth anniversary of the 'big' treaty on 15 February 2004 was celebrated in Kazan without much publicity, but already in October of that year a new working group was formed for the purpose of discussing and preparing amendments in the 'big' Treaty. The delegations from Tatarstan and Russia were headed respectively by the Speaker of the State Council of the Tatarstan Farit Mukhametshin and the Plenipotentiary Representative of the Russian President in the Volga federal district Sergei Kirienko. The proceedings were kept all but secret, but one can imagine what heated debates were going on behind the closed doors, especially on the subject of Tatarstan's limited sovereignty.

However, at the end of 2005, Tatarstan's State Council approved the provisions of the amended treaty as presented by the Republic's President Mintimer Shaimiev. 'Times are a-changing', so it is said, but the fact also is that the Treaty did indeed require amendments reflecting the political, and, moreover, economic realities of Russia in 2005. The Russian Federation grew much stronger politically and economically and, importantly, her economic development since the beginning of Putin's presidency ever more resembled the innovative ways of Tatarstan. In this atmosphere, the interests of the republic and her *Realpolitik* really did dictate that Tatarstan harmonize its laws with the federal legislation.

Nevertheless, President Shaimiev gave due credit to the 1994 Russia-Tatarstan treaty by saying:

> ... in the complex political situation of those years the Treaty clarified and stabilized the relations with the federal centre. It also proved to be an important stabilizing factor in Tatarstan herself. Precisely from 1994 Tatarstan entered the period of constructive political activity and economic growth. During the period of our transition to a market economy we, very importantly, accomplished the division of property with the federal centre, determined the ownership of mineral resources, worked out our privatization policy, addressed social security measures for our population, and began to address the programme of liquidating our ramshackle dwellings, develop our policy of foreign activity and established certain traditions linking us with the outside world. At the beginning of 1990s we openly said that our policies of 'soft entrance to the market' would be temporary, after which we would join the common legal and taxation framework of our country. The transition period in Russia is now almost over – the time has come to sign a new treaty.

The treaty approved by the State Council of Tatarstan and sent to the Russian presidency reflects the amendments in the republic's constitution, but still retains the spirit and main achievements of the 1994 treaty in securing Tatarstan's right to her own resources and economic policies, including those in the international sphere. It also safeguards the rights of the indigenous population in relation to the development of their culture and upholds the constitutional provision that the president of Tatarstan should be a fluent speaker of both the Russian and Tatar languages.

In losing some independence as regards macro-economic decisions, Tatarstan used the new treaty to secure federal commitment to particular problems of the republican economy, including the problems in the oil and industrial sectors which are crying out for technological rejuvenation and renovation requiring massive capital investment. In making her way along the thorny road of transition, Tatarstan with all her evident successes recognizes the importance of benefits accruing from economic cooperation and coordination with the federal centre, which is now awash with money for viable investment programmes, in which Tatarstan has little to learn from other regions of Russia, having pioneered many such programmes on her own soil.

Politically, the new treaty may seem a far cry from the previous one. But, crucially, Tatarstan has managed to include in the preamble of the new treaty the condition that it is being concluded 'on the basis of the people's will expressed in the 21 March 1992 referendum and on the basis of the historical, socio-cultural and other peculiarities of the Republic of Tatarstan'. By this, Tatarstan confirmed and highlighted the fact that her demands and requirements in the context of Russian federalism are justified – not by some caprice of 'the elite', but by her democratic right to grow and develop as her multi-ethnic population sees fit.

This momentum of the Tatar statehood, so long latent in the conscience and aspirations of the Tatar nation, will be carried far beyond the 'Shaimiev époque' by his successors, but his towering political figure will surely be remembered in the annals of not only Tatar, but all-Russia history. His will be the story of a man who never lost his head and power of reason in the most adverse period of recent Russian history and skilfully and courageously maintained the only thing he was there to maintain – the drive of his people to secure and express their right to independent thinking and cultural development based on economic and political freedom to create 'the common good'.

It will be interesting to see how this momentum is used in the yet most important undertaking of Tatarstan in the twenty-first century – the resurrection of her capital as one of the economic and political centres of all Eurasia, which will be the next topic to be addressed in our book.

NOTES

1. V. Chernomyrdin, interview, *Moscovskyi Comsomolets*, 29 June 2001.
2. Raphael Khakimov, 'Prospects of Federalism in Russia: A View from Tatarstan', http://federalmcart.ksu.ru.publications/khakimov2.htm.
3. Edward W. Walker, ibid.
4. Ibid.
5. Raphael Khakimov, ibid.
6. V. Likhachev, 'On the Path of Law and Fairness', Moscow, 1997.
7. The terms for different federal territories of Russia.
8. R. Khakimov, ibid.
9. M. Shaimiev, speech to the State Council of Tatarstan on 30 August 1996.
10. M. Shaimiev, ibid.
11. 'President of Tatarstan Will Press for Complete Divorce Between the Regions and the Centre', 'The Business Press' internet portal, 1 January 2001, http://www.business-press.ru

CHAPTER 4

KAZAN GATEWAY

> For a city consists in men, and not in
> walls nor in ships empty of men.
>
> *Nicias (c. 470–413 BC)*
>
> Everything should be made as simple as
> possible, but not simpler.
>
> *Albert Einstein (1879–1955)*

From the beginning of the eighteenth century, Russia always presented two faces to the outside world, which corresponded to the culture and way of life of her two capitals, Moscow and St Petersburg. Depending on circumstances, the historical emphasis shifted from one to the other, which in turn engendered a certain sense of rivalry between these two great cities. Thus, Moscow, today, is now perceived as the Russian state capital of power and wealth, whereas St Petersburg, the *northern* capital, is acknowledged as Russia's capital of cultural enlightenment and reformist traditions.

At the onset of the third millennium of Russian history, however, it is the city of Kazan that increasingly is being called the third, *Oriental* capital of Russia. Historically, it was, of course, the ancient Russian gateway to the East, yet since the 1990s it has become a new, ever more widening gateway to the less evident, but immensely important multi-ethnic reality of Russian life.

Try as I must to remain neutral in assessing the Tatarstan model in the transitional phase of her centuries-long history, I am bound to say it is particularly difficult for me to offer a truly dispassionate view of Kazan's history. This is partly because I am myself a Kazanian – an example of the flesh and blood of this city, the significance of which for Russian and world history is much higher and considerably deeper than it is usually presumed. Certainly, however, it is much less to do with me as a person, than with realities of history. In my conscious life, I have witnessed only half a century of the millennial life of Kazan, but even that has been enough to realize her extraordinary capacity for change, whilst retaining the inner core of her traditional values, and immense creative drive enabling her to survive the vicissitudes of history and address the challenges of the future.

I recently wrote a book which traces the story of Kazan as a city with a heart and soul of her own.[1] Her heart is, of course, the ancient Kazan Kremlin, yet her soul is, in my view, the soul of an emancipated, modest, hard-working, compassionate, beautiful, and at the same time naturally imperious and proud Tatar woman, whose common sense is always there when it comes to keeping peace in the family.

The true story of Kazan may be an unexpected eye-opener for anyone seeking to understand the history of Russia. In fact, Kazan's standing in Russian history is best described with the suggestion that, given other circumstances, she could have become the capital of Russia rather than Moscow – an assumption, which is actually not so far-fetched.

Indeed, Kazan was first identified in the middle of the tenth century as a trading post on the Kazanka river, close to its confluence with the Volga, and soon became a bulwark against the persistent Viking drive down the medieval Great Volga Waterway.

During the eleventh and twelth centuries Kazan became a northern frontier town of Volga Bulgaria – a prosperous and peaceful Islamic polity located on the borders of present-day Tatarstan from the ninth until the beginning of the thirteenth centuries, when, as we have seen, it fell prey to the Mongol onslaught from the Far East. The Turkic tribes of the Volga Bulgars, whose direct progeny Kazan Tatars are, built a great civilization which is easily discernible in the cultural and economic features of the Kazan Tatar nation, and there is a bitter irony of history insofar as the Mongol assault, which ruined the growing Volga Bulgar economic and cultural dominance in the region, subsequently came to be called *the Tatar invasion* in both Russian and foreign annals and chronicles.

Be that as it may, during the thirteenth and fourteenth centuries, Kazan, having embraced the flow of refugees from the burnt-down and destroyed Volga Bulgar cities, became the capital of a separate princedom within the framework of the Golden Horde. Her favourable geopolitical location made Kazan a rightful heir to the Volga Bulgaria markets and, after becoming in the middle of the fifteenth century the capital of the Kazan khanate, Kazan soon prospered economically and culturally, thus becoming a formidable political rival and economic competitor to the growing Moscow princedom.

With this continuing economic and political rivalry, at the end of the fifteenth to the beginning of the sixteenth centuries, the historical fate of today's Russia long hung in the balance, but was finally shifted towards Moscow after the bloody conquest of Kazan in 1552.

History has no 'ifs', but in the middle of the sixteenth century Kazan was indeed much larger and more economically prosperous than Moscow, and the influence of the Kazan khanate reached much further to the east and south of today's Russian Federation than Moscow's influence to the north and west of it. However, with the conquest of Kazan, the Great Duke of Muscovy assumed the crown of Kazan khans and, with it, the kingly title and status of the Russian tsar.

Thus, Kazan and its khanate had formed the historical nucleus of the Russian empire and today's Russian Federation. Despite being called 'the Gateway to the Orient' by its conqueror Ivan the Terrible, and then by a succession of Russian emperors, including Peter the Great and Katherine the Great in the eighteenth century, in the nineteenth and twentieth centuries Kazan was reduced to the status of a Russian provincial town, even if during the Soviet period it bore the not-so-meaningful title of 'the capital of the Tatar

Autonomous Soviet Socialist Republic'. And yet, as we will see, the city never forgot its erstwhile history and always reticently and warily entertained the dream of regaining at least some features of its former grandeur and glory.

The lofty title of Oriental capital, though long coming by way of recognition, was repeated many times during the August 2005 millennium celebrations, if not officially, then at least in spirit. It was especially appropriate, of course, on the occasion of the millennium of the foundation of the city of Kazan, which was marked as an all-Russia state event according to the consecutive official decrees of President Boris Yeltsin and his successor, President Vladimir Putin.

The new *de facto* status of Kazan was further reinforced by the fact that on 26–27 August 2005, the meeting of the Russian State Council and the CIS (the Commonwealth of Independent States of the former USSR) summit was held in this city, when important issues of international importance concerning the Russian state were discussed. The issues on the agenda included the CIS Single Economic Space agreements and the resolution of long-standing conflicts like the conflict in Nagorny-Karabakh and the Trans-Dniestr region. The August 2005 meeting also meant that all heads of the Russian regions and the leaders of the CIS states (with the notable exception of the leader of Turkmenistan who sent an official to represent him) were present at Kazan's grand jubilee.

There was much for the leaders to see in the Tatar capital, and accordingly a special programme of events and sightseeing was hosted by the President of the Republic Mintimer Shaimiev. During this much-publicized celebration of his republic's achievements, he wisely took a low profile – in the true time-tested Tatar fashion of not boasting about what is really dear to you, not least because the republic's self-evident success could easily have provoked unnecessary jealousies among his fellow heads of the Russian federal regions. There was no need of special publicity, nor a high-profile advertising campaign on the part of the man who, curiously, made virtually no major mistakes during his tenure as the leader of Tatarstan, despite the fact that his responsibilities as leader in this capacity were completely unprecedented for any politician before him.

Indeed, the transfiguration of Kazan over the last fifteen years was indeed striking not only to its guests, but also to its ordinary townsfolk who, understandably tired of daily hardships like road closures and muddy detours, were relieved that the job of rejuvenating the city's infrastructure was finally and successfully completed. Comparing the time-scale and order of magnitude of this job, it would be not too fanciful to repeat President Putin's conclusion that 'in recent years Kazan has changed more than in the previous one thousand years'.[2] Indeed, the magnitude of this urban metamorphosis is truly amazing. Ahead of its millennium Kazan underwent not just a simple, though still very expensive, face-lift, but an almost complete overhaul of her urban infrastructure. What happened to Kazan was less of a renovation, but more of a true resurrection of the city. Of course, without a great deal of laborious preparatory work and massive political persuasion this could not have happened in any country, let alone such a mistrustful one as Russia.

Since 1 September 1999, when President Boris Yeltsin signed his decree 'On commemorating the 1000-year-anniversary of the foundation of Kazan' and, further, since 28 January 2000, when the then acting President Vladimir Putin became the chairman of the all-Russia Commission for the Kazan Millennium, the entire Russian Federation has contributed towards this revitalization of Kazan as 'one of the most ancient cities of the country and a large political, research-and-production and cultural centre of Russia, which has made a great contribution to the treasury of world civilization'. The fact that, upon becoming the bona fide President of Russia, Vladimir Putin did not delegate his responsibilities as the Chairman of the said Commission to anybody else, reveals the importance he and his entourage placed on this event. A complex federal programme of preparations of the city for the millennium was then devised and put in place with the closest possible cooperation of the Tatarstan authorities and the Moscow federal centre.

Within the framework of this federal programme, twenty Russian ministries were involved in preparations for the millennium, together with the participation of representatives from forty-four states and eighty-three cities worldwide. Respective agreements were concluded with more than ten different international organizations, including the Council of Europe and the International Centre for Studies of Islamic History, Art and Culture (ICSIHAC), who actively participated in the millennium preparations.

After a meeting in June 2003 in the Kazan Kremlin, President Mintimer Shaimiev and the UNESCO Secretary-General Koitiro Matsuura signed a Protocol concerning UNESCO's participation in Kazan's millennium preparations. In October 2003, the general conference of UNESCO in Paris included Kazan's thousand-year anniversary as well as the bicentenary of Kazan State University into the Calendar of UNESCO's Memorable Dates. And that was not the only example of recognition of Kazan at international level.

In Spain, in April 2003, the Administrative Council of the Organization of the Cities of World Heritage decided to create the Euro-Asian branch of this organization with headquarters in Kazan. In April 2004, under the joint resolution of the World Organization of the United Cities and Local authorities and the Congress of municipal formations of the Russian Federation a constituent session of the regional branch of the World Organization of the United Cities and Local authorities of Russia and the CIS was held in Kazan, which resulted in the establishment of the regional Euro-Asian branch of this organization with headquarters in Kazan.

In June 2004, the International Conference of the Cities of World Heritage of Eurasia took place in Kazan. Appealing to the participants of this conference, the President of Tatarstan again spoke about the role of Kazan as a model of inter-religious and cultural understanding, especially noting that 'on the territory of the Kazan Kremlin a Christian cathedral and a Muslim place of worship stand side-by-side, presenting a symbol of peaceful co-existence of various creeds and cultures'.

The latter event was inextricably linked to the much broader objective of maintaining and developing the economic, scientific and cultural relations of Kazan internationally. One such example is the series of international conferences entitled 'The Great Volga Waterway', which have been held in Kazan annually since August 2001, playing an especially important role during the millennium years. As a result of this international scholarly work, in 2003 the General conference of UNESCO passed a resolution to include the sub-theme of

'The Great Volga Waterway' into the interdisciplinary scientific project of the ongoing development of the Volga-Caspian region.

The growing global recognition of the significance of Kazan was expressed, among other things, in the fact that, in 2002, Kazan received in the Moroccan city of Marrakech the UNESCO award for Promotion of Peace, and, in 2003, on the Greek island of Rhodes – a diploma for her contribution towards the preservation of World Heritage.

For all the relevance of the international appreciation of Kazan, her all-Russia significance as the centre of the government of the Tatarstan Republic and a large economic, scientific, cultural and sports centre of the Russian Federation has particular importance. During the period immediately preceding the Kazan millennium, huge efforts and finance were directed towards making the capital of Tatarstan worthy of her anniversary. Town-planning efforts, the like of which Kazan had never seen, brought their results in a very short time against all economic odds and in spite of many hardships arising in the all-Russia transition from centralized Soviet planning to a multi-layered market economy. The results of these combined efforts are now clearly visible and tangible as far as many new governmental, public, educational and cultural buildings of Kazan and her residential and transport infrastructure are concerned.

THE STORY OF THE URBAN RENEWAL

As already noted, such town-planning achievements on an unprecedented scale in the centuries-old history of Kazan could not have been carried out by the republic and the city alone. They required massive federal assistance, albeit that the original impetus towards the transformation of the capital was initiated in Kazan as early as in 1996 with President Mintimer Shaimiev's decree entitled 'Concerning the Programme of Demolition of Slum Housing and Reconstruction of the Residential Quarters of Kazan'.

Of course, such things as presidential decrees are undoubtedly important. In fact, there were dozens of decrees regularly issued throughout Russia during those murky years. But, as with everything in the 'Tatarstan model', there are special features to the Tatarstan way of doing things. The main characteristic of this model is undoubtedly the combined approach for achieving a cohesive solution to the many necessary tasks of the day, based on a thorough assessment of the republic's real needs judged against her actual capabilities. The said programme had several key elements – social, economic and political dimensions, of course, being the most important amongst them.

In those days, more than a decade ago, President Shaimiev was still regularly being called a former communist who allegedly preferred quasi-Socialist approaches to the 'highly advisable' market measures being pursued elsewhere in the Federation. His catch-phrase, uttered at the very outset of the botched all-Russia privatization process, that 'reforms are worth nothing, if they cause unnecessary suffering of the people' was then perceived as cheap populism and die-hard Socialist conservatism. He was, of course, a former communist, as were the overwhelming majority of state officials in those days, but he was also something else, and this 'else' would sadly not fit into any cliché of the shrewdest observers and watching minds either in Russia, or abroad.

It is not that these people were not shrewd enough. True to their books and political theories, they were looking mostly for Machiavellian-type secrets and the post-modernist culture of liberated greed in his political thinking. What they failed to grasp was that his was not a transitional philosophy, but a philosophy of transition. The latter is, alas, less comprehensible to a post-industrial urban scholar, than to any sensible farmer in Norfolk or Iowa. The farmer will artlessly tell you that you cannot reap before you have sown and you cannot get decent or, indeed, any fruits from a tree, before it has matured. But such revelations of the workings of Nature mean little to today's consumers who are destined to see their 'fruit and veg' only in supermarkets.

Indeed, the President of Tatarstan stubbornly refused to follow the 'shock therapy' methods practised in the rest of Russia which caused the population untold misery. This stubbornness was perceived as nothing but a fit of nationalistic separatism, a threat to Russia's integrity and the 'coming Russian boom'. But was it sensible to bleed people empty of the last penny as a result of super-inflation and ever rising prices and then expect them to willingly contribute their potential to the reform process? One recalls here the proverbial gypsy who tried to teach his horse not to eat. The gypsy was sure to succeed, but the horse sadly died before the experiment was over. The meaning? Feed your horse or let others feed it, before you place any bets on it. Or is it only horse-loving Tatars who understand such down-to-earth things?

Later, we will have the opportunity to take a close look at the Tatar President, but one thing became clear quite early on in the last decade-and-a-half: a populist in a derogatory political sense he is not. If anything, he is a populist only in the sense that populism can be defended, and that is 'on the basis that it constitutes a genuine form of democracy, intermediate institutions tending to pervert or misinterpret the people's will'.[3] To refine this description with regard to President Shaimiev, we will, however, have to add in the fact that the role of the intermediate institution in the case of Tatarstan is played by the all-Russia State Duma, whereas the will of the Tatar people must be viewed in its wider historical perspective.

But, returning to the presidential housing programme, it must be said that the issue of poor housing was much more pressing in Kazan than in many other Russian cities. If, on average, a little more than one per cent of the urban population across Russia subsists in slums, in Kazan this was six times higher. Obviously, in market conditions, when prices for decent housing rose sharply and continued to rise, thousands of Kazan families were doomed to live in slums for generations to come and thus be completely excluded from any potential gains from market transition. It was this gloomy perspective that was highlighted by President Shaimiev, when he stressed *an absolute need* to relocate the inhabitants of Kazan slums, saying that, under emerging capitalist circumstances, the dwellers of the ramshackle houses will never be able to improve their living conditions, unless the Tatarstan government helps them out of their misery.

In branding President Shaimiev a cunning populist politician looking only to broaden his electoral base, the all-Russia and Tatarstan opposition media often chose to overlook the fact that the entire liquidation of ramshackle housing programme was based on the assumption that the new quarters in central

Kazan would be built through the sale of the freed urban land and successive private investment into its development, thus balancing the governmental expenditure of constructing new residential housing on the then edge of the city.

The government-supported dynamics of this *social market* programme has successfully survived even the all-Russia state default of 1998: by the year 2000, more than 14,000 families had moved to new comfortable flats from slums and communal housing. In 2001, 180 blocks of flats, or 1108 thousand square metres of residential housing, were constructed, and 18,282 families had moved there. By the spring of 2004, 35,000 Kazan families had been housed. Overall, by the end of 2004, almost 50,000 Kazan families were enjoying greatly improved living conditions.

It has to be said, however, that under the circumstances of a general catastrophic slump in production, fiscal mismanagement and the ensuing all-Russia financial crisis, it was indeed extremely hard to implement the rehousing programme, the practical fulfilment of which fell to the lot of the Tatarstan Government led by Prime Minister Rustam Minnikhanov and the City Administration under the direction of the then Mayor of Kazan Kamil Iskhakov. Just before the millennium anniversary, the implementation of this presidential programme went ahead on schedule, and in the provision of residential housing Kazan led all other cities in Russia.[4]

In 2004, almost 1.6 million square metres of housing accommodation in Tatarstan were delivered to new occupants and it meant that the provision of housing in the republic reached 19.4 square metres per capita. Of course, this may not be that much compared with, say, Germany or Canada, but it is still a significant step forward from Soviet times, and the whole idea of transition was to make people's lives better, was it not?

Some people hate anniversaries because of their artificiality and dismiss them as mere show-up occasions, and, undoubtedly, many anniversaries turn out to be just that. Whilst replying to inquisitive journalists during the international forum 'Kazan – a world city' in August 2003, the President of Tatarstan, true to his early catch-phrase, stated that 'the millennium of Kazan must become a matter of celebration first of all for her own residents'. The successful fulfilment of the Kazan housing programme was certainly proof that these words regarding 'the good of the people' were not articulated in vain. But by the same token, what is also important, is that this drive for major infrastructural improvements was not just limited to Kazan. In 2004, the President of Tatarstan announced:

> We are not constrained by the tasks of preparing just this celebration. Kazan is an ancient city. Many houses have decayed so much that a simple face-lift will not do any more. And what pleasure can the anniversary bring, if people do not have decent housing? Imagine houses without sewerage, with the toilets in the yards – and all of that in the very centre of the Republic's capital! Therefore, eight years ago we initiated a programme for replacement of slum housing, which has no parallel in Russia. This programme first of all concerns Kazan, but not only her.

It meant that Kazan will not remain the only beneficiary of Tatarstan's will to improve: other towns and rural settlements are already benefiting from the improvement programme.

'New' replacing 'old' is a two-sided equation. It was much easier and considerably cheaper to pull the whole of central Kazan down, than engage in a painstaking process of retaining her historical image. For all the nostalgia, which is evoked in the hearts of older residents of Kazan by the change of the external appearance of the familiar buildings, her rebuilding, as well as the many basic town-planning changes in the former character of the city, call, first of all, for a philosophical re-thinking of the very essence of these urban changes. Kazan has changed its appearance many times during her thousand-year history; such alterations were dictated not by the whim of the city authorities, but by the imperatives of urban development and by the change of Kazan's role in the process of her evolution as an urban and administrative centre. Previous generations of Kazan citizens, and this is apparent from reports gleaned from old newspapers, also complained about urban changes, the results of which we now consider to be historical and thus untouchable. But let us look at Kazan through the eyes of future generations – in what shape will we leave the city to them as our legacy?

Nostalgia for the past is, of course, the nostalgia for one's youth, when everything seemed more reliable and one, as a rule, did not feel acute estrangement from the society fed and motivated by one and the same fairy-tale. This fairy-tale of a just and understanding society, built on mutual brotherhood and equality, represents the quintessence of all of humanity's social Utopias, and it is not so easy to dismiss this. Today, when fairy-tale hopes have been rudely taken away from the people and they, like children growing-up, have felt a sense of disappointment at the discovery that Santa Claus does not actually exist, such nostalgia for a common fairy-tale still, however latently and unconsciously, persists in the minds of many people. In some, the resistance to changes is fuelled by the childish hope that another Utopia will appear as a new motivator and bring people together. In November 2005, I put it to President Shaimiev, whether this hope might have some validity? He replied:

> No. The past is gone forever. Nostalgia is a tricky thing, because it tends to create bright mirages of the past, while hiding the not-so-bright past realities. We remember how it was, and we would not like to repeat that. Real people should build real societies, and motivation lies in realistic objectives, even if they seem less unattainable today because of the many difficulties of transition. The main thing is to thoughtfully define the goals and then set out to achieve them come what may. Nostalgia is the wrong companion for doing that.

Indeed, the continuing metamorphosis of the city preserves only what can be preserved and what, in its restored shape, will be pure decoration for the Kazan of the future, because this city is a place for the living and not a museum of past memories. And yet, some architects, historians and other inhabitants of Kazan have accepted many of the recent urban changes with regret. Their reaction is understandable – the loss of the traditional appearance of the Kazan streets, squares and houses brought heartache to many people in Kazan as if one was losing one's present-day memory itself.

No period of robust building and development can avoid excesses, which in time people come to lament. At the same time, many Kazan houses, for all their nostalgic and historical value, could not be saved in the condition that they were. This does not mean that a considerate attitude to Kazan's past was taken off the city council's agenda. The then Head of Administration, K. Iskhakov, spoke many times on the importance of recognizing the fragile equilibrium between the historical shape of the city and its new architectural imperatives:

> Kazan is not simply an historical city. It is one of the most ancient cities of Russia. Here the original features of ancient planning, original architectural ensembles and complexes of olden times were preserved through the ages. We are lucky that in the past our historical centre was not destroyed and built up with Soviet council houses, as was the case in many other Russian cities. Unfortunately, it was not possible to save all the buildings included in the Presidential Programme for the redevelopment of slum housing, as many of them simply collapsed. But we do tend to take into account the particular historical stylistics of the location and to restrict the number of floors for new buildings in the downtown area. 'The golden mean', a harmonious combination of the past and present is the principle which guides us in the definition of town-planning landmarks.

This principle of 'the golden mean' is very peculiar not just to Kazan's reconstruction and other historic towns in the republic. Basically, this idea of retaining durable things from the past and combining them with things of the present underlines the entire philosophy of the Tatarstan model. It is also just a common-sense philosophy of sensible ownership. Indeed, why pull down and completely dismantle a well lived-in house in order to make inside-out improvements, especially when you still have to live in it, while all the improvements are being made? Obvious as this question may seem, the start of the all-Russia transition was based on a totally different premise of completely doing away with the past; not surprisingly, Tatarstan was involved with a lot of painful resistance to ensure she did things her own way.

Disputes regarding the urban development boom in Kazan will echo for a long time in the conversations of her inhabitants. For example, a particularly heated debate flared up over plans for the reconstruction of the Gentry Assembly building, which during its implementation evolved into a new architectural reality – namely, the Urban Town hall, or the Capital's Rathaus.

The story is also a good metaphor for Kazan's transition from her past into the future.

The new name of this great edifice, which until 1997 was called the House of Officers of the Kazan garrison, reminds one of the historical Tatar Trade Rathaus of the eighteenth and nineteenth centuries, as well as the building of the City Merchant Magistrate located then in the Kazan trade quarters.

The latter building, by the way, was for a long time occupied by the Kazan bakery plant. Among the plans for its further use was also a plan to renovate it in order to house the State Hermitage Rooms, as regular exhibitions of the State Hermitage have already become one of Kazan's newer scientific and artistic traditions. However, the State Hermitage Rooms eventually became a constituent part of a new National Picture Gallery in one of the restored buildings of the Kazan Kremlin. This gallery with its Hermitage Rooms became a welcome addition to Kazan's art museums and show-rooms, among which a special place is still held by the Kazan Museum of Fine Arts,[5] since 1959 housed in the former private residence of the former commander of the Kazan military district General Sandetsky. Meanwhile, this link between St Petersburg and Kazan is not a one-off occurrence. The anniversaries of St Petersburg and Kazan have pulled the two cities much closer together. In St Petersburg, there is now a Kazan (Kazanskaya) street, whereas one of the ancient streets of Kazan, pedestrianized and completely re-arranged as a gift of St Petersburg to Kazan on the occasion of her Millennium, now bears the name of Petersburg (Peterburzhskaya) Street.

During the preparation for the 300th anniversary of St Petersburg and the 1000th anniversary of Kazan both cities exchanged ideas on the question of the restoration and reconstruction of historical buildings, one of which, the aforementioned Gentry Assembly, provoked the hottest architectural and philosophical debates in Kazan. As a result of this restoration, the original structure of the building was preserved. And yet, the deterioration of its interior fabric and the portico, under which in April 1999, there was a spontaneous collapse of soil into a cavity, as well as the question of a new functionality of the building, called for a fundamental alteration of both its external elevation and interiors. The refurbished building received a grand hall with 280 seats for official occasions and international meetings, and a banquet hall with 100 seats, as well as many auditoria and a winter garden under its new dome.

In this way the Kazan Gentry Assembly building, which served as a military hospital during the First World War and later became the Soviet House of Officers, was reconstituted as the capital's Rathaus (town hall), and it is in this Rathaus, that the summit of the CIS leaders took place on 27 August 2005, thus designating it as a permanent venue for important official and cultural events.

Immense as the achievement of ridding Kazan of her centuries-old shabby houses was, it was only one aspect of the overall transmutation of Kazan. The life of a city of more than a million strong is defined not only by its external appearance and availability of recreational facilities. Every city has to sustain its own economy, and a state-of-the-art urban economy directly depends on the existence of a reliable transport network. Thus, the most important construction project ahead of Kazan's millennium was the construction of the metro underground network, a project, which was from its outset branded impossible by a great many people.

THE STORY OF THE KAZAN METRO

The project was also a legacy from the USSR, as the story of the Kazan metro began in 1983–84, when a Kazan complex transport scheme was approved and an initial geological feasibility study had begun. The plan was approved by the USSR Ministry of Transport in 1987, but, in 1989, when the Soviet economy finally stalled, the USSR Council of Ministers issued a secret decree stopping the financial backing of all metro projects throughout the USSR. The work on the Kazan metro slowed down drastically, but never stopped, being kept alive by a tiny flow of funds from the city budget.

In 1995, the Kazan metro survived a second attempt on its existence. The Kazan city authorities learnt that the Russian government had compiled a list of nine cities, where construction of a local metro network could be considered. Kazan, however, was not among the designated cities. A delegation hastily despatched from Kazan to Moscow and 'remotely controlled' by President M.

Shaimiev and the Mayor of Kazan K. Iskhakov, managed to achieve the nigh impossible: Kazan became the tenth city in the list!

This is only one example of the Kazan power of persuasion. There are two aptitudes that Kazan and Tatarstan have in abundance – audacity and the courage to strive for seemingly unattainable goals, as well as the political shrewdness to exploit any legal opportunity or loophole to succeed in doing so. When during the controversial all-Russia presidential campaign of 1996 Boris Yeltsin visited Kazan, a possibility arose to ask for federal sponsorship of the metro project. This chance was not missed, and thus the Tatarstan authorities revived the project as one of the key projects in the development of the Kazan transport network. In 1997, despite mounting criticisms that the federal money could be better spent on social needs, President Shaimiev insisted on implementing the metro project (but then the tax relations between Moscow and Kazan were different, of which we shall speak more later). The initial stages of construction were courageously financed by 58 billion roubles of the republic's own money. In 2000, however, Tatarstan succeeded in persuading another Russian President, Vladimir Putin, of the importance of building a Kazan metro in the context of the federal programme for the Kazan Millennium.

The first line of the Kazan metro cost 10.7 billion roubles (330 million US dollars) to build, and its three lines due by 2023 will have cost at least 55.6 billion roubles (1720 million US dollars). It is serious money to be spent in one city by any, let alone Russian, standards. Against all odds, the first line of the Kazan metro opened for business, as planned, on 27 August 2005. This alone would surely be an amazing achievement for any unsuspecting foreigner – not least a Londoner!

The Kazan metro, the construction of which was faced with not only financial and logistical difficulties, but, with many geological problems under Kazan, linked to the necessity of meeting rigid global regulations for the construction of tunnels. Its construction, carried out in cooperation with key specialists in the field of domestic metro construction, was, by definition, a huge challenge for all concerned. The technology applied in the construction provided sealed and dry tunnels, created by special cutting tools capable of driving through in the hydro-geological conditions of the local soil. In the spring of 2004, at a technical conference of the international 'underground' association, the architectural and planning solutions applied in the Kazan underground received high praise from all participants.

The initial section of the underground totals five stations on the first line, which are Kremlevskaya, Tukai Square, Cloth Mill Settlement, Ametyevo and Gorky (Small Hills); the overall distance of seven kilometres will be covered in only twelve minutes. While discussing the cohesion of Tatarstan's economic and social projects, we must mention that Kazan's erstwhile shabby housing-dwellers who initially complained of being moved away from the city centre, are now able to reach the innermost Tukai Square from Ametyevo and Gorky in just a few minutes.

The network of the Kazan underground envisages, as we said, the construction of three lines, and the second phase of the first line will provide connections from 'Small Hills' to 'Avenue of Victory' and from 'Kremlevskaya' to 'Zarechnaya' (Cross-River) covering the distance of 17 kilometres.

The second line will be the 'Azino' (Railroad station) route for a distance of 12.5 kilometres; finally, the third line will connect four Kazan districts – Privolzhskyi, Moscovskyi, Novo-Savinovsky and Kirovskyi.

The metro, far from being a luxury for this ancient city, is an urgent necessity for the economic development of Kazan and a welcome relief for her commuting inhabitants. Designers have carefully thought out the structure of the metro, so that its stations have been combined with entrances to the large trade complexes of Kazan in the centre and suburbs. The existence of the metro changes the appearance of central Kazan and the functioning of her main shopping streets.

The first pedestrian shopping street in Kazan was the Baumana, formerly, Big Prolomnaya street. Its reconstruction demonstrated the full extent of the Kazan architects' and engineers' imagination and historical memory, who received high praise at the international and all-Russia exhibitions in Leipzig and Moscow in 1998. The design and reconstruction of the pedestrian zone in the historical trading quarters of Kazan began in 1997, and during the reconstruction not only the historical buildings, but the entire underground communication systems were completely renovated. The street space has also been imaginatively redesigned – along it, street fountains and sculptures were erected, including a unique bronze sculpture of the historical carriage, in which Katherine the Great toured Kazan in 1767. As a result of these efforts, the street became a magnet for the public, which further stimulated the inflow of private investment towards reconstruction and the restoration of historical buildings in the adjoining quarters.

Another memorable building which underwent reconstruction but met with many legal difficulties during the initial transition period was the House of Tatar Cuisine, opposite which there is the Tea House, where one can sample traditional products of the extremely imaginative and delicious Tatar national kitchen. Once in the centre of Kazan there were only two cafés frequented by young people – the 'Rest' cafe in the classical Alexander Arcade and the 'Little Fir-Tree' café in Baumana street. Today, along with dozens of new restaurants and cafés with strange names requiring a knowledge of world geography, Kazan returns to her former favourite establishments under the old names, but with completely new, state-of-the-art interiors. The 'Sail' restaurant – once a floating two-storey landing stage serving as a restaurant, which was moored to the Kazan Kremlin embankment until 1973, is one such example. In its place is a restaurant complex under the same name designed as a cascade of sails. In the former 'France' hotel converted in Soviet times into communal flats, the hotel and pizzeria 'Giuseppe' has long since become a popular venue.

The famous Kazan landmark, the Alexander Arcade, which since 1883 has had to contend with cavities below ground washed out by the water of the neighbouring Chernoe (Black) lake, has also been restored to its pre-revolutionary glory. This dazzling building revealed its first underground flaws in 1890, and further flaws appeared in 1920 and 1945. But in 1977 a real catastrophe befell this unique building – the Black-lake section of the Arcade collapsed, and all attempts to restore it during the Soviet years came to nothing. At last, in 2003, a tender for the restoration of the Arcade was won by the Polish company 'Budimeks', which under the supervision of Tatarstan's Scientific and

Methodological Council of the Ministry of Culture started the laborious work of reconstructing the building with a view to preserving its functionality as a hotel and entertainment complex.

Certainly, in recent years a number of hotels have already appeared in Kazan – the multi-storey 'Safar' hotel on the bank of the Kazanka-river, the five-star 'Mirage ' hotel built by the Italian architect Marko Piva who designed a hotel at the request of the Prince of Monaco and built the 'Laguna Palace' hotel in Venice. On a broader scale, prior to the millennium Kazan was and still is in great need of new hotels: barely half the demand is being satisfied, which presents an obvious opportunity for potential investors.

Even this brief overview of what the new Kazan offers would be inadequate, if we did not mention Kazan's sports facilities. Kazan always was a city of sports with several stadiums and a multitude of sports schools and clubs, the pupils of which frequently became Russian and world champions, excelling themselves in international competitions.[6] Nor is it surprising that Kazan sportsmen excelled in water sports with so much water available thanks to the Volga, and the Kazanka river and the three city lakes. Just on one of them, the central Kaban lake, a whole galaxy of outstanding masters of boat racing and champions of international regattas has been brought up. The city has long established herself as a venue for many international competitions and sports festivals, but prior to her millennium Kazan had become a sports centre known throughout Russia. And not for nothing.

The 'Ak Bars' ice hockey club under the chairmanship of the Chairman of Tatarstan's State Council, F. Mukhametshin, is the leader of the Russian championships. The 'Rubin' football club, which until late 2005 was chaired by the then Head of the City Administration K. Iskhakov, in 2003 became a bronze winner of the Russian championship. The 'Unix' basketball club, which in 1998 at the request of the President of Tatarstan was taken under his care by the Director of the Tatarstan National bank, E. Bogachov, became bronze and silver winner of the Russian Super League. Consequently, basketball today is one of the most popular sports in Kazan alongside the Kazan hockey and football teams. Basketball, in fact, became so popular that the hall of the Palace of Sports became too small for its fans and, at the end of 2000, construction began of the 7500-seat Kazan Basket-Hall on the banks of lake Kaban, which was opened in 2002.

In recent years, the number of sports facilities both in Kazan and in the entire Republic has significantly increased. In Kazan, the Palace of Sports was reconstructed and hosted the all-Russia figure-skating championships in December 2005. Despite having modernized the Palace of Sports, Kazan has also managed to acquire a brand new Ice Palace – the largest and most technologically advanced of its kind in the whole of Russia.

It is already clear from the above that the Tatarstan authorities take great interest in various sports, recognizing that this not just a welcome pastime for city residents, but also a great way to promote Kazan worldwide.

The Kazan car-racing circuit 'The High Mount' is recognized as one of the best in Russia and vies for lead position in the European auto-cross championships. The Prime Minister, Rustam Minnikhanov, who incidentally is the Russian champion in car-races of the 2nd division, announced in 2004, that Tatarstan and Kazan had begun to pay significant attention to youth politics and sports, and called on the sports authorities to nurture sportsmen for master teams at home, instead of recruiting them at great expense from abroad[7].

In Kazan and around the city, more possibilities move and open up for the development of sports. In 2004, on a slope going down to the banks of the Volga, a state-of-the-art skiing complex known as 'Kazan' opened, where skiers train on two routes from 730 up to 1,046 metres with an over-fall of heights from 130 up to 165 metres. The number of skiing routes is to be increased to sixteen or seventeen, and the complex offers a wide range of services, including the sale and hire of skiing equipment and snowboards, café and restaurant, hotel and rental accommodation, a fitness-centre, aqua-park and tennis courts.

At the time of opening this skiing complex in January 2004, President Mintimer Shaimiev repeated his belief that:

> ... despite all hardships, the republic continues to progress in all directions. With all the positive changes in our society, we now comply with most of the daily needs of the people. In Tatarstan, large sports structures are under construction, and mass and professional sports develop simultaneously. The main task now, especially for children, is to be engaged in physical culture and sports from an early age. It is necessary to create for the next generation all the conditions for an active lifestyle. It is a vital formula, and we shall do everything to achieve this purpose.

There is now a future for Kazan, which even day-dreamers could not anticipate twenty years ago. The city develops in many directions, becoming one of the finest-looking and, as far as job-creation and housing facilities are concerned, one of the most attractive cities in Russia. But, as we have seen, the thousand-year anniversary of Kazan was not an end in itself. Many projects initiated before the anniversary are being pursued in the wake of the celebrations, because, for all the accompanying political and economic reasons, the main beneficiaries of this work are still the people – the residents of Kazan and her many guests and business visitors.

How can one sum up the achievements of Kazan at the time of her millennium? One way is to look at Kazan from a bird's eye point of view, as she is seen by visitors arriving at the new Kazan airport from cities in Russia, and also on 'Lufthansa' flights from European countries and the wider world.

Below, we will take a look at the city with her white-stoned Kremlin enclosed by water, with its most recent mosque of Kul-Sharif and all the ancient Orthodox temples, the 'UFO'-shaped Kazan circus and the geometrically harmonic 'Pyramid' complex rising among new places of interest on the embankment of the arrow-straight Bulak channel with its many bridges. We will identify the newest and most interesting buildings of the city placed in her ancient architectural landscape, town gardens and parks, theatres, stadiums and sports halls. Here are some statistics:

KAZAN AT A GLANCE

Kazan today is a city of approximately 400 square kilometres with a population of 1.2 million people representing more than 100 different ethnic groups.

The city is famous for her industrial potential, and is well-known for her machine industry and metal-working, avionic and instrumentation technologies, chemical and petrochemical enterprises, light industry and food-processing plants and factories. The city produces the Mi-8 and Mi-17 helicopters (Open Share-Holding Society KVZ), aeroplanes Tu-214 (Open Share-Holding Society KMPO and KAPO named after Gorbunov), compressor and refrigerating machinery (Open Share-Holding Society Compressormach), polythene and other petro-products (Open Share-Holding Society 'Kazan plant of synthetic rubber'), medical (Open Share-Holding Society KMIZ) and optical instruments (Open Share-Holding Society KOMZ), washing powder (Open Share-Holding Society 'Nefis-Cosmetics') and medicines ('Tatchimfarm-preparaty'), a significant share of which goes for export. One of the leaders of the Russian food-processing industry is the brewing concern of the Open Share-Holding Society 'Red Orient'.

In the city, there are 653 consumer services establishments, employing 7,000 people. The range of supermarkets has grown and a wide choice of goods is ensured by 2,782 trading enterprises and public catering establishments accounting for some 350,000 square metres. In the city, there are seven large markets, including the reconstructed Central market and the 'Savinovo' market occupying in all some 20,000 square metres with 1,112 trading days.

The system of taxation in Kazan makes the city attractive to business, and in this sphere an important role is played by the so-called 'Kazan model' of support to urban commodity producers, when the Kazan government makes agreements on socio-economic cooperation, providing grants from the urban budget to approved projects. Banks and shopping centres accept credit and charge cards from Visa, Mastercard, STB, Union Card and American Express.

In the city, besides wire and radio telephone, a net for cellular communication via GSM-900, CDMA, DAMP, and MNT-450 has been developed.

In today's Kazan there are 759 ancient and cultural monuments, eighteen museums, five show-rooms and art galleries, seven large theatres, three of which are Tatar ethnic theatres, two Philharmonic societies, the Conservatoire of Music and the Great Concert hall – the second-largest in Russia.

In the city, there are fifty-five musical and art schools, 300 libraries, a circus, twenty palaces and houses of culture, the national cultural centre 'Kazan', and the House of Friendship of Peoples. At Kazan University alone there are six thematic museums: the university history museum, museums of Kazan chemical school, archaeology, ethnography, zoology and a geo-mineralogical museum.

After Kazan University, which celebrated its bicentenary in November 2004, there are thirty high schools and twenty-three educational institutions in which 120,000 students study. Up to 10,000 young men and women graduate from Kazan high schools annually.

In the city, there are many annual arts festivals: the F. Chaliapin International Opera Festival – the most representative in Russia, and the International Festival of Classical Ballet named after Rudolf Nureyev. Also, there is an annual international 'Europe-Asia' festival of modern music, the 'Piano-Forum' festival of piano music, the 'Tatar song' competition, the 'Nauruz' festival of Turkic theatres, the young ballet dancers competition, the theatrical festival named after K. Tinchurin, as well as organ, chamber, jazz and classical music festivals. In 2001, the first festival of modern music of the former Kazanian and nowadays world-famous composer Sofia Gubaidulina took place in Kazan and the Centre of Modern Music was opened.

In Kazan, there are 141 religious organizations, including sixty-five Muslim, forty-four Orthodox Christian, twenty-five Protestant, two Roman Catholic, two Judaic, and also some organizations of non-conventional religions. In the city, there are twenty-nine functioning Orthodox churches, three Old Believer's temples, a Roman Catholic chapel, a synagogue, prayer houses of Baptists, Seventh Day Adventists, Krishnaites and Bahais, and thirty-one mosques.

In addition, there are two higher theological educational institutions – the Kazan theological seminary, the Russian Islamic university, the 'Muhammadiya' high madrassa and the madrassa named in commemoration of the 1000th anniversary of the acceptance of Islam.

There are also many annual scientific and cultural meetings and conferences, among which a special place is occupied by the World Congress of Tatars, which in 2002 was held for the third time. There are almost 100 travel agencies offering diversified tourist, educational and health-improving programmes. As regards media, there are five broadcasting companies and television studios, fourteen radio stations, 150 newspapers and journals, twenty publishing houses and eight press services. These are the figures with which the capital enters her new millennium; of course, they constantly vary, evolving as Kazan evolves.

And yet, there is something else in Kazan, which a bird's eye view would fail to see, namely real men and women who made all of the above possible and, in the process of achieving their objectives, learnt how important it is to take forward their new know-how and understanding far into the future. The lessons of the Tatarstan model and the Kazan millennium, however bitter and disappointing they have been or continue to be at times, will never be wasted on the people of Tatarstan, because in every initial struggle for survival there are always necessary steps that have to be taken in order to lay down firm political and economic foundations to ensure a successful outcome along the path of transition.

Striving for 'the good of the people' does not by definition guarantee that the people will be completely satisfied, especially with their leaders. Wise leaders will understand this perfectly. But it is a welcome relief for all those genuinely wishing Russia well that in recent years certain aspects of Tatarstan's reform processes are being applied elsewhere in Russia. The rapid promotion of Kazan Mayor Kamil Iskhakov to the post of President Putin's Representative in the Far East region of Russia is proof enough that his work and achievements in Kazan were noticed where it matters.

At the same time, President Shaimiev's know-how, experience and pragmatic approach has been increasingly welcomed and applauded at the federal centre in Moscow.

At the end of 2005, the Russian government at last took a number of practical steps towards bringing about the long-awaited implementation of four strategic national projects: 'Modern Healthcare', 'Quality Education', 'Affordable Housing' and 'Effective Agriculture' with a budget totalling 180 billion roubles. We will see later how Tatarstan has approached these critical issues on its own soil, but it is no coincidence that at the State Council meeting in the Moscow Kremlin in December 2005 it was President Shaimiev who presented to the members of the Council Tatarstan's practical experience in the housing sphere. His programme of the liquidation of slums was the show-case of his presentation. But President Shaimiev also spoke about the most recent measures aimed at providing the population of the republic with affordable housing in the new market conditions. The essence of these measures was in the so-called Programme of Social Mortgage Lending designed in Tatarstan, which is, in his words, 'a symbiosis of share-owning mechanisms, leasing and mutual credit societies', but the main attraction of this option was that it was thirty-three per cent cheaper than all other mortgage schemes and much simpler and easier to manage for the borrowers and lenders alike.

Under existing circumstances state support for such ventures is imperative, he said, especially in view of the house-building requirement, the infrastructure – especially roads, public amenities, schools, kindergartens, medical and sports facilities, as well as caring for the environment.

Russia's strategic social projects are financed from the surplus state income generated by oil sales and the expenditure will be strictly controlled by the relevant authorities. Even so, there is much debate taking place concerning the very principle of the state participating in the provision of housing and other elements of Russia's internal markets. Some are already accusing Russia of reneging on her market economy pledges, in the same way as some are criticizing her for suppressing democratic freedoms. It is not the objective of this book to enter into these debates. But the question of the role of the state in a market economy is still a valid one, although it is surely evident that, especially in the process of market transition, such a role is beneficial provided that the state handles it sensibly. As for the so-called 'state-regulation-free' economies, where the global financial controllers are located, it is interesting to consider the following observation:

> Here's a statistic for you: The capitalization of corporations owned by the US federal government exceeds $2.85 trillion. Add to this the state and locally-owned operations, like water systems, and the total invested in public enterprises eclipses the investment in the New York Stock Exchange, making the US one of the most socialized nations left on this sad planet. If you're not American, you wouldn't probably know that. And if you are, you probably wouldn't know that either.[8]

It only sounds simple and straightforward said President Shaimiev when one talks of the Russian state participating in the creation of commercial housing, because the national project of 'Affordable Housing' should neatly and intricately balance house prices and people's incomes as well as the interests of the state, the regions and municipal organizations, corporate players and financial institutions.

As for the Tatarstan model, the Programme for Social Mortgage Lending was covered, in 2005, by 3.6 billion roubles of the Tatarstan budget and an additional 1.5 billion roubles from public down payments and other sources, which provided for the construction of 6,100 flats with all necessary amenities. In 2006, the republic will make available a further 3.2 billion roubles from the 5.5 billion of combined investment, which will help 6,500 families to get onto the property ladder for the first time. To keep housing affordable, the republic plans an annual increase in the volume of residential construction and by 2010 to reach the level of 2.2–2.5 million square metres, which will require an additional investment of 11.6 billion roubles.

At the same time President Shaimiev suggested that the project of all-Russia 'Affordable Housing' should be financed by both the federal government and the respective regions. This suggestion provoked heated debates in the State Council. Indeed, the Russian federal regions are very different in many aspects; many of them subsisting on government subsidies and are happy just to go with the flow, wherever it may take them.

Of course, experience and organizational skills are very important in any major project. But, to make the entire process of transition successful, one first of all needs a vision, even if the essence of this vision escapes the scrutiny of many people – foreign and domestic scholars and journalists all too often being amongst them. Again, it is not because they are somehow biased or less knowledgeable, but only because they often try to gauge things with their own tools which they profoundly believe to be the only proper tools anywhere in the world.

But then – try measuring a soul, be it a human soul, or the soul of a nation? It may sound odd and eccentric, but, interestingly, the result may prove much more practical and useful, than that of any other approach, however scholarly and value-free it may pretend to be.

NOTES

1. Ravil Bukharaev, 'Saga of Kazan', Slavia, St Petersburg, 2005.
2. President V. Putin.
3. Andrew Heywood, ibid, p. 178.
4. In 2005 President V. Putin noted: 'if the problem would be solved at such rates in other cities, including St Petersburg, we would consider our task in this regard completed'.
5. Among the treasures of this museum are the works by F. Rokotov, D. Levitsky, V. Tropinin, K. Bryullov, I. Ayvazovsky, V. Perov, A. Kuindzhi, I. Levitan, I. Repin, N. Roerich and many other famous Russian artists. A distinctive place in the museum is occupied by the works of N. Feshin and V. Kandinsky. The works of Tatar artists are also widely represented – from the *chef d'oeuvres* of ancient Volga Bulgar craftsmen to the masterpieces of B. Urmanche, H. Jakupov, L. Fattahov and many other masters of Tatar painting and engraving arts.
6. Olympic, world and European champion wrestler A. Kurynov, fencer E. Bayanov, fencer O. Knyazeva, football player O. Kolotov, figure skater A. Fadeev and many other well-known sportsmen and sportswomen began their life in sport and acquired international fame while living in Kazan.
7. The practice is yet on-going, however. During the lull in the NHL championships in the USA and Canada, for example, the best and highest-paid ice hockey players came to play for the Kazan 'Ak Bars' hockey club.
8. Greg Palast, *The Best Democracy Money Can Buy*, Robinson, London, 2003, p. 361.

CHAPTER 5

'VILLAGE CULTURE'

回

> Liberty cannot be preserved without a general knowledge among the people, who have a right . . . and a desire to know; but besides this, they have a right, an indisputable, inalienable, indivisible, divine right to that most dreaded and envied kind of knowledge, I mean of the characters and conduct of their rulers.
>
> Henry Brooks Adams

I was born and educated in the city of Kazan, and recall what precious little (mostly cosmetic) change the city underwent in the forty years of my own life – before the arrival of the 1990s. From the middle of the 1970s, I had been living in Moscow and each time, I returned to my home city after a long absence, I hoped to see some interesting architectural and other changes; but, alas, it was always the same, and apart from one or two buildings here and there, the shape of the city never seemed to improve for the better.

It was a city that suffered chronic deficits of everything, except the seemingly never-ending years of one's childhood and youth. As a child, I still remember how my then post-graduate father once brought home from Moscow a bottle of Vietnamese pineapple juice. Usually, he used to bring fresh pineapples, which were never on sale in Kazan. But the juice – it was such a sweet and beautiful rarity that my younger brother and I made it last for a whole two months, enjoying a small sip of it each day. I still remember its taste and shining clarity with a touch of gold, and how each of those small sips sparked my imagination, causing me to muse about distant countries, monsoon rains, jungles and much more, which after many years, finally encouraged me to travel and see it all for myself. This probably was one of those many imperceptible and seemingly accidental reasons why I became a creative writer. Of course, that discovery of such a special taste can never be repeated today because of today's abundance of all kinds of fruit juice in Kazan. This childhood recollection reminds me time and again, that it is not the abundance of everything, but the happy realization of a unique personal desire that really counts.

Is it more than a little sad that today's consumer abundance rarely stimulates the sort of challenging thoughts that can bring about positive, enduring change in people's lives? Instead, it tends to suppress all thought, slowly but surely turning *Homo sapiens* into *Homo consumeris*, whilst hailing such change as the peak of human history. Yet, history itself started with the process of thinking – so is it to negate human free will to think that that signifies it has achieved its peak? Of course, such views seldom arise in countries where consumer goods are in short supply, and thus one surely has to get a taste of what abundance means before getting philosophical about it.

The Kazan of the not-so-distant past was a place where any unregulated talk of the medieval trials of Tatar history or an ingenuous interest in Christianity or Islam would soon become a matter for the KGB, since not only materialistic, but also spiritual desires were often not fulfilled. For all the innocent joyfulness of youth, and despite rather good schooling,[1] the idea of travelling to London, Milwaukee or Salt Lake City was simply unimaginable, as if these were phantom cities only seen in the cinema and on TV. This is not to say that my generation was not, in principle, aware of all the cultural trends beyond the Iron Curtain: we knew much more than is still presumed in the West about our awareness. Maybe, because of that by the 1980s this feeling of being 'caged' became all but unbearable, albeit mostly in the 'academically vague' spiritual sense.

At the beginning of the 1980s everyone, including the cleverer communist authorities, had already guessed that the country had lost the plot and, with it, its destination. The gloominess of central Kazan with its ramshackle houses that had no running water and, sometimes, a single lavatory for forty families, only added to this mounting civic despair. The Kazan Kremlin, then housing some minor ministries and governmental departments, was not the tourist marvel it is now; furthermore, because Kazan was a city full of military-industrial plants it was closed to foreign visitors until the beginning of the 1970s.

The historic channel of the Bulak built in earlier times to link the central lake of Kaban to the Kazanka-river and thus to the great Volga waterway, was then used as a dump for discarded tyres and other rubbish rotting in the puddles of its shallow waters. Its two thoroughfare embankments, straight as they were, were as warped by ruts and potholes as any of the streets in Kazan, while the historic houses on both sides of it seemed abandoned for ever, as the city and 'borough' authorities never had enough funds to maintain them.

Fortunately, this cheerless portrait of Kazan no longer exists.

In early September 2005, after the two week-long celebration of the city's millennium had finally subsided, I came out with my wife Lydia onto the Bulak embankment close to the Kazan Kremlin after a party with friends. It was a warm, calm, quiet, starry night. The completely restored and rejuvenated Kazan Kremlin with its floodlit medieval white-stone walls was akin to a fairy-tale castle, revealing in the dark the airborne golden-blue cupolas of the ancient Orthodox Cathedral of the Annunciation and the soaring minarets of the newly and most exquisitely built Kul Sharif mosque, both of which now endow Kazan with a real sense of a magic city.

Behind us, on the grassy slope between the Kremlin and the long-standing John and Paul Church with its open-work crosses with the sign of the crescent beneath, there was a newly decorated entrance to the Kremlevskaya station of the Kazan metro – a breakthrough achievement in the development of the city transport network. Another major accomplishment is the brand new wide bridge over the Kazanka-river with the illuminated capital 'M' of its main pier pointing to the millennium of the city which joins both sides of the river further along from the place where we stood. Along with the Kazan metro and several new underpasses this bridge greatly increases the movement of goods and people across the city, as dozens of modern office blocks and trade complexes have appeared in the last five years on both sides of the river, and Kazan, almost in the wink of an eye, became the second Russian city after Moscow shopping area on a per capita basis.

Opposite the Kremlin with its festive floodlit illumination, across the vastly enlarged 500-year-old market square of Tash Ayak,[2] there stands in the place of the familiar squalid buildings of the Soviet epoch the new entertainment and conference complex of the 'Pyramid' in the shape geometrically true to its name. Adjacent to it, there is the five-star 'Mirage' hotel, which only a day earlier strangely reminded me, of all cities, of Milwaukee, when a black Cherokee jeep habitually went down its elevated ramp. This recollection proved prophetic, because only two months later, on 7 November 2005 in London, it was Milwaukee that Kazan was to lose to in the final stage of the World Leadership Forum competition for the best urban reconstruction programme. That, however, seemed a bit unfair, given the context and circumstances in which the reconstruction of Kazan has been achieved. Impressive though the development of the Lake Michigan frontline in Milwaukee is, Kazan could, in all truth, set that off with a range of comparable developments, having done so with completely incomparable financial resources.

The Kazan transfiguration, showing itself in the glowing lights of that memorable night, was indeed remarkable. The thoroughly renovated and refurbished classical nineteenth-century houses on both sides of the Bulak channel (now almost all privately owned) suddenly awoke in our minds yet another reminiscence – that of St Petersburg, so fresh and solemn they looked with their colourful mirror images glimmering in the water. The night, as I said, when everywhere was very calm and quiet, suddenly, as if out of nowhere, two Porsche cars went by, revving at full throttle, along the Bulak embankment and in a matter of seconds disappeared into the dark in the vicinity of the Kaban lake.

One has to be a seasoned Kazanian, let alone a former Soviet citizen, to fully appreciate the impact that it had. I am not a big fan of cars, let alone luxury cars, and far removed from judging the general wealth of society by the number of Mercedes and Porsches seen on the streets of a capital city. One has to agree with the notion that 'a traffic jam of Mercedes in a country with a per capita income of $4,730 (as it was in 1997) is a sign of sickness, not health'.[3] Even if one knows that, in 2004, car sales in Russia already grossed 18 billion US dollars and the projected sales for 2005 total over 21 billion, it is still too early to say that Russia has turned the corner in this respect.

With today's monthly *cash* income per capita in Tatarstan averaging, in the rouble equivalent, of just under $250 (domestic energy, water and other subsidies not included), the presence of deluxe Jeeps and Porsches says nothing of how the general public fare. In August 2005, according to the data published by the State Council of Tatarstan, the average cash income per capita was 6,340.8 roubles, while the consumer basket of essential foodstuffs cost 1,142.4 roubles. Later that year, the Tatarstan government fixed the average living wage in the republic at 2,460 roubles.[4] Despite the fact that real income per capita in Tatarstan grew in 2005, year on year, by 24.5%, it is still a far cry from making any pricey goods affordable, let alone a Porsche car![5]

But the cars were there to impress no one, as the streets were blissfully empty. Being just a finishing touch, as it were, to my perception of Kazan that night, they went down the embankment so routinely, as if its finely improved surface had been there from time immemorial, and a Porsche in a once dilapidated Kazan was entirely normal. And so, it seemed, it was – now, after only fifteen years of common-sense policies, which, for all the problems of the deepening social divide, have saved the multinational population of Tatarstan from the worst excesses of the Russian 'shock therapy' years. But, also, it has to be said, this Porsche outing reminded me of a conversation I had with a leading member of the Kazan City Administration just after the actual date of the millennium celebrations.

I asked him, how on earth was it possible to accomplish all the feats of the Kazan urban renovation programme in such a short time even with the, for once, uninterrupted flow of federal investment and the complete dedication of the local authorities to the task, which even six months earlier seemed well nigh impossible. Money, of course, is important, but money is not all, as the story of the London Jubilee Line extension clearly demonstrated. In Russia, as in any other country, the sheer volume of investment does not presuppose that the funds will be handled and put to work properly. Good organizational skills and official pressure, as well as public enthusiasm, also go only so far, otherwise the USSR economy, constantly pressurized 'from above', would not have failed so miserably in delivering 'the good of the people'.

The answer of my interlocutor was as simple as it was enlightening. He said:

> About a year ago we achieved the thing that we wanted the most. We succeeded in awakening the self-interest of private investors who, having been at first very reluctant and wary of official appeals for participation, were in the end completely swayed by the sheer momentum of the millennium project. Seeing the finesse and zeal with which the public projects were being accomplished, they stopped economizing on renovation and refurbishment of their own properties and started to invest heavily in land development, because they finally realized the potential value of this capital investment. It also goes for corporate investors – many privatized enterprises of Kazan and the republic made substantial contributions towards the general success of the Kazan urban development programme.

The latter remark was especially noteworthy, because it brought to mind many things – the attitude of the president and the government of Tatarstan towards big business being one of the most interesting of them. On the authority of the president, an additional tax of one per cent was levied for the giant republican enterprises which was accumulated in a special fund for the reconstruction of Kazan. As these enterprises were already private businesses, albeit sometimes with large government stakes, such a move might seem like unnecessary state interference in the Tatarstan market. But again, all the steps taken by President Shaimiev's government should be looked at against the reality of the transition period and against the background of the emerging Tatarstan capitalist society.

One major thing that hinders the capitalist transformation of Russia is the public perception that the de-nationalization of the Soviet economy lacked any semblance of social justice. In Russia at large, the mistakes made at the dawn of the all-Russia privatization, which created the infamous oligarchic structure of the Russian economy, are now being rectified at a huge cost to the Russian state. The vast private holdings are being bought back from the Russian oligarchs, the most well-known example of this policy being the buy-back from Roman Abramovich, who sold his Russian interests for the sum of seventeen billion US dollars. In this process of apparent re-privatization the mammoth Russian oil and heavy industry enterprises are not being nationalized (anathema to Russian, as well as Western players), but the Russian government affirms its interests in the country's economy by purchasing back what it gave away during the madness years of 1992 to 1996 and floating that on the national market for everyone to buy into.

In an atmosphere where the public perceives all the large private capital in Russia to have been appropriated unfairly, such moves, however costly, are generally seen as leading to a more just society and therefore generally positive. We may argue to what extent the 'social market' and 'state regulation' trends in recent Russian economic history will prove to be beneficial in the long run, but one thing at least is certain: namely, that the Russian public understands these trends in the light of the re-emergence of the idea of social justice in the country, where such a notion was barely ever mentioned previously.

In Tatarstan, with her policy of a 'soft entrance' to the market economy, when prices for essential goods were subsidized in the early years of the transition and the policy of privatization was drastically different from that of Russia, the idea of social justice and 'the common good' never completely left the scene of the reform process. Still, in the unprecedented task of the re-structuring of the entire system of property ownership, there were, statistically, only a few winners and too many losers, and any common-sense government would take the resulting social frustration into account. But again, how does one go about the task of, as it were, of re-distributing wealth in the interests of the entire people, without shaking the foundations of the new society, where, as a rule, all property rights have been gained lawfully, as was the case in Tatarstan?

In this light, the levying of an additional tax on the colossal privatized enterprises of Tatarstan with the proceeds being immediately invested into the capital's reconstruction fund which was also intended for the improvement of people's living conditions is, of course, a regulatory measure, but, in the peculiar philosophy of Tatarstan's transition, it was also a means of rectifying any possible shortcomings of the status-quo wealth distribution in the republic in the eyes of her citizens. It is believed that such measures in the transition period are indeed necessary to re-create a vital sense of justice in the society, without which no successful transition and no real feeling of participation in such a transition are possible.

The major programme of replacement of slum housing was at the heart of the revitalization of Kazan. The President of Tatarstan at a session of the Kazan municipal council of People's Deputies in March 2004, once again underlined that this business of re-housing people from their dilapidated dwellings was a task for the entire republic and her big enterprises and corporations, stating:

> Into the non-budgetary housing fund for the replacement of slum housing one per cent of turnover was contributed by all businesses of our republic. According to the 1 January 2004, data, the Republic has a GDP of over 250 billion roubles, and Kazan – over 52 billion roubles. It is already a positive moment. Consider, that 90 % of this fund has been generated by all our commodity producers and our oilmen because the oilmen of the republic were taxed for these purposes by a special addi-

tional Tatarstan excise. Therefore, in approaching the millennium of Kazan and being proud of the positive changes in the capital, we should be grateful to all the commodity producers of our republic.

But large corporations were called to do even more towards bringing Kazan's historical quarters and architectural monuments into shape for the millennium. One example of big business involvement in the reconstruction of Kazan was the modernization of one of the major city attractions – the hundred-year-old House of Kekin carried out by the Open Share-Holding Company 'TAIF' led by its Director General Albert K. Shigabutdinov. The building commissioned by the affluent Kazan merchant Leonty Kekin in 1903 to 1905, and built by the famous Kazan architect Henrich Rush, has long impressed the townspeople and visitors to Kazan with the singularity of its design, combining a wide range of architectural styles. The composition of the building with its prevalence of Gothic motifs and the external appearance of facades with numerous little balconies, lancet and round-headed windows, porticoes and tents, the bulbs of domes and sharp-headed turrets with spikes always singled the House of Kekin out from the surrounding buildings. The house, which is advantageously located at the intersection of Little Lyadskaya and Big Lyadskaya streets, was used by the owner as a trading house, in which there were also shops, offices, educational and official establishments. In the Soviet period, the upper floors of the building were used for residential housing, but, as is common in that period of neglect, the house also remained neglected, and by 1998 had reached a pitiable state and fell into disuse. In a short time, the ancient architectural masterpiece of Kazan, with its walls deformed and cellars full of water, would have simply collapsed. Under the circumstances, when the financial possibilities of the state with regard to the restoration of historical buildings and monuments of architectural interest were, and are, extremely limited, private capital fortunately came to the rescue. Having taken on the responsibility for the preservation of the historical and architectural originality of this unique Kazan building, the new owners respected every aspect of its original features, and in its restoration the best architectural skills of Kazan were involved who, after the well-known architect F. Zabirova, called the House of Kekin 'a metaphor' for and 'a puzzle' of the enchanted capital.

The restoration of the House of Kekin was not only an example of the participation of private capital in the revitalization of Kazan, but, in many respects, also a charitable undertaking. It is because the restoration of historical and cultural monuments burdens the investor with many rules and regulations, thus constraining the building work and incurring heavy costs, especially in the reconstruction of engineering communications. The company 'TAIF' conducted the reconstruction, in the words of the mayor of the city, 'to the detriment of its financial interests', and therefore the reconstruction of the House of Kekin may be seen as an example of the company's genuine Kazan patriotism, which is also involved in building state-of-the-art apartment houses within the framework of the presidential programme of the replacement of slum housing, as well as fine office buildings. The cultural and entertainment centre 'Pyramid' near the Kazan Kremlin, in which there are a concert hall and one of the best restaurants in Kazan, offering everything from masterpieces of Tatar cuisine to the delicacies of the French and Japanese kitchen, is also owned by the company. But this is only the tip of the iceberg which is TAIF, Tatarstan's largest private corporation. Its very foundation and business activities may offer useful insight into present-day capitalism in the republic.

Introducing TAIF (Tatar-American Investment and Finance company), *Forbes* magazine wrote that the company holds stocks of the most successful Tatarstan enterprises, including the Tatneft Oil Company, the Kazanorgsintez and Nizhnekamskneftekhim petrochemical plants, the Nisznekamskshina tyre and the Almetyevsk Pipe-casting plants. In addition, TAIF has a controlling interest in the 'New Age' satellite television channel, the 'Avers' bank and 'Avers' insurance company, the 'Kazan' contruction company, and just recently has sold its interest in the Tatarstan mobile phone network. In the words of its Director General A. Shigabutdinov, TAIF today consists of thirty-eight companies in five economic sectors – oil-drilling, oil-refining and petrochemicals; securities and the financial market; construction; telecommunications, and customer services, employing in all 30,000 people.

The Tatarstan press, especially the most inquisitive and irreverent parts of it, often openly calls TAIF 'the property of the Shaimiev family', because the President's son, Radik Shaimiev, owns a twenty per cent stake in the company. This fact itself is hardly enough to maintain, as *Forbes* magazine does in its May 2005 issue, that Radik Shaimiev occupies 91st place in the list of the richest people in Russia and is worth 340 million US dollars, if only because this sum represents the total capitalization of the entire company. At the same time, even the most outspoken critics of the president's policies have said that, in all fairness:

> ... despite the fact that *Forbes* magazine has made it known who the father of Radik is thereby removing all questions, the fact is that the questions still remain. Of course, one cannot seriously analyse his 'path to success', because he was destined to enter the Russian business elite on the very day when he decided to go into business. He did not have to struggle with bureaucratic barriers, seek ways to approach officials or work with his hands. All of that was done for him by the name and the post of his father. And yet, he himself is not an ordinary man, but a man with a character. This is evident at least in the fact that in his youth, having had the chance to 'skip' the army draft, he never used that opportunity and truthfully served his conscription period, and not as a military clerk, but as a commando at that. His sporting successes – after all, he is a European car-racing champion! – also cannot but inspire respect. However, be he a super-talented businessman or a super-purposeful man, he hardly would be able to control *de facto* the assets of TAIF, if his father was not Mintimer Shaimiev ... [6]

This characterization of one of the president's two sons by the former press spokesman of the Tatarstan presidency Irek Murtazin was published on the Russian internet site of compromat.ru, which is an interesting collection of some real facts mixed with intense gossip about what is going on in Russia. Russia is also a peculiar country in this respect. While accepting that the Tatarstan model has its valid criticisms, it is also fair to say that there are many things that are presumed 'self-evident' in the atmosphere of social distrust created by the turmoil of the all-Russia transition. A fact taken out of context is the weapon most frequently used in polemics not only by indignant parts of the Russian press, but also by some Western scholars and observers who are so keen to get 'independent opinions' about the realities of what is taking place in Russia. Strangely enough, however, once one begins to trace 'an independent opinion', it almost invariably brings one into the network of some presidential hopeful working towards his own hold on power in Tatarstan. These hopefuls and those who voice their sometimes valid discontents have every right to be in opposition in a democracy, but why call their opinions 'independent' and base their 'value-free' research on them? The 'self-evident' presumption that the president's son is a crony player on the Tatarstan business scene is part of a much wider-ranging prejudice towards Russian business culture, and this is not always helpful. The same observers, who would not mutter a word about the Bush family network in the USA, would be only too happy to point out the family connections in Tatarstan and in Russia at large. Imagine a situation when presidential elections in Tatarstan are most narrowly decided by one region, where the head of the region is a close relative of the winner. What kind of self-righteous outcry would then follow in the USA, of all places!

In November 2005, when TAIF and the Russian-British oil giant TNK-BP signed a memorandum of understanding on deliveries of TNK-BP gas supplies to the Kazanorgsintez plant, worth about 300 million US dollars, the most impertinent, if sometimes populist, newspaper 'The Evening Kazan' published a big interview with TAIF's Director General sparing no direct questions about the nature and essence of the largest private corporation in Tatarstan.[7] Predictably, one of the questions concerned the role of the president's son regarding the activities of TAIF – the question, which is often put to the president himself, for instance in the magazine *Oil and Life*.[8]

> QUESTION: Not so long ago *Forbes* magazine included your son Radik Shaimiev in the list of richest people in Russia. His worth was valued at 340 million US dollars.
>
> ANSWER: Some write about 340 million, some – about 140 million, but I do not think it is that much. Radik is a wealthy guy, but also a civilized businessman. He is not fond of money, just like Airat, the second of my sons. They are both independent and modern people. They both successfully participate in auto rallies, both are European champions. My principle is not to interfere in the business of being complete men. As far as his wealth is concerned, I do not know how it is calculated. Maybe, they include the shares in the ownership of the founders of the TAIF company. I once read the memoirs of American billionaire Armand Hammer, who started his business with Russia at the time of Lenin. And so, in 1992 he wrote that 'at last, I had 300,000 dollars of free money'! He then bought a farm and started breeding a special kind of ox renowned for its 'marble' meat. I will tell you this: I like how Radik is doing his business – he does it in a civilized way. However, he rarely briefs me about his business affairs. In TAIF, there is a strong team of professionals, and a clever Director General. They are engaged in over twenty lines of business.

This interview, one of many, should be enough to show the relative openness and inquisitive freedom of the Tatarstan press and the ease with which the president himself answers this direct question, always saying that he never instructed his son to be a businessman, but neither did he prevent him from taking that path in life.

The truth of the matter is that the president's son was a founding member of the TAIF company at the very start of its existence. Radik Shaimiev, who became acquainted with the present Director General of TAIF during the Soviet-time campaign of 'student construction teams' and both participated in the construction of one of the installations of the giant Nizhnekamsk petrochemical plant, approached A. Shigabutdinov, already the head of 'Kazan' – a successful construction company – with the proposal of investing in the Nizhnekamsk infrastructure. It was the beginning of the 1990s, and the economic situation in Nizhnekamsk was rather tense, as anywhere in Russia. This was the beginning of the rise of TAIF, further closely linked to Tatarstan's attempts to establish its financial base in the stormy years before large-scale privatization. As A. Shigabutdinov recalls:

> Privatization in Tatarstan started in 1992–1993, and as far as the Nizhnekamsk petrochemical plant was concerned, it was decided to distribute 51% of the shares among the workers and management of the plant. According to the privatization plan, they had to buy those shares from the state in cash, requiring five billion 'old' roubles, but had no funds for that. So, they came to us, to our company 'Kazan', for help. In those days all share companies were a novelty, and there was a need for the establishment of a market for both private and state-owned shares. At the same time, the shareholders had to manage their newly acquired plants, and only a few people knew how to go about it, so, for the most part, it was done only formally. At the beginning, we also took wrong turns and had to engage in a lot of negotiations with banks and Western partners. Eventually, there emerged a proposal from our American partners to the state Property Ministry for the establishment of a structure which would create a share market in the republic. We needed money. The Americans gave ten million dollars and the state invested a small part of its shares – 9% of the Nizhnekamsk Petrochemical Plant, about 4% of Tatneft, 3% of Orgsintez Chemical plant and so forth. This was the beginning of TAIF.

Today, as we said, TAIF is one of the largest and therefore most influential private corporations in Tatarstan, but its story is very characteristic of the way in which Tatarstan successfully tried to retain the most valuable industrial property in the hands of state investors at the beginning of the 1990s. Tatarstan did not create her own oligarchs and never allowed Russian oligarchs to swallow those juicy pieces of her economy. Whatever can be said about the workings of Tatarstan's capitalism, de-nationalization of state property in Tatarstan was undertaken with much more foresight and discipline than in the rest of Russia, and the role of the president in this process cannot be overestimated.

As the head of the republic, who had to lead her through the most difficult political and economic circumstances imaginable, President Shaimiev has also had to withstand a lot of criticism from the republican press. In February 2006, I walked into one of the big Kazan bookshops and immediately saw on the shelves a book entitled *Shaimiev: Real and Virtual* by the outspoken Tatarstan journalist Lev Ovrutsky, who is also a frequent source for foreigners researching on Tatarstan. The book is a compilation of his own articles published in the Tatarstan press over the years and, if anything, this book alone demonstrates the democratic 'reality' of the local press towards the president and his policies. However, the author himself states that in his book:

Irony melted into sarcasm, the colours were laid on thick, and criticism towards some sides of Shaimiev's regime, it seems, had transformed into a total negation of 'Mintimerism'. I do not believe that in reality things in Tatarstan are as negative as they may appear. Be it the other way round, how would it be possible to have published all these articles in the pages of the *MK in Tatarstan* and other Kazan newspapers? My personal attitude to Mintimer Shaimiev is twofold. I sense the historical scale of the role he played. I am sure that he will deserve a monument as a man who did for Tatars the same that Ben-Gurion did for Jews – returned them their self-esteem. At the same time I do not see any reason preventing me from systematically subjecting him, as indeed any other public politician, to a critical scrutiny.

At least, this kind of critical scrutiny comes from a journalist who understands the realities in which the president had and has to work during a real-life, and non-academic transition process. For many positive foreign evaluations of the Tatarstan model under President Mintimer Shaimiev, and they are indeed a-plenty, we sometimes see attempts to fit the reality of Tatarstan as part of the larger all-Russian economic and political scene into the Procrustean bed of post-modern 'imaginative' social science, where academics try to reverse their theory into reality, and not vice versa. In this way, many things are considered self-evident, like the presumption that all power structures in Russia are corrupt by definition, and therefore it is permissible to call politicians 'corrupt' without even bothering to bring forward any substantiation or proof to that effect. When one reads works like *Islam in post-Soviet Russia* edited by Hilary Pilkington and Galina Yemelianova,[9] where the latter is so at ease with calling the president names, one recalls the words of the British poet Humbert Wolf (1886–1940):

> You cannot hope
> to bribe and twist,
> thank God! the
> British journalist.
>
> But, seeing what
> the man will do
> unbribed, there's
> no occasion to.

Out of the many approaches to the business of analysing the present state of affairs in Russia, or, for that matter, Tatarstan, the 'elite theory' is one of the most popular. Apparently, this theory came out of the academic vacuum left by the failure of economic and political Marxism with its once most convenient division of society into classes according to their economic standing. Today, it seems, the idea that the analysis of one's political standing is the key to unlocking the fascinating workings of post-Communist societies gains preference over more elaborate approaches based on the causes and realities of the transition process itself. Those foreign works based on the 'elite theory' vary in their depths and power of insight, but, despite the fact that even some Tatarstan political scientists have taken this theory as their instrument of choice, the postulation of theorems upon which the elite research is often built, sometimes show how little even an honest researcher from abroad understands the raison-d'etre of Tatarstan. For example, the substantial research work of Linda Røysi of the University of Bergen[10] in the part dealing with the Tatarstan political elite starts with the assumption: 'I claim that harmony of interest between the elite and the periphery within the republic of Tatarstan and harmony between the ethnic groups within the republic strengthens the Republic *vis-à-vis* Moscow. I also argue that the regional elite was *well aware of this, and used this knowledge as an instrument to gain power.*' [Emphasis added.]

If the main thesis of Linda Røysi is right, then the entire statehood history of the Tatar people should be put away for the sake of academic theorizing, which, as it happens, can always devise proof to meet a conveniently localized task. In the present atmosphere of political disbelief reigning throughout the world, the thought that the historical idea of statehood may be the engine of politics and may therefore bring forward politicians for its defence and development even in our age of political distrust and disillusionment might seem naïve and far-fetched, but, nevertheless, it is at least as valid as the presumption that politicians do everything only for their own sake.

The term *regional elite* used by political scientists in the way a pathologist employs a scalpel, always fascinates me when applied universally to all non-Western societies. If, by definition, elite is 'a minority, in whose hands power, wealth or privilege is concentrated, justifiably or otherwise',[11] the Western perception is that, in countries undergoing transition, the position of elites is less justifiable. When one reads that 'the main purpose of the representatives of the elite layers is to hold leading positions within a given society and to expand their own sphere of influence',[12] one wonders whether the 'good of the people' is indeed a mirage and all that matters is the elite's self-interest, which propels this canny maintenance of society's *status quo*. By placing firm emphasis on the self-interest of the Tatarstan elite and by presuming that it is the members of the elite who create real-life demands and not vice-versa, Linda Røysi seems to transpose primary and secondary goals of the Tatarstan elite, when she goes on to say that along with the fulfilment of the principal purpose of their own survival and growth 'they seek to carry out measures directed towards upholding political, economic and social stability, towards expanding interregional and international relations of the territory, and towards upholding stable relations with the federal centre'.[13]

In this view, whatever happened to Tatarstan since the beginning of the all-Russia *perestroika* in 1985 is a result of a cunning self-promotion of the elite, notwithstanding the fact that the philosophy of 'the Tatarstan model' is far older than Soviet history itself. It is also older than the appearance on the scene of the present-day regional elite, the members of which, as it is said, 'have mobilized around joint values (such as religion and language) in order to establish equilibrium in the periphery'.[14]

What has been said above does not, of course, completely refute the honest attempt of the scholar to debunk the phenomenon of the Tatarstan model by using the surgical instruments of the 'bonapartist' and 'elite' theories. At the same time, it may be argued that it is the elite that are created by the movements of History, and not History by the elite. The fact that these social theories are more easily understood by the Western mind does not imply that they bring one any closer to the truth, than the author's suggestion that the enigma of the Tatarstan model is best resolved by examining the driving forces of the whole of Tatar history, and not only the post-Soviet period.

I may agree that among the Tatarstan elite, if and when the term can be satisfactorily defined in relation to this particular country and its rather complex social and ethnic circumstances, there are some representatives who just enjoy their position as compared to the 'less lucky and less canny' general population. But, in my experience of looking at how some members of this elite work in reality, I might suggest that not everybody would swap places with them – for example, with my above-mentioned interlocutor who explained the enigma of Kazan's rapid rebirth at the beginning of this chapter.

He gets up before dawn and works until very late resolving the all too many mind-boggling and nerve-racking difficulties of this complex age of transition, whilst bearing full responsibility for their successful resolution. He has a nice house, but it is indeed rare for him to return home before midnight. Often, there are no days off at the weekend, because the huge demands of the volatile transitional economy dealing with a whole host of pressing social issues, often inherited from the Soviet past, could not wait until Monday. In short, the process of the establishment of a working market democracy on the ruins of the Soviet economy, further aggravated by the necessity of creating an appropriate legal base and of the constant need to overcome the Soviet mentality in post-Soviet society, is not a process that produces pleasure. In the majority of cases, the Tatarstan elite are real men and women of Tatar, Russian, Jewish and other ethnic origins who have already proved capable of usefully and fruitfully toiling under such difficult circumstances, and it is simply not fair to group them together just as another self-indulgent 'regional elite' for the sake of yet another PhD.

It is true that I do not want to distance myself from the people who, for all that might be said of them, have transformed the republic and, to an extent, the society they live in. Looking at them, I become only stronger in my conviction that people receive their roles from history and it is up to them how powerfully they understand and fulfil these roles. If a society still has a sense of history, it will produce men and women to realize it, and they will often sacrifice themselves to do it, because a person is to be judged by his or her preparedness to forfeit for the common cause, even if this person just follows the momentum, having no time for any philosophy of a higher order.

In my view, the President of Tatarstan throughout his working life presented the quintessential example of a Tatar person chosen for his understanding and for developing the momentum of Tatar statehood throughout the USSR period and the all-Russia politics. The vision of Tatarstan as a self-sufficient democratic country, where inter-ethnic harmony and economic justice are the beacons of social development, is the main vision of the president, which he had to embody relying not only on his acute political talent and sense of direction, but also on his life-long experience of daily life in the republic. His common sense, which empowered him to take vital steps in the political and economic turmoil of the transition period, may be, of course, ascribed to his hereditary village background, for there is no person in the world who is more judicious than a farmer who always stakes his livelihood on his common sense. But even in this respect, President Shaimiev just reflects the historical path of his people after they lost their official statehood in 1552. This story of national survival is unique in world history, but before turning to the indispensable part of the Tatarstan 'can do' culture, let us yet again cite the work of the Norwegian scholar Linda Røysi who repeats the charge of many other political scientists that:

> The coherence of Tatar elites is secured by the predominance of rural elites. Two-thirds of the Tatar elite originate from rural areas. Agrarian bureaucrats headed by Shaimiev constitute the nucleus of political power, with the military-industrial complex as their junior partner. They have brought with them a 'village culture' which characterizes all relationships within the elite. This culture's characterizing features are: traditional customs of servility; disdain for dissent and opposition; favouritism towards people from the same milieu, especially nepotism; distrust for strangers, particularly urbanites and the more educated stratum of society; self-righteousness and narcissism (Farukshin). This culture is clearly anti-democratic at its very core. In general, it is easier to mobilize and manipulate votes in rural rather than urban areas. As a result, rural elites are more adept in gaining votes, thereby increasing their political voice. Consequently, the agrarian bureaucracy of Tatarstan, with its origin in the old regime, was even further strengthened under the new regime.[15]

It is strange that this harsh indictment of the Tatarstan elite by the Norwegian scholar is based on the works of the leading Tatar politologue Dr Midhat Farukshin who is able to voice and publish his opinions in the republic and abroad without any obstruction on the part of this 'terrible' regime. He is also a source of choice for many scholars on Tatarstan and is always presented as the most objective observer in the republic. Interestingly though, he is also a leading front-bench member of the so-called 'Party of Life' headed by the former mayor of the town of Naberezhnye Chelny, Rafkat Altynbaev, one of the main pretenders to the post of President of Tatarstan and therefore its most vocal critic of President Shaimiev. How it is that the political adversary of the president can become the most objective source for Western academic research, is beyond my comprehension. Both R. Altynbaev and M. Farukshin know that President Shaimiev never relied on the rural vote alone for his vast electoral and social backing, but then, politics is politics, even if projected as impartial scholarship.

One may agree with some observations about the structure of the Tatarstan elite, although Linda Røysi herself states a little earlier in her research that, 'almost all members of the ruling elite in Tatarstan are highly educated men. In contrast to other regions, the authorities of Tatarstan inherited the pre-1990 cadre policy and rejuvenated cadres in a planned manner. Subsequently, the leaders are younger than average in the Russian regions'.

But what I cannot agree with is the description of 'village culture' in Tatarstan as something backward by definition and possessing the predominantly negative features listed in the above quotation. If Linda Røysi can be excused for not knowing the history of the Tatar nation in its 'village period' of 1552–1800, than Dr Farukshin is bound to know it, if he did not completely swap history for political science as the instrument of politics. If he did, he, alas, cannot be considered an objective observer, because the momentum of

Tatar development was not only preserved, but also developed during the historical 'village exile' of Tatar urban civilization.

THE STORY OF TATAR VILLAGE CULTURE

After the fall of Kazan in October 1552, all her Tatar inhabitants were exiled beyond the city limits, and her original urban population was forced to settle in the countryside. For a radius of thirty kilometres around Kazan there are no historical Tatar villages and settlements even today. Throughout the sixteenth and seventeenth centuries Tatars were not allowed to settle any closer to their former capital. However, the economy of Kazan after the banishment of Tatar merchants and handicraftsmen began to fall into decay, and her new authorities were compelled to bring in some Tatar traders in the vicinity of the city in the so-called Old Tatar, and, later, in the New Tatar settlements. However, all over the former Kazan khanate Tatars were forbidden to live and trade in towns, as well as to settle along the big rivers – the Volga and the Kama.

In this way the sedentary and highly urbanized Tatar nation was forcefully turned into a nation of wanderers. Only in 1678 were the Tatars permitted to settle near the ruins of the cradle of their civilization, Bolgar-on-the-Volga: we know of this from the life of the poet and philosopher Bairamgali Kulyev, or Maula Kuly as it was he who was entrusted to supervise this resettlement – one of many. However, in 1699 the Tatar settlement at Bolgar-on-the-Volga was ordered to be populated with Russian immigrants, and the Tatar population of the village was compelled to move to the bank of a small river, the Sheshma, where they founded the village of Old Ishtiryak. Maula Kuly's descendants still live in this village, but the earlier story of his wanderings is extremely characteristic of the plight of the Tatars of the former Kazan khanate in the seventeenth century. The poems by Maula Kuly, as, indeed, the poetry of his Kazan predecessors of the sixteenth century Kul Sharif, Garif Bek, Ommi Kamal and, certainly, the great Muhammedyar, provide the most valuable sources on the history of Kazan-Tatar culture and philosophy after the forced village exile. It is no coincidence that in an earlier book I viewed the medieval verses of Tatar poets as historical documents at a time when the main body of the original historical documents of the Kazan khanate had apparently been destroyed in the capture, and some of them went missing together with the library of Ivan the Terrible.[16] It also did not help the state of Tatar historiography of the fifteenth to the seventeenth centuries that, besides the storm of 1552 and other afflictions, Kazan suffered two all-devouring fires in 1672 and 1694. Only a small part of the official archives of the Kazan khanate, including some samples of the official acts of the Kazan khans, avoided complete historical oblivion. But all that did survive is an account of the tireless efforts of the urban-turned-village Tatars who not only saved them in their dwellings, but also continued the task of recording their history under the new order.

The Tatar inhabitants of Kazan still had no right to enter the Kremlin even at the beginning of the eighteenth century. John Bell, who visited Kazan in 1715, left us the following interesting observation:

> This town ... has a formidable location and is protected by a castle built of bricks. In the fortress there stands the cathedral, the archbishop's and governor's quarters

The President of the Republic of Tatarstan Mintimer Shaimiev

2

Tatarstan leads many Russian regions in sustained agricultural development

3

National traditions and customs of many Volga ethnicities flourish in the rich diversity of Tatarstan's multi-ethnic culture

The New Year – new plans and hopes!

With Kazan's famous cinema and theatre actress Chulpan Khamatova who is of Tatar origin

6

President Mintimer Shaimiev sports a sailor's hat while holding a look-alike miniature at the opening of a new seafood restaurant in Kazan

7

At the newly refurbished Kazan railway station. The Kazan-Moscow 'Tatarstan' train now reaches Moscow in just 10 hours, 30 minutes

'Tug of War' – one of the great spectator competitions of the Tatar traditional Sabantui (plough) festival

9

The revered icon of 'Our Lady of Kazan' is handed over to the Tatarstan's President by the Moscow and all-Russia Orthodox Patriarch Alexis II to forever remain in Kazan as the place of its appropriation in the sixteenth century

10

President Mintimer Shaimiev with the Moscow and all-Russia Orthodox Patriarch Alexis II (left), the Chief Mufti of Tatarstan Gusman Iskhakov (right) and the Speaker of the State Council of Tatarstan Farit Mukhametshin (behind) in the Kul Sharif mosque of the Kazan Kremlin

The Kul Sharif Mosque in the ancient Kazan Kremlin

12

Tatarstan's President with former Russian Prime-Minister Victor Chernomyrdin (right) and former Russian Privatization Tsar Anatoly Chubais

13

'And I say – we can do it!' President Mintimer Shaimiev with the Prime-Minister of Tatarstan Rustam Minnikhanov

Kazan's 'Pyramid' concert hall and entertainment complex

15

At the opening of the Hermitage Rooms in the Kazan Kremlin. President Mintimer Shaimiev with the St Petersburg Governor Valentina Matvienko (centre), the Director of the State Hermitage Museum Mikhail Piotrovsky and the Vice-Premier – Minister of Culture of Tatarstan Zilya Valeeva (left)

16

The former Human Rights Commissioner of the Council of Europe Alvaro Gil-Robles (right) and his successor Thomas Hammarberg enjoying a relaxed moment in Kazan

One's youth is the time of dreams and hopes: Mintimer Shaimiev and his newly-wed wife Sakina

The love of horses is a life-long passion of the President. The new Kazan hippodrome, considered one of the best in the world, staged the final of the prestigious World Cup races on 30 August 2006

At the official opening of the St Petersburg Street during the Millennium celebrations in Kazan

At the Shaimiev parental house in the village of Anyak

Mintimer Shaimiev and his wife at the grave of the President's father

22

The leaders of the Commonwealth of Independent States (CIS) in the Kazan Kremlin during their August 2005 summit

23

President Mintimer Shaimiev hosts the presidents of the CIS countries in the rejuvenated Kazan Kremlin

President Vladimir Putin is a frequent guest to Kazan

25

The ancient Suyumbika Tower in Kazan

26

The Spasskaya tower of the Kazan Kremlin at sunset

The Kazan Kremlin – an aerial view

The leaders of the 'United Russia' political party (from left to right): President Mintimer Shaimiev, the Moscow Mayor Yuri Luzhkov, the Speaker of the Russian Parliament Boris Gryzlov, the Minister for Extraordinary Situations Sergei Shoigu and the Parliamentary Vice-Speaker Vyacheslav Volodin

President Mintimer Shaimiev with the Culture Minister of Azerbaijan Polad Byul-Byul Ogly (right) and the former Vice-President of Tatarstan Dr Vassily Likhachev

Traditional Tatar wrestling is the main contest of the ever popular Sabantui festival.

31

Kazan as the birthplace of the great Russian singer Feodor Chaliapin boasts his first and only monument in the world

32

Planting trees in the new Millennium Park in the centre of Kazan

33

Tatarstan's President with the former Mayor of Kazan, now the all-Russia Presidential Representative in the Far East federal region Kamil Iskhakov (far left), and the new Mayor of Kazan Ilsur Metshin

34

President Mintimer Shaimiev hosting the Iranian Ambassador to Russia Golam-Reza Ansari in the Kazan Kremlin

35

Mintimer Shaimiev, President of the ancient, yet dynamic Tatarstan Republic

The ancient Tatar tea-ceremony

The Motherland Memorial in the Kazan Victory Park – a gift by the President to the city of Kazan

Not-so-ancient history: Presidents Mintimer Shaimiev and Boris Yeltsin negotiating the first bilateral treaty between Tatarstan and Russia

President Mintimer Shaimiev with the former USSR President Mikhail Gorbachev and the Speaker of the Russian Parliament Boris Gryzlov

New medical facilities and general health care is a long-time priority of Tatarstan

President of Kazakhstan Nursultan Nazarbaev (front centre) was impressed by the achievements of Tatarstan's aviation industry

42

There are so many students in Kazan!

43

Do these children know that chess is a favourite game of President Shaimiev!

The future of Tatarstan sports

There are over 100 ethnicities in Tatarstan!

46

Tatar beauties

47

Triumphant common sense springing from village life: Tatarstan has long since been fully self-sufficient in all basic foodstuffs

Tatarstan is still rich in oil. President Mintimer Shaimiev and the Director General of the Tatneft Oil Company Shafagat Takhautdinov

The great contemporary writer, the Plenipotentiary Ambassador of Kyrgyzstan to the Benelux countries, Chinghiz Aitmatov, is also a recipient of the medal 'In Commemoration of the Millennium of the City of Kazan' from the Tatar President

The world famous tennis player Marat Safin happens to be a Tatar

51

American Ambassador William J. Burns has called Tatarstan a model of inter-ethnic and inter-religious accord for the entire world to see and learn from

52

Politics is a matter of knowing and understanding human nature

53

The ancient market square near the Kazan Kremlin is now used for major concerts and other public events

54

The Millennium Bridge across the Kazanka River is one of the main achievements of the grand Kazan jubilee

Tatarstan – the face of the future

and the district chancellery. A ditch and a fence surround the town. In the suburbs, there live craftsmen, save one or two streets, where live the Mohammedan Tatars born in those parts: they live rather tidily and are independent in their worship, and they enjoy many liberties. They are involved in trade with Turkey and Persia and other countries, and some of them are very rich.

In fact, the educational tradition of the Kazan Tatars, preserved through their exile, became the greatest of their riches. Instead of disappearing in the countryside, the centuries-old urban civilization of the Tatars survived and flourished through hereditary entrepreneurship, hard work and, of course, their love of learning. In every village, alongside the mosque or a smaller house of worship, there was a school for boys and girls run by the rural mullah or his wife, called *abystai*, respectively. This was, in a way, only natural as the thirst for education resulted from the teachings of Islam, in which one of the oft-repeated prayers says: 'O Allah, increase me in knowledge!' The Holy Prophet of Islam who always was and remains a human ideal for believers, urged the faithful to seek knowledge even as far as China, and also said that 'the ink of a scholar is dearer than the blood of a martyr'. Although the educational system of the Kazan khanate suffered a setback along with Tatar statehood, it did not, however, disappear altogether. It happened because the need for education was never imposed on the Kazan Tatars 'from above', but was always generated at the grassroots, being, from time immemorial, one of the basic driving forces of Tatar society. Professor of Kazan University Karl Fuks (1776–1846) in his book *Kazan Tatars in Statistical and Ethnographic Profile,* marks this thousand-year-old tradition and gives credit to the Tatar mullahs who 'try to spread Oriental education not only in towns, but also in the poorest and smallest villages, and are rather successful in doing so':

> The fact that Oriental education has spread in villages as much as in towns, can be seen as soon as one enters almost every Tatar village. Between small, often collapsed huts, you will see some beautiful small houses; you will by all means want to enter them. Enter, then, you will be met by the owner, in a calico white shirt and in Bukharan camisole; the mistress, tidily dressed, covers her face with a Zilan (shawl) like any urban Tatar lady. You will see on her a considerable set of silver and turquoise ornaments. The room is very clean; the samovar and a tea service stand in a cupboard; on the wide Podmara (wide bench), there lie folded feather-beds and pillows, and second-hand Persian carpets are spread on the floor. Judging by a Russian peasant's way of life, you will think that this Tatar is rich; – no, he is a farmer, little richer than his neighbour, but his life does not any more resemble the life of a peasant. He reads spiritual books every day with his family, and come the night, he puts on a turban and goes to the mosque where the mullah ordinarily sits with the elder Tatars and deliberates with a sense of importance about him ... Not to mention the famous Tatar ladies, even those less well-to-do and village ones are literate and derive the utmost pleasure in chanting the Surahs from Al-Quran. Every Tatar lady executes the spiritual rules of her religion with surprising strictness and diligence.

In his life, K. Fuks did a great deal to enlighten the Russian people about their thousand-year-old neighbours, the Kazan Tatars, and one of his most well-known citations is the following:

Every visiting person will be, undoubtedly, surprised to find in the Kazan Tatars a nation, broadly speaking, more educated than other nations including the European. A Tatar unable to read and write is despised by his fellow countrymen and, as a citizen, does not command any respect from others. That is why every father tries to enlist his children as soon as possible in a school where they will be taught to read, write and learn the tenets of their religion. For facilitating this, at each mosque there is a school under the special supervision of the akhun (head imam); the mullah of the mosque is the teacher there, daily engaged in teaching all these subjects. In both of the local Tatar settlements there are eight mosques, and, at them, only four schools, which, however, are attended by many pupils.

If the aforesaid could be to some extent understood as an expression of 'Kazan patriotism' by K. Fuks, the nineteenth-century 'Description of All Peoples Residing in the Russian State' also gives a favourable summary of the Tatar education system maintained in the Tatar villages and townships:

> The Kazan ... Tatars ... take great and creditable care of the decent education of their children. They not only accustom their children to diligence, thrift and other ancestral traditions, but also take care in teaching them to read, write, know the Arabic language and their faith. Ignoring such care is considered a great sin for the parents, and, therefore, in each of their villages, too, there is a special prayer house and a school ... in their settlements (sloboda) and large villages there are schools for girls in similar fashion. At the same time, children are taught some understanding of their own history ... Many Tatar peasants (muzhiks), and, more frequently, merchants possess small libraries of written texts and a very considerable knowledge about current affairs – not only their own, but also those of neighbouring countries, and, on the top of that, know their ancient history quite well.

From the above it is becomes clear that the struggle against Islam permeating sixteenth-seventeenth century Kazan history, was, for the Tatar, not only a struggle against their system of education, but also against the very history of the nation. Remarkably, even in the seventeenth century – one of the most difficult periods of Tatar history – in Kazan, that is, in the Tatar settlement somewhat removed from the city, there were many Tatar schools. We know about this because the previously mentioned poet Maula Kuly at the beginning of this troubled century studied in Kazan at the school of one mullah Mamai who, by the way, was also a Sufi poet and philosopher. Here, alas, we must remind ourselves of the conditions, under which Tatar education proceeded in the sixteenth and seventeenth centuries, however sad it might be for us. But we must always remember that 'those oblivious of their history are doomed to re-live it'.

Let us recollect then, that for two centuries Islam as the basis of Kazan culture was effectively banned, and people professing it were subjected to inconceivable spiritual and physical burdens, double taxation, soldiering and a complete lack of rights. Surviving and preserving one's cultural origins and mother tongue under such adverse circumstances is nothing short of remarkable: the Tatar nation preserved itself as an ethnic and cultural reality, even despite the fact that this nation with its thousand-year-old written literature was not only 'reduced to village culture' until the beginning of the nineteenth century, but also forbidden to publish its own newspapers and magazines until 1905.

Thus, Tatar urban culture, persecuted and impoverished, found its safe haven in villages all over their former country and in the city settlements. Here, alongside wooden and, later, stone mosques, schools were built. Learned people and scholars known throughout the Muslim world, – Kursavi, Nasyri, Mardzhani, – worked here. Here also the great poets Utyz Imyani, Gali Chokry, Kandaly, Gabdulla Tukay were born... Here the truth of history was saved, and ancient books and manuscripts, which had by some miracle survived the flames, were industriously copied. Here the Kazan Tatars preserved what their ancestors had not given up despite the pain of death and all kinds of terrible deprivation: their epic poetry and samples of calligraphy of the Bulgar and old Kazan times, their way of life, their patterns and ornaments, their songs. Here, in the suburbs, Kazan saved and preserved her soul which is alive today.

As for the 'anti-democratic' nature of the Tatar 'village culture', it is in the villages that a unique and particular kind of Tatar historical democracy was born in an environment lacking aristocratic power structures, which disappeared with the demise of the Kazan khanate. Spiritual compulsion, aggravated by economic pressure and the deprivation of Tatar rights to land, urged the Tatar aristocracy, which had already had blood ties with the Russian nobility for two centuries, to accept baptism in order to preserve their privileges. Thus, many Russian aristocratic families were born: the echoes of Tatar descent sound in the family trees of such representatives of the Russian cultural *crème de la crème* as N. Karamzin, G. Derzhavin, A. Radishchev, K. Ryleyev, A. Chaadaev, S. Rachmaninov, D. Mendeleyev, A. Kuprin and A. Skriabin.

So, for centuries, contrary to the state policy of the alienation of Tatar culture, the ancient Bulgar-Kazan culture not only cooperated, but from time to time even merged with Russian culture. But, in the villages, the role of leaders fell on the shoulders of the 'elders' or, in Tatar, 'abyzes' chosen by the majority of their respective communities and representing their interests *vis-à-vis* the Russian authorities. Interestingly, in the atmosphere of religious, and thus cultural, intolerance on the part of the Russian authorities, this Tatar leadership was, effectively, elected and endorsed by the common people.

The popular institution of *'abyzes'* presented a rather peculiar form of political leadership which evolved under conditions of continuous restraints, limitations and outright persecution of the Muslim Tatars in the area under Russian Orthodox control. The Tatar *abyzes* were the real elected leaders of their respective communities, on the one hand fulfilling the duties of the supreme religious authority, and on the other, undertaking a representative role when dealing with Russian governmental structures. The authority of such leaders was based on several factors, the most important being their faithfulness to Islamic traditions, religious knowledge and social fairness. 'A just leader is a shelter of God', says one of the utterances of the Holy Prophet of Islam. If anything, the adherence to the Prophet's example perpetrated the idea of social justice among the oppressed, but still charismatic Tatar communities. Wealth earned through the worldly enterprise and personal charisma of the *abyzes* also played an important role in the process of their rise to a position of prominence within their respective communities. Moreover, such people undertook not only the immense task of preserving and safeguarding Islam against all odds, but, also, and more significantly, the duty of further spreading and propagating

Islam in Russia. At the same time, it is to those Tatar elders that Russia owes the establishment of her historical trade links with the Muslim South and India.

As one of the many examples of such self-sustaining Tatar village communities in the historical Tatarstan and Russia at large, the history of the Kargala settlement near Orenburg is particularly instructive. In 1783, in his account of a 1751 sojourn to India and the Middle East, one Ismagil Aga of the Sayid Settlement near Orenburg wrote: 'By the will of Allah written in our fate (*taqdir*), mullah Nadir and mullah Yakub, and Ismagil, and Gabderahman, and one of the servants of Nadir mullah, all five of us were sent by Sayid the Elder to the city of Bukhara for trade purposes.'[17] Here, the word 'mullah' is used in its usual sense in the Tatar language, bearing the connotation of a 'learned person well-versed in religion'. Sayid the Elder in this record is a historical personality who, with the permission of the high Russian authorities, in 1745 led a group of other Volga Tatars, weary of religious and economical restraints, from the Kazan province to that of Orenburg. Here, he founded a settlement, from which he then expanded his trade to Bukharan, Khivan, Kashgarian and other Asian markets.

The Sayid Settlement, known also as Kargala, with the passage of time became one of the most enlightened centres of Islam in Russia, as well as a prosperous commercial centre. In a recent book on the history of Kargala,[18] it is rightly observed that with its autonomous rights of economic activity and relative cultural and religious freedom, Kargala in the thirty years since its establishment had grown into a rich trade and crafts city resembling 'an Islamic republic'. The example of Kargala sheds a bright light on the capacity of the Tatar people, when they are left to their own devices within greater Russia. Besides conducting successful trade and engaging in industrial activities, which created a considerable share of 'Tatar' capital in eighteenth and nineteenth century Russia, charismatic Muslim leaders such as Sayid of Kargala and his successors travelled all over Russia, establishing communal settlements with mosques, schools and prosperous enterprises. Little village education establishments later grew into the world famous *medreses* of 'Hussainiye' in Orenburg, 'Muhammediye' in Kazan and 'Galiye' in Ufa, which, by the beginning of the twentieth century, were among the most, if not the most, prominent, innovative and far-sighted centres of Islamic education in the Muslim world.

The political role of the *abyzes* should also not be underestimated. The report by the Russian military commanders Kirillov and Rumyantsev, who were given the job of suppressing Muslim revolts in the area between the Volga and Ural Mountains[19] says:

> In all of those villages, the Tatars who moved from the Kazan district live in the capacity of mullahs and abyzes. All of them are learned and intelligent men. Their word is received by the population as the word of a prophet. For that reason, Tatar mullahs and abyzes should be expelled from the Ufa district, their religious schools (*medreses*) should be closed, their students should be used as interpreters, etc.[20]

The popular democratic institute of *abyzes* ceased to exist after the Russian Empress Katherine the Great instituted the Muslim Spiritual Board in Orenburg in 1789. Since then, the Muslim leadership was appointed by the Russian authorities and ceased to be a representative institution of the people. The officially established Muslim hierarchy, for the most part, served the ruling authorities from which they received their appointments 'by edict'. The rule of dogma prevailed among those '*mullahs* by edict', and yet, the traditional educational and cultural drive of the Volga Tatar nation eventually overcame even this grave obstacle, which played such a negative role in the cultural and economic decline of other countries of the Islamic world during the nineteenth century.

So, when I see the term 'Tatar village culture' used in a derogatory or contemptuous context, I always remember that it was the educational, spiritual and economic drive of this unique culture that had not only safeguarded the entire Tatar nation from extinction, but also made it what it is today. There would be no political, economic and inter-ethnic 'Tatarstan model' known all over the world without this 'village culture' with its inherent qualities of the commonsense perception of things, economic and trade industriousness and a sense of historical destiny. It is only fair that Tatar 'village culture' returns to the cities with their former Soviet-style cosmopolitanism diluting all the national features which are so vital in making things happen in Tatarstan. In this chapter, I do not even refer to the issue of the Tatar mother tongue, which historically survived only in the villages, whereas the Tatar constitution demands that the President of the Republic should be well versed in both Russian and Tatar.

NOTES

1. I was able to speak English and German fluently and knew Shakespeare by heart at the age of eighteen, although these language skills were never called for until after *perestroika*.
2. Literally, the Stone Leg – the name of the square in Kazan during the fifteenth and sixteenth centuries.
3. Joseph E. Stiglitz, ibid, p.154, referring to Russia as a whole.
4. 2,713 roubles per capita for people in work, 1,761 roubles for pensioners, 2,442 roubles for children. The decree of the government of Tatarstan No. 17, 25 January 2006.
5. There are some positive signs though: in 2005, consumer credit loans of Russian banks totalled 1 trillion roubles, or 30 billion US dollars, and many goods, including cars, TV sets and even mobile phones are being bought through consumer credit facilities.
6. Irek Murtasin, www.compromat.ru/main/shaimiev/forbes.htm
7. *The Evening Kazan*, number 201 (3143), 2005, www.evening-kazan.ru/printart.asp?id=20686.
8. *Oil and Life*, 6 (18), 2005, the interview first published in *Tribuna Weekly* in Tatarstan.
9. *Islam in Post-Soviet Russia. Public and Private Faces*, edited by Hilary Pilkington and Galina Yemelianova, RoutledgeCurzon, Taylor & Francis Group, London & New York, 2003.
10. Linda Røysi, 'Explaining the political autonomy of Tatarstan', Russian Centre and Periphery, Thesis submitted in partial fulfilment of the Candidata Politicarum Rerum Decree, Department of Comparative Politics, Faculty of Social Sciences, University of Bergen, May 2004.
11. Andrew Heywood, ibid, p. 167.
12. Røysi, op. cit.
13. Ibid.
14. Ibid.
15. Linda Røysi, op.cit.
16. See, *Historical Anthology of Kazan Tatar Verse* edited by D. Matthews and R. Bukharaev, Curzon Press Ltd, 2000.

17. A. Aleeva, 'Sojourn of Ismagil Aga', in *Quests, Thoughts, Findings*, Kazan, 1989, in the Tatar language.
18. R. Iskandarov, A. Iskandarov, *The Sayid Settlement*, Tatar Publishing House, Kazan, 2005.
19. V. Imamov, 'The Akay-Kilmek Uprising', *Idel Monthly*, No. 10–11, 1991, Kazan, in the Tatar language.
20. The commander's report also advises the limiting of the term elders to one year, the placing of Russian Orthodox settlements alongside Muslim villages and the impeding of procreation among Muslims. Indeed, the activities of *mullahs* as religious teachers and *abyzes* as religious and political leaders brought about results highly unwelcome to the Russian authorities. 'If, in the period before 1719 the overall number of christened Tatars in the Kazan district amounted to 13,322, in the twelve years thereafter this number reduced to 2,995.'

CHAPTER 6

'WE NEED MILLIONS OF PROPRIETORS'

The system of private property is the most important guarantee of freedom, not only for those who own property, but scarcely less for those who do not.

Friedrich August von Hayek (1900–92)

Private property is a necessary institution, at least in a fallen world; men work more and dispute less when goods are private than when they are common. But it is to be tolerated as a concession to human frailty, not applauded as desirable in itself.

R. H. Towney (1880–1962)

From my rare conversations with President Shaimiev I do not believe that this visionary leader of Tatarstan's economic, political and social transition formulates his vision of the republic's destination, and especially his particular policies, in terms of a fairer wealth distribution (mentioned in the previous chapter). If anything, his motto is common-sense wealth creation, but, again, doing so in the interests of the entire people he is there to serve and protect.

Interestingly, in one of my recent meetings with the president, he started with a quotation from, of all things, the last writings of Lenin – those from his New Economic Policy published in the mid-1920s. In Kazan, as it happens, one cannot avoid Lenin: the city has the ambiguous honour of still having his museum, because his grandfather on his mother's side had land possessions in the vicinity of Kazan. Kazan also saw the beginning of Lenin's revolutionary activity, when he was kicked out of Kazan University for staging a student protest. However, the later writings of this communist Machiavelli were already full of remorse and re-evaluation of communist policies of total rejection of private enterprise. The Lenin of his later days was still enough of an economist to realize that the revolutionary policies of the young Soviet state brought about a colossal fall in industrial production and more than doubled the tax burden of the Russian farmers. His dying revelation that 'We need millions of private proprietors', is the only advice from the father of all-Russian misery that President Shaimiev is keen to follow.

Today, after fifteen years of transition, almost one-fifth of Tatarstan's working population are proprietors of their own enterprises, totalling over 300,000 people. Half of them are owners of small and medium-sized businesses, of which 16,000 are commercial farmers and over 160,000 are entrepreneurs in various partnerships. The latter provide almost four-fifths of all services in the republic in the spheres of residential refurbishment and construction, photo and hairdressing services, as well as furniture production, food, juice and mineral water production, clothing manufacture, etc. They also represent nine out of ten of all tourist agencies and provide four-fifths of legal services in Tatarstan. The most profitable services in Tatarstan today are transportation, housing and letting, advertising, health and photographic services, as well as commercial audit, communications, auto services, restaurants and the entertainment sector. At the start of 2006, the wages in the small private sector of Tatarstan's economy were higher than in the large- and medium-sized enterprises, averaging 7018 roubles per month, which is 65 per cent higher than in 2004. At the same time, the growth in wages in large businesses averaged just 25 per cent.[1]

Of course, Tatarstan is not yet a society of the 'millions of private proprietors', but the trend is well under way. In 2005, the joint turnover of small businesses in Tatarstan reached 139 billion roubles, or 18 per cent of the turnover of all enterprises of the republic. The tax revenue from small businesses grew in 2005 by 30 per cent year on year, totalling 11 billion roubles. Such growth became possible partly because small enterprises all over the republic are benefiting from the renovation of the cities and transport infrastructure in part financed by the mammoth oil, petrochemical, machine and aircraft building and likewise privatized enterprises of Tatarstan. Socially-oriented expenditure of these large plants, holdings, corporations and even the National Bank, for instance in the sphere of professional and amateur sports facilities, create the necessary conditions for the growth of the services sector not only in Kazan, but also in the relatively remote parts of the country, in towns such as Bugulma, Almetyevsk and Elabuga. Huge and thoroughly modern sports installations like the outstanding Basket Hall and Tatneft Ice Arena in Kazan, the racing circuit and alpine skiing resort in the vicinity of the city are matched by smaller, but no less important sports installations in other parts of the country. The involvement of the president in such projects also reflects his vision of developing the whole of the republic in a social sense – increasingly less at the expense of the government and more investment of large enterprises, so that private ownership could work for the benefit of the entire population and not for the lucky few.

At the same time, the government is there to create favourable conditions for the growth of small and medium-sized businesses by way of providing sustainable credit investment. The lack of readily available and cheap credit was, and to some extent, is the Achilles heel of the entire Russian economy, which is still struggling with stubborn annual inflation. However, in 2005, 986 small firms and companies in Tatarstan received 266 million roubles in credit from the Investment Venture Fund of Tatarstan. Since October 2005, the Leasing Company for Small Businesses is functioning in Tatarstan, which has already financed small-size projects to the sum of 440,000 roubles. These sums may not seem big in themselves, but one has to take into account the real circumstances on the ground and consider that, as recently as 1998, Russia experienced total financial collapse when the state defaulted on debt payments; Tatarstan also suffered, but to a lesser extent. This lucky escape was due to the fact that since the beginning of the 1990s Tatarstan struggled to build her own financial base never allowing big Russian speculative banks into her playing field. So, when these commercial banks, which heavily speculated in the all-Russia GKO government bonds and thus participated in building the state financial pyramid, defaulted, the people of Tatarstan suffered less pain from yet another haemorrhage in their life savings. Even so, after 1998, many small businesses in Tatarstan also had to start everything afresh and therefore all positive signs of sustainable growth are to be welcomed and nurtured in today's climate.

When, therefore, we talk about President Shaimiev's vision of the 'country of millions of proprietors', we must remember that the entire process of private wealth creation in Tatarstan had to be started from scratch. For people in the West who take for granted the existence of large and small private enterprises and the prospect of inheriting from close and distant relatives, it may be difficult to appreciate that citizens of Tatarstan, as well as the all-Russia citizens, had almost nothing in their private possession at the beginning of 1990s. Even the properties in which they lived did not, as a rule, belong to them with the exception of rural areas. So, how do you create proprietors in a country where everything used to be in state ownership?

There were two main approaches to addressing this crucial issue, the first being advised and sponsored by the IMF and the World bank. We may call this the 'Chubais approach', the main feature of which was the speed of de-nationalization of the Russian economy. Anatoly Chubais was then the chairman of the Committee for State Property and he argued that the team of the 'young reformers' or the 'Chicago boys', as they were called in those days, had to act rapidly to seize the moment and privatize everything before the Russian parliament came to its senses and intervened. The Russian parliament did indeed intervene, but was silenced by the artillery bombardment of 1993. Interestingly, the acclaimed Russian reformers of the Yeltsin era, who boasted of their presumed knowledge of the workings of the market economy, approached privatization not from the economic, but rather from ideological point of view. Their main excuse in selling colossal industrial wealth to those who happened to be near to them at the time, at a fraction of the real cost, was that the rapid privatization should make any return to a command Socialist economy impossible. The result of this swift privatization of 1992–93, involving a most dubious decision to practically give away the Russian budget and the most juicy stock of the Russian oil, aluminium-production and similar key industries to the country's commercial banks in 1996 in the scam of the 'privatization auctions', was disastrous in the sense that it completely spoiled, in the eyes of the Russian citizens, the entire idea of private ownership and, along with it, the very idea of a democratic market economy. The rapid and rather thoughtless de-nationalization of the Russian industrial and mining sectors created a layer of oligarchs and unjustifiably concentrated the country's wealth in the hands of a few businessmen and, what's more, almost for free.

It is not the place here to examine the 'Chubais approach', not least because today it is the very consequences of this erstwhile approach that hinder the economic and social development of Russia, whose citizens never accepted this crony wealth distribution as just and fair.[2] Of course, its excesses can be attributed to general ignorance of the market economy in Russia in those days, but then, Western examples and patterns of privatization were widely available for the 'Chicago boys' to emulate; they always said that economic laws work in the same way in any economy of the world, be it Poland, Bolivia or Russia. It would have been enough to examine the preparations and precautions taken, for instance, in the process of privatization of British Steel, which took five years in the long-established market economy of the UK! Even then, other examples of the privatization and price liberalization in the UK and the USA show that even the most well-meaning market-oriented measures can result in economic failure. The rapid privatization of the Russian economy, with its huge military-industrial sector demanding sustainable state orders for its existence, was adventurism on an unprecedented scale, a veritable catastrophe in the making, which, maybe, only Russia with its vast natural and human resources could survive. Suffice it here to say that the experiment achieved exactly the opposite result, causing the Russian people to become totally disillusioned with the entire process of 'oligarchic' transition, which made them destitute, devoid of rights and socially frustrated without opening many new avenues for personal growth. Their participation in the market transition was seemingly assured by the 'voucher scheme', according to which each citizen of Russia received a nominal voucher for his or her share in the country's wealth. These vouchers were intended for buying into the emerging market economy, but because of the lack of information and market knowledge and, especially, any valid legislation, the voucher scheme became the scam of the century. I still have three shares in some strange enterprise called 'Hermes-Finance' bought by my family's vouchers. This firm, like others of its kind, was established with the sole objective of collecting people's vouchers and, like all such 'companies-for-a-day', rapidly disappeared into thin air. Russian people, robbed of all their life savings by the hyperinflation that was subsequently unleashed and rudely deceived by the voucher scheme, could only watch, in anguish, as the country's wealth, created by enormous efforts of the entire people of Russia, passed into the hands of a few shady entrepreneurs whose only virtue was complete lack of conscience and an inside knowledge of the Russian economic labyrinth. In any civilized country the results of such de-nationalization would be a matter for the courts, but the West only applauded with delight at the 'death of Communism', which in fact proved to be the death of the Russian economy and even the Russian 'capitalist dream'.

The economic regime, which reigned in Russia in the wake of privatization, was so hateful to the average Russian citizen that today's economic policies aimed at macroeconomic and social stability seem to them a welcome relief from the earlier total frustration. Yet the most colossal task facing today's Russia is not a question of just achieving economic growth. Its biggest task is re-establishing social trust and a sense of participation in the economic future of the country which has been completely destroyed by the previous chaotic years of the all-Russia transition. For all high-flying economic theories, the most vital things in life and the economy are very simple. There can be no good enjoyed by the people, if the people are thrown out of the equation, which was done by the 'Chicago boys' period of the Russian transition. People have to embrace the reforms as their own, if the country is to achieve something. The 'Chubais approach' could be summed up in the formula 'people for the economy', when people are expected to bear all hardships and even die as a result of collateral damage for the sake of an economic theory. Nobody really understands how Russia survived her last economic experiment of the twentieth century. Its very existence since then is something of a miracle.

But what about the 'Shaimiev approach'? First of all, it did not and does not expect any miracles to occur with this particular vision of the market transition. Its formula, if anything, is an 'economy for the people'. When in the heat of the all-Russia rabid privatization President Shaimiev refused to toe the Moscow line and chose instead the method of the 'soft entrance to the market', he was criticized for his apparent Socialist beliefs from all sides, including Western observers. In the uproar surrounding his policies of subsidizing the cost of basic foodstuffs and his bold decision not to participate in the all-Russia voucher scam, few people heard the main argument voiced by the president and even less understood its significance. This argument was simply stated in his words 'reforms are worth nothing, if they bring unnecessary suffering to the people', and contained the essence of the 'Shaimiev approach', viz., during market transition, one must create conditions, in which the people will accept reforms as their own and not as foisted from above in the saddest of Russian historical traditions. The people have to perceive their own good in everything that is happening on the economic front and this is impossible without maintaining a sense of economic and social fairness. Major changes in the transformation of the economic system cannot be achieved overnight, because these changes must first take root in the social conscience of the people and this takes time, even if time is the most precious commodity in the challenges of transition. In short, there can be no market without a significant degree of social approval and the establishment of a market culture associated with democratic market economy.

Under the circumstances of declining industrial output and political uncertainty throughout Russia, President Shaimiev consistently advocated his gradual approach to vital economic reforms – principally the crucial task of creating private wealth in the republic. Here, his earthy philosophy and village background played no less an important role than his reliance on sound economic advice and the learning curve he had embraced concerning the intricacies of the market economy.

For it is not enough to come into possession of something to become a responsible owner of it. In the lottery of the all-Russia privatization fiasco, large and middle-sized enterprises fell into the hands of the people who only wanted to milk them to death and then dump them, because one does not value anything, which almost comes for free and by chance. Such a proprietor is not interested in developing his business, as he is motivated only by greed: all the Russian money which was siphoned from the country over the years and turned into luxurious yachts and real estate abroad, is proof enough of the above observation. Such people are not masters of their property, but at the most parasites dwelling on it.

It is in this sense that President Shaimiev is the master of his republic who understands what responsible ownership means. Yet, any semblance of such a sense of responsibility during the Soviet years remained only at the level of village culture, which, as Lenin would resentfully say, 'each day and minute creates a class of proprietors'. It is because of the implicit truth of that observation that Russian and Tatar farmers experienced such an ideological onslaught and outright robbery on the part of the Soviet state from the dawn of its existence. For all the fine-sounding communist slogans like 'the land to the farmers', the October Revolution in Russia actually changed the life of the Russian and Tatar village for the worse: during the years 1922–24, for instance, real taxation on the Soviet farmers grew twofold compared to 1913.[3] The Stalinist 'collectivization' was meant to render the last blow on the 'eternal village quest for private ownership' and it almost succeeded in depriving the country's farmers of any economic and even civic freedom (Soviet farmers did not have passports until the 1950s and were effectively chained to their land). The agricultural sector came to be considered 'the black hole' of the Soviet economy, and such an attitude prevailed among Soviet and later Russian economists well into the twenty-first century.

Here again, it was Tatarstan under the Presidency of Mintimer Shaimiev that declared the republican agricultural sector to be one of the economic priorities of the transition period. Some observers and political scientists would immediately ascribe this decision to the president's village background. Indeed, he himself often speaks about this background with reference to his long-gone and immediate ancestors. His grandfather Shagimuhammad, who was called Shaimi by his fellow-countrymen, was a well-off farmer who got 'dekulakized' – dispossesed of all property and forced to wander with his family looking for accommodation in alien households – during the Stalinist collectivization period. This man, from whom the Shaimiev family got their family name, was a representative of a long-established Tatar village culture that knew the worth of the native land and the responsibility of caring for it.

Tatars, by the way, never were serfs in the old Russian serf system. They always were so-called 'state farmers', free men under governmental taxation, even if their freedom was often violated by the additional burdens like a foisted responsibility to provide transport and labour for the extremely hard 'Lashman' work – felling and carrying wood for the old Kazan dockyards in the eighteenth century. Still, Tatar farmers successfully carried their agricultural traditions originating from the times of Volga Bulgaria and the Kazan khanate well into the twentieth century, and knew only too well the worth of their land and livestock.

The Soviet system of collectivized agriculture hit into the heart of this centuries-old tradition. President Shaimiev's father, Sharifulla Shaimiev, became the chairman of the collective farm (Kolkhoz) despite his own father's sad fate, and worked in this capacity for twenty-six years, with only one interval, when he spent a year on the Moscow front during the Second World War. In today's 'post-modern' world, that is to say, in the prosperous countries of the West, the majority of people are unable to imagine, the extent of the hardships which were endured by the Soviet people during that war, let alone understand the way of life and dire conditions in Russian and Tatar villages at that time. The war effort would take away everything the farmers produced and the village people would live on the verge of starvation. President Shaimiev still remembers that time of his childhood when a pancake made of the frozen potatoes would seem the richest dish in the world. Such recollections, which are very much alive in the memory of Russian people, always remind them of the real worth of such things as daily bread as opposed to the post-modern culture of 'seeking entertainment and pleasure' and 'self-gratification'. President Shaimiev still remembers how his father got arrested in the spring of 1949, when, during imminent famine in his village, he gave away to the villagers two quintals (1 metric quintal = 100 kg) of seed millet for food. For that, he was accused of misappropriating 'the Socialist common property' and almost got ten years imprisonment. He was interrogated until the autumn of that year, when it appeared that, actually, the crops in his Kolkhoz were better than in neighbouring villages, and he was left alone.

Was it then that the idea that providing for people rather than using them as soulless tools is good economics entered the future president's mind? However, the thought that it is people who are the most precious asset of any economy, subsequently became the main inspiration in his economic and social thinking.

At the dawn of the *perestroika*, there were deafening calls to immediately dissolve the Kolkhozes and give land to the farmers, thereby creating the foundations of a market economy in the agricultural sphere. As usual, such calls were voiced by the people who barely knew the real situation on the ground and had no idea that farmers need not just land, but also technical assistance, means of transport, and fuel for their tractors and cars, but, most of all, sustainable credit facilities and a functioning market for their produce, none of which they had in Russia. All of this had to be thoughtfully planned, provided for and substantiated legally, but, as it happens, it was Tatarstan which was the first to start along that path, in the face of a storm of disapproval from the side of 'market reformers'.

Here, the president's experience as a former farmer and director of a rural technical assistance facility became invaluable. Knowing that nothing will grow out of nothing, he never advocated the immediate dismantling of the republican collective farms, even if the farmers were given a free choice and could leave with their plot of land if they so wished. Few were willing to leave, because the Tatar villagers realized that they will be unable to logistically and financially provide for themselves and their farms in the first years of market transition. Instead, the government of Tatarstan started investing heavily in the agrarian sector, providing rural areas not just with funds, but also with the necessary infrastructure, roads and agricultural machines. The great help given to the farmers and rural population also included the complete gasification of the Tatarstan countryside, which saved the villagers time and effort in stocking wood for the long Tatarstan winters. Such support, which some would call 'state involvement in the market', paid off handsomely, despite all the prophesies of doom.

Despite being in the zone of risky agriculture, Tatarstan steadily improved its harvest – in 1996 the harvest was 30 per cent higher than in 1991. As a result, Tatarstan moved from fifth to second place among all Russian regions in cereals production and sustained her agricultural growth despite the adverse weather condition of 1998. Moreover, in 2005, Tatarstan achieved unheard-off yields of main crops, which delivered on average 33 quintals per hectare of cereals in the zone, where 13–16 quintals were always considered an acceptable norm. Due to the presidential policies of sustained investment in agriculture, by 1996,

Tatarstan was completely self-sufficient in basic foodstuffs, which saved the republic a great deal of hard currency after the 1998 default, as she did not need to import food products to anything like the extent of other less far-sighted regions of Russia. Since then, food imports into Tatarstan have not exceeded 10–12 per cent of public requirements, and these imports are mainly of produce not available in Tatarstan itself, such as southern fruits, Western soft drinks, etc. This advance in agricultural growth has been sustained into the twenty-first century as well, so much so that the all-Russian national project on agriculture has included many features of Tatarstan's pioneering agricultural practices.

Despite all the accusations of the 'market reformers' who still believe that market conditions can be created simply by dictat, in 1998, Tatarstan was the first region in Russia to adopt the Land Code allowing the purchase and sale of land. Land in Tatarstan can be bought and sold not only by the citizens of the republic or those of Russia at large, but also by foreigners and persons without citizenship, although foreigners can only buy land from the State Reserve. As far as agricultural land is concerned, it can only be bought by the people who understand agriculture and are prepared to work to develop their land.

In short, in the agricultural sector President Shaimiev has remained true to his main economic credo: do not act on impulse and ideology, but always create the necessary conditions and legal basis for further reforms. Do not take another step, before you have fully accomplished the previous one, is a lifetime motto of President Shaimiev. Since 1998, Tatarstan has actively encouraged the creation of private farms, because the conditions are now ripe for such liberalization. In 2000, the number of private farms grew threefold compared to 1993. The pace of this transition is, however, hindered by the fact that those leaving the collective farm take with them their share of the collective farm's debt, which is not always conducive to a successful start as an entrepreneur in the private agricultural sector. But then, we all have to live in the real world and nobody is being forced to make individual life choices. In 2006, on the eve of the all-Russia agricultural census, the data from Tatarstan show that the share of private farms in the republic's agriculture is less than five per cent, yet their joint production in 2005 grew by one third compared to 2004. Remarkably, this growth is higher than the respective growth not only in the collective farms, but also in the village personal estates, with their gardens, vegetable gardens and livestock. In order to sustain the growth and further develop cereals and livestock, Tatarstan also welcomes large private investment into the agricultural sector, for instance, by the young brewer tycoon, Airat Hairullin, the former owner of the 'Red Orient' brewery, who recently sold 92.34% of his brewery interests to Efes Breweries International N. V. for $360 million in order to concentrate on his agricultural interests. Already in 2003, the 'Red Orient' Brewery, the fifth largest in Russia, bought 100,000 hectares of agricultural land, of which only 12% was used for barley. The rest was used for other cereals and, importantly, for establishing modern dairy farms equipped with Western machinery and freezer installations. The company 'Red Orient Agro' became the world's largest producer of milk and pedigree cattle with an investment of eight billion roubles, yet its owner then complained that not many corporate investors are keen to invest in agriculture, mainly because of the lack of all-Russia governmental support for agricultural development on an industrial scale. The situation may improve with the all-Russia national project for developing agriculture based on many features of Tatarstan's experience in this sphere, but the results remain to be seen.

However, today, it is a fact that over half of all agricultural land in Tatarstan is in the hands of large corporate investors like 'Tatarstan Milk', 'Red Orient', 'Kamazzernoproduct' and others. In 2005, they invested over 260 million roubles into Tatarstan's agricultural sector and this investment as well as preferential credits, are used for buying top quality seeds, machinery and fertilizers. The cattle-breeding and poultry-farming, which severely declined during the Soviet years, need and do receive special attention. For example, in 2005, the poultry farmers of Tatarstan achieved a record output of 4,400 tons, which was 26 per cent higher than the previous year.

Considering that Tatarstan belongs to what might be called the zone of risky farming, it is indeed surprising that republican farms occupy the top places in the list of the best agricultural enterprises of Russia. For example, in the rating for the 2002–2004 period the agricultural complex named after Sindryakov of the Nurlat region of Tatarstan occupied third place after two farms of the southern Krasnodar district with the unbelievable harvest of 68 quintals per hectare. A further nine farms of Tatarstan are also listed among the 100 best in Russia. If only the Russian cereals market would be more transparent and less prone to insider preferences! The Russian government keeps its buying prices low, whereas the farmers have to pay ever more for fuel and logistics. In such circumstances, Tatarstan has to seek ways of accessing foreign markets, and in 2001 the republic for the first time sold 300,000 tons of cereals to the countries of what is known as the 'far-abroad'.

It would be naïve to think that by paying special attention to the agricultural sector the president simply indulges his nostalgia for his village youth. Tatarstan is soon to compete on a global scale in the context of the WTO, and thus it will have to compete with Western farmers who are receiving tens of billions of dollars in farm subsidies. Is President Shaimiev wary of that? To this question he replies that the WTO is just another market and one has to find one's place in it, whereas Tatarstan is not a novice in world markets with her industrial production. There are other things, which disturb the president in the light of globalization, but of that more later. After all, I am a witness to the fact that quality of the food in Tatarstan is much better than that on average of, say, the UK and all of this wonderful food is organic: come and taste it for yourselves and prove me wrong! Tatarstan is not afraid of competition provided it is fair, but she still makes all the necessary moves to sustain and develop her agricultural future.

Being a world-class politician rubbing shoulders with many world leaders, President Shaimiev still seems in his element when it comes to agriculture, the source and engine of his political wit and common sense. Given the choice of all of Kazan's many restaurants, he still advises his visitors to try a new restaurant and entertainment complex in the centre of Kazan constructed in a shape of a village, where one can try wonderful traditional Tatar cuisine. I did and I was not disappointed.

Tatarstan, as we have seen, fought hard to retain her right to pursue a separate economic policy and the former bilateral treaty with Russia gave her enough leverage to do so. Basically, we may say that this is an ongoing policy and covers two major periods in Tatarstan's economy. The first of those was the period of de-nationalization and the establishment of the foundations of a market economy without falling into the abyss of irreversible contraction in its economic output. In the circumstances, when most former USSR supply and distribution links were broken, the government of Tatarstan had to re-establish these links within Russia, the CIS and the 'far abroad' and, simultaneously, secure vital industrial orders, among others those for her large machine and aircraft construction enterprises. All of this had to be done almost in a the blink of an eye, as even the most successful industry can die very quickly if it has no orders and no market for its finished products. The years 1992–1994 were crucial market in this respect, and I will challenge any economist to dispute the macroeconomic and social steps taken by Tatarstan at this time.

For all the delirious assumptions elsewhere in the Federation that the free market would immediately establish economic order in a highly centralized economy with 70 per cent share of the state budget order-dependent on military-complex enterprises and lacking not only market institutions, but even basic market legislation and any knowledge of a market economy, Tatarstan, surprisingly, clearly saw the ways in which its economic order could be restored and developed despite the chaos of the all-Russia neo-liberal 'reforms'. President Shaimiev and his team, the famous 'Tatarstan elite', very quickly realized the priorities, towards which all economic policy should be directed. Those included: halting the slide in oil and industrial output, creating a legal base for privatization and private ownership, the 'soft entrance into market' through subsidizing basic food prices for the population, and pin-pointing help directed at the poorest layers of society, and, last but not least, privatizating state property, but in a most thoughtful and moderate manner. All of this had to be done simultaneously, in a very short period of time and against a background of political confrontation with Moscow given the lack of any meaningful treaty-based relations between Tatarstan and the Russian Federation. If President Shaimiev had only led his country through this dark labyrinth of complete economic and political uncertainty and concluded the 1997 bilateral treaty with Russia, ensuring the leading position in the all-Russia process of privatization and the first shoots of economic growth, even then his legacy at this point in the history of Tatarstan would have been assured for all posterity. But he, as we know, achieved much more, making Tatarstan the show-case of the Russian transition for all the world to see.

In 1992, the overall industrial decline in Tatarstan reached 12.6% (9.8% in the enterprises under the jurisdiction of Tatarstan) and the oil output declined by 8%. The biggest decline of 25% was recorded in the sphere of the military-industrial complex, as Russian federal orders decreased by 47.4%. But in 1992 on the world markets Tatarstan sold 1.7 million tons of oil, 40 thousand tons of diesel fuel and a number of heavy-duty trucks from the KAMAZ plant, worth $100,000, which went straight into agricultural grants, and food/transport subsidies, as well as to help maintain wage levels in the budget sector of the economy. The government of Tatarstan also introduced a common-sense system of rationing, limited to the citizens of Tatarstan, whereby everyone had preferential rights to buy about twenty different kinds of foodstuffs. Without strict controls, neighbouring regions would seek to avail themselves of Tatarstan's subsidized prices at a time when all-Russia price liberalization and inflation was running at over 1,000 per cent. At the same time, the government of President Shaimiev introduced the system of the so-called 'addressed' support of the most vulnerable layers of society – pensioners, students, families with children – 2,400,000 people in all. Was this a legacy of Socialist thinking? Not exactly.

While supporting the people through the most desperate times in their post-Second World War memory, the government of President Shaimiev was looking much further than simple survival. They established a fund for the structural re-building of the economy, which accumulated, first of all, hard currency proceeds from the sale of oil and petrochemical products from the largest sector of the republic's economy. This fund formed the material basis for the measures aimed at halting the decrease in industrial output, which proved rather successful, as in 1992–93 the decline in Tatarstan's industrial output was lower than in other Russian regions. In 1994 there was a slump in output, but even by 1995 industrial output grew by 2% and in 1996 by 3.5%, whereas in the rest of Russia the slump continued. Since then Tatarstan's economy has grown year on year, continually strengthening its market foundations despite less than perfect market conditions.

The privatization process in Tatarstan was aggravated by the fact that many large enterprises in the republic were federally-owned or had a shared Tatarstan-Russia ownership. During the Second World War, many large USSR plants, factories and design offices were evacuated to Tatarstan, which later made the republic one of the main hubs of the all-USSR machine-building and military-industrial complex. Later, with the development of Tatarstan's oil fields and the construction of the huge petro-chemical plants like Nizhnekamsheftekhim, Nizhnekamskshina, Orgsyntez and others, as well as construction of the giant Kamaz heavy-truck plant, Tatarstan became one of the largest world producers of petrochemicals, trucks, military and civil-use helicopters and other aircraft. In order to survive and prosper, these plants needed not just sustainable state orders, but also new markets within Russia and the CIS, as well as in the 'far abroad'. Thus, Tatarstan made it a priority to re-establish the broken industrial links of the USSR on her own by creating joint enterprises with companies in Ukraine and other former USSR republics. The same purpose was served by establishing trade representative offices in such countries as the USA, France, Turkey and others. Such multifaceted policies in the completely unprecedented circumstances did not just save Tatarstan's industry from mortal decline, but also secured the former and opened new markets for her products: for example, Tatarstan still produces a large percentage of the synthetic rubber and other petrochemicals made in Europe.

Of course, these juicy pieces of the Tatarstan industrial pie continue to trouble the imagination of the Russian oligarchic circles. But, being the leader of his nation and master of his house, President Shaimiev could not allow the republic's riches to be squandered in the bacchanalia of the all-Russia privatization hurricane. Moreover, at this time his common sense dictated that the major industries of Tatarstan would have to be privatized later – in circumstances of relative economic and political stability and for real money, and must be based on solid legal foundations. Thus, the first stage of Tatarstan's privatization concentrated on the smaller companies and enterprises in the service sector, and even then with all possible care and consideration.

This approach, however, could not be effected without a decree of independence in taking vital economic decisions and this was one of the main reasons why Tatarstan simultaneously tried to persuade Moscow of the validity and justice of her claims to limited sovereignty. From the interviews given by President Shaimiev at that time it becomes clear that his decision had to be taken in the context of an ongoing debate with the Russian government which was already persuaded by the ideology of rapid privatization. In one of his interviews in the mid-90s President Shaimiev later said:

> In all our choices we orient ourselves not at political or ideological preferences, but at firm pragmatic interests. That is to say, at the laws dictated by market conditions. Instead of the ill-fated 'voucherization' effected by the federal authorities of the Russian Federation, we, upon meticulous scrutiny of the peculiarities of the existing agro-industrial complex in Tatarstan, introduced additional categories of privatization cheques and opened in our banks the inscribed privatization accounts for each of the republic's citizens. In order to safeguard the population in those years of galloping inflation, when people were forced to sell their privatization shares to the light-fingered second-hand dealers, we reserved the right of our state to effect a temporary moratorium on share dealings with those inscribed accounts. This measure proved sufficiently effective and today no one can rebuke us for having been stripped of his or her share of privatized property and that the privatization process in Tatarstan turned to yet another propaganda exercise allowing a narrow group of those close to power to receive super-profits. Today, when the pace of inflation has slowed down considerably, we removed the strict limitation on the sale of privatization cheques. But again, as long as on the world bourses our shares are not getting their real value, we will consciously restrain their entrance to the share market.

The special features of the Tatarstan privatization programme were: 1) The evaluation of the state property according to its approximate *market value;* 2) effecting privatization mainly through the workforce of the privatized enterprises, which at the first stage of the privatization process preferentially bought large stock packages of ordinary (voting) shares for their privatization cheques and inscribed privatization deposits; 3) safeguarding the vulnerable parts of the population according to the Presidential Decree entitled 'On Social Protection of Separate Categories of Citizens of the Republic of Tatarstan In the Process of Privatization' from 10 December 1993. In all, Tatarstan valued her industrial property at 25–30% higher than the Moscow Kremlin and, along with the Tatarstan's own privatization cheques, at the first stage deposited in inscribed bank accounts, the republic also recognized the validity of the all-Russia vouchers, which gave the population of the republic additional buying-in power. As the Russian magazine 'Business People' later reported, 'The Voucher auctions in Tatarstan were held according to a special scheme, thanks to which the shares of the Tatarstan enterprises largely remained in the republic, and consequently the state control over the economy was assured. The auctions proceeded in an orderly manner. The authorities did all they could not to allow the shares of the national holding companies getting into 'alien hands'. Share quotas were introduced, and the controlling packages remained in the hands of the state. Not everyone was allowed to take part in the auctions. But those who did were obliged to purchase the local inscribed vouchers sold in specialized shops at the coefficient of 2.7 to their nominal value. The Moscow guests soon realized that it was not at all profitable for them to buy Tatarstan shares. Therefore, as the (then) Minister of Economics Damir Bikbov remarked, 'privatization in Tatarstan avoided shooting and bloodshed'.

Is it not common sense that the state should obtain maximum possible proceeds from the privatization of its property in the interests of the wider population whose social rights and, with those, the market future, may be safeguarded only by the state? But what an onslaught of the 'market philosophers' ensued after the president and the government of Tatarstan went along their own path of privatization! In 1992–94 Tatarstan indeed lagged behind the rest of Russia in the volume of privatization, but in 1995 she already was a leader of this process inviting foreign investors to buy into large Tatarstan holdings in the full security of the well thought-over local legislation. By October 1995, 60% of Tatarstan enterprises were privatized, among which were the most economically essential companies of the republic such as 'Tatneft' (the fourth largest oil producer in Russia), Nizhnekamskneftekhim (petrochemical giant), the Kazan Helicopter plant and the famous Chistopol watch factory 'Vostok'. The pace of the Shaimiev-style privatization was well measured: from 1992 to 1995 the republic privatized only 489 enterprises. The structure of privatization also significantly differed from that of the rest of Russia. In 1993, for example, 61.9% of all privatized enterprises belonged to the trade and services sector – shops, restaurants, workshops, etc. In 1993, only 11.9% and 2.4% of enterprises in the industrial and construction sectors, respectively, were privatized. Yet, in 1994, 54.7% of all privatized companies belonged to the industrial sector, 19.6% – to the construction sector, and only 14.5% – to the services sector. In 1995, the ratio was restored: 35% of enterprises were privatized in the services sector, 24% – in the industrial sector and 11% – in construction. As a result of privatization, on its first stage 41% of the joint statutory capital remained under state control and 43% belonged to the workforce of more than 800 privatized enterprises. Sixteen investment foundations were registered in Tatarstan uniting 480,000 people in their participation in the privatization process. Overall, 95.68% of the population made do with their inscribed privatization cheques, and the unused cheques were directed to support the poorest among Tatarstan's people.[4]

Such a measured approach to privatization has continued in Tatarstan up to the present day, but always dependent on working within the right legal basis, especially regarding the sale of land and the willingness of the enterprises to be sold at their highest market value. In 2005, Tatarstan proceeded to privatize her postal services (not without an argument with the federal postal service), the energy grid (Tatelectroset), radio and TV communications (Radioteleset) and other enterprises such as the republican bakery plants, the trading house of 'Kazan Central Department Store', the Zelenodolsk Veneer Factory, some large transport and construction enterprises, and others. In 2005, Tatarstan earned some 4.2 billion roubles from oil refineries (state owned) and consolidated its role in the republic's economy with a view to proceeding to privatization through the further selling of shares in the large and medium-sized state enterprises. In 2006–7 it is planned to sell a further 250 packages of government-controlled stock to private investors. Special attention is paid to the sale of state-owned land, which continues to increase in value and the government of Tatarstan is projecting that soon it can obtain three times more from the sale of land, than at the present time (2006).

According to the president, Tatarstan's economy is a socially-oriented market economy, in which, at least during all the uncertainties of the unprecedented market transition, the role of the state cannot be over-estimated. This credo, hateful as it may be to neo-liberal academicians and 'wild Russian capitalists', has proved right over and over again in recent years. The state regulation in Tatarstan is not a goal in itself, and we can observe how it changes over time. In my opinion, this role is validated by two main peculiarities of Tatarstan as a 'state within the state' of the Russian Federation. Firstly, as we have seen, the Tatarstan state had to take upon itself the crucial task of re-creating conditions in which the production of the colossal Tatarstan industrial enterprises could be assured and at the same time secure its markets both within the Russian Federation and abroad. This thorny path, exacerbated by the many political and economic shocks of nascent Russian capitalism and, for all the sweet talk of globalization, veritable obstruction on the world markets, was taken by Tatarstan not only by her own free will as a self-dependent state, but also out of economic inevitability in the circumstances, when the Russian state would not bother to think about its own industrial and agricultural producers.

One of the most striking examples of such a contemptuous attitude is the story of the Tatarstan-produced Tupolev Tu-214 civic aircraft, which is still struggling to find its way into the Russian aerospace market despite being the most advanced machine of its kind, meeting all the regulations of the world market. Even after causing a stir at the 1996 Farnborough air show, it was still sidelined by the Russian government in favour of Boeing aircraft at the very same show. The first Russian civic aircraft of the post-Communist era designed and built since 1992 by Kazan's aviation plant, despite the most adverse economic conditions, is further clear proof of the resolve and skill on the part of Tatarstan producers as well as a credit to Tatarstan's economic management. And yet, even after state certification in 2000, the aircraft cannot go into mass production because of the unwillingness of the privatized Aeroflot company to purchase the home-produced aircraft instead of second-hand Boeings.

Why? Well, I remember myself speaking with one of the representatives of the Russian government some years ago. Sitting in his comfortable chair in the former headquarters of the Communist Party on the Staraya Ploschad' in Moscow, he was telling me that Russia should forget about being an industrial producer in sectors such as aircraft and automobile manufacture, and fully concentrate instead on being a producer of raw materials and an energy supplier to the West. 'We should understand that we are not able to compete, then why bother', was his attitude then shared by most policy-makers at the top of the all-Russia elite. And, sadly, it was useless to ask him what all the colossal, but investment-hungry Russian enterprises should do and how they are supposed to pay wages to their highly-qualified and experienced workforce numbering tens of thousand of skilled people? Such questions never entered the minds of the people who were called 'Russian reformers'. Were they indeed to be so faithfully subservient to foreign economic interests as to give up all idea of competition, which is, after all, the very engine of the market economy they were so vocal in espousing? But, thank God, this attitude was never present in Tatarstan, with its sustained and wisely regulated production and sales of the world-famous Mi-17 multirole helicopter and the further development – in the uncertain time of transition! – of the new helicopter models ANSAT, AKTAI and Mi-38. In the atmosphere, where Tatarstan aviation-manufacturers had to produce and market their goods against all odds, they came up with the idea of the Financial Leasing Company, which helped finance the orders, promote and organize the sales of Tatarstan aircraft to Russian and overseas consumers like the Administration of Khabarovsk District and the 'Dalavia' company in the Russian Far East, 'Transaero' company, Slovak Airlines and other large consumers. However, most recently prices for Tu-214 components, including the engines made by Perm Motor Plant, went up 8.25%, which threatened to destroy the competitive edge of the Tatarstan aircraft and bring the cost of its production close to that of Boeing machines. The Tatarstan government headed by Prime Minister Rustam Minnikhanov and, of course, the president of the republic naturally voiced their concerns and, in their usual way, argued that it was not market forces that triggered the price hike. Yet, despite all concerns, which in 2005 made President Shaimiev insist on the substantially increased federal participation in investing in Tatarstan's aircraft production industry, in 2006 Tatarstan signed an agreement with China for the delivery of five Tu-214 aircraft with an option of delivering another ten. There are also plans to develop a new aircraft, Tu-334, for which Tatarstan anticipates foreign investment. In early March 2006, a cooperation agreement was signed in Tatarstan with The Fearthainne Group and LBG Global Funding. It was on this occasion that President Shaimiev famously insisted that Tatarstan is not only an oil-producing, but also an aircraft-manufacturing republic. Basically, it is Tatarstan that provides Russia with its wings by producing a large share of her civic and military aircraft and it is only good sense that the federal centre should pay more attention to this uphill struggle of the Tatarstan enterprises.

Paradoxically, in 1995, when the Russian economy was still far from being stable, the Kazan Motor-Building Holding was awarded the prestigious prize of the 'Birmingham flare' (torch) for successful development in adverse economic conditions. The Director General of this huge enterprise, Alexander Pavlov, in his recent interview proudly said that 'even in hardest years further production development remained for us an indisputable priority'. Besides all the other achievements in the years of transition, the maintaining of the various technically-advanced plants and factories of Tatarstan, was due to the fact that the ongoing skill base of its workforce was underpinned by its own excellent technical education system. While in many other parts of Russia qualified specialists were forced to change their trade for unskilled labour, industrial Tatarstan paid a lot of attention not just to maintain the high skills of her workforce, but also encouraged young people to come into the industrial production field, choosing it over other occupations. Without that, Tatarstan's large enterprises would soon be devoid of qualified specialists; it goes without saying that to produce a skilled worker is not the same as a shop assistant in the republic's growing service sector.

At the beginning of the 1990s, Tatarstan's aviation production sector, which delivered aircraft of the 'Antonov' series, the first ever Tu-104, the intercontinental Il-62 and the strategic Tu-160, was left to its own devices and all but completely forgotten by the federal authorities. Tatarstan always had a number of strategic enterprises, occupying the most essential niches of the all-Russia industrial base. In effect, the whole process of keeping these industries afloat, finance, keeping and educating the workforce, developing new designs and models, marketing and selling the end product in the all-Russia and world markets fell on the shoulders of Tatarstan's management which was under the overall supervision of President Shaimiev. Not bad for a 'village culture', may I say! During his regular visits abroad, President Shaimiev also personally promotes Tatarstan's industrial production and it is also due to his power of reasoning and persuasion shared by the members of the government and the top managers of Tatarstan's industry that Tatarstan's industrial goods find their way to the markets of Turkey, Egypt, Malaysia, India, Finland, United Arab Emirates and many other countries. As President Shaimiev said in his 2006 Annual Address: 'Tatarstan, jointly with a number of private enterprises, has managed to invest over 500 million US dollars in her aviation industry, which is more than the total federal budget allocated for the entire Russian aviation production over the last five years'. It is also due to such commitment, supported by the president, that the Kazan helicopter plant still supplies its helicopters to more than eighty countries worldwide.

The story of the KamAZ heavy-truck factory, the largest in the world, also illustrates the role of the Tatarstan government in creating conditions enabling the market economy to flourish. There is an anecdote that when Henry Ford IV came to Tatarstan to look at the construction of the KamAZ plant in its early stages, he vowed to become a communist if the project were successful. It was a massive project envisaging the construction of a super-plant, which would supply heavy trucks to satisfy the needs of the entire Soviet Union. It took colossal investment and colossal labour input to construct this conglomerate of several large units supplying parts to the main assembly plant. But, as often happened with gigantic USSR projects, it continued in production despite mounting additional costs: who was interested in counting the public money in those days of uninhibited Soviet-style enthusiasm? In December 1976, the main conveyer started to move: the projected capacity of the entire plant was 150,000 heavy trucks and 250,000 engines annually. KamAZ did indeed supply its trucks to every sector of the USSR economy increasing its output year in, year out. Again, its real overhead costs were kept secret, but some observers wondered, what was the real cost of a truck, some smaller parts of which were being airlifted daily from Belorussia? In the 1980s, this type of high cost, low value, production started to experience difficulties along with the rest of Soviet economy but somehow managed to crawl through the times of *perestroika*. Output from the plant was decreasing year after year: by 1990, it barely reached 100,000 vehicles. Eventually, in the heat of *perestroika*, the Soviet government decided to turn it into a share-holding company, but, as it proved to be, in the typical Soviet way. By special decree, all six major plants and nine subsidiary factories of KamAZ were transformed into a pseudo-privatized share company with a capital value of US$1.5 billion and 3.7 billion roubles (not forgetting that those were still Soviet roubles with an official nominal value of 0.60 per US dollar).

This Soviet type of half-measure did not improve the standing of the company, and in 1993 things were made much worse by a devastating fire in the engine plant. If, in 1990, the plant still produced about 100,000 trucks a year, in 1994 its output had decreased to about 20,000 a year. The major headache for the Tatarstan government was that there was no 'genuine proprietor' of this enterprise, despite a large number of shareholders. KamAZ sank into debt, despite various controversial measures to save it from bankruptcy, which involved the participation of the American Investment Company KKR (Kohlberg, Kravis, Roberts & Co), which acquired a 49% stake in the company in return for attracting investment to the tune of US$300 million. In 1994, KKR, with a view to restructuring KamAZ, suggested creating a consulting firm, KamAZ International Management, in which KKR would have a 51% stake, 10% would go to the top managers, KamAZ, two 7.5% stakes would be taken by the governments of Tatarstan and Russia, two 4.5 per cent stakes would go to the firms Cummins and American Reinsuans, brought in by KKR and one 4.5% stake to the financial company IMAG, with 10% remaining as a reserve.[5] It was all in vain. KamAZ proceeded to sink deeper into debt, the stakeholders quarrelled blaming each other for the failure. The credit of the European Bank for Reconstruction and Development, brokered by KKR, was wasted and partly squandered in dubious deals by the plant's management. As the results of the audit showed:

> There was an impression that an attempt was made to depreciate the enterprise. As the analysis of the financial situation in the enterprise has revealed, in the course of three years the enterprise was being artificially devalued ... The former management of the KamAZ Company lost control over the factories and share stakes belonging to the company, having misspent considerable part of the liquid assets. The controlling stake of the company has been practically estranged to the benefit of alien organizations, and deals, rather dubious from a legal point of view as well as in terms of their effectiveness, were struck involving large stakes in the company. Despite having problems with its own turnover, KamAZ invested its means in dubious projects, throwing away almost 2.4 trillion non-denominated roubles.[6]

The situation became economically outrageous, which was all the more depressing since Tatarstan had such a small stake in the company, the welfare of which affected the whole city on its territory. Things had to change. In 1996, with KamAZ under threat of bankruptcy, Tatarstan paid the plant's tax debt to the federal government and, in 1997, decided to take the ill-fated plant under its wing by paying the debts of the plant in return for an increase in its stake in the enterprise. The emergency shareholders meeting in March 1997 approved the transfer of a 40% stake in the company to the Tatarstan government, and the former KamAZ director general, Nikolai Bekh, was sacked from his post. In May 1997, he was also sacked from his position as the chairman of the board of directors, pending criminal investigation, as the special commission of the Tatarstan law enforcement ministries uncovered evidence of criminal mismanagement and outright fraud. In May 1998, Tatarstan as a major stakeholder put nine of its representatives onto the board of directors of the company and announced the possibility of cancelling the contract with KKR. In January 1998, in London, major creditors of KamAZ agreed not to undertake any actions leading to the bankruptcy of the enterprise and, in February of that year, a new board of directors, agreed with the creditors, was set up. Its make-up clearly signified that the Tatarstan government was assuming control of the company. Since then, the plant's position has improved dramatically and KamAZ has slowly regained its leading position in auto-production in Russia. In 2005, the company sold 32,200 heavy trucks, which was 14% higher than in 2004. In cooperation with the German company, Friedrichhaven AG, KamAZ formed a company known as ZF Kama producing gear-boxes for KamAZ trucks from the components made in Tatarstan. In 2005, KamAZ and the government of Tatarstan sold their stake in the daughter company ZMA, which produced the small 'Oka' cars for the consumer market on the base of the KamAZ conglomerate. The new owner of this production line, Severstal-Auto Ltd, has already started producing 'Rexton' cars and their variants with the aim of producing 5,000 cars in 2006 and 10,000 cars annually thereafter. Severstal-Auto also signed an agreement with Fiat Auto to start, in 2007, the production of Fiat Paleo and Fiat Albeo cars for the Tatarstan and Russian consumer market. Special attention in the republic is paid to production of auto components (Alnas Ltd), which supplies its end products to such Russian auto giants as Gaz, Autovaz and Izhevsk Auto Plant and holds cooperation talks with such well-known producers as Benteler (Germany), Iveco (Italy), Fiat (Italy), Continental (Germany) and Ford Focus (Russia). As for KamAZ trucks, in recent years they were indisputable winners of the Paris-Dakar desert rally, which only increases their popularity on world markets.

The fascinating story of how Tatarstan saved and developed her large enterprises against the overwhelming adversity of the transition period and how she managed to tame and convert her mammoth military-industrial complex could easily fill a large book in its own right. Sometimes one wonders, why this colossal and very educative experience of the republic is not more widely known around the world? Is it because 'good news' is 'no news' in our media culture? When talking of Tatarstan, however, everybody remembers that the republic is the only European source of oil in the Russian Federation. Some lesser leaders than President Shaimiev would perhaps rely on the benefits of the republic's oil to enjoy their political life while it lasts. But the major decision taken by the president at the beginning of transition was that the prosperity of the republic should not become oil-dependent and should rather rest on the development of her industrial and technological base. Still, the republican oil extracted in the east of the republic was and is like blood for its economy, especially in the situation of Russian financial disorder. Due to the earlier agreement with the federal centre, in 1999 out of about 26 million tonnes per annum, some 5 million tonnes remained at the republic's disposal, and this amount served as a natural collateral for any foreign economic activity in Tatarstan. It comes as no surprise, therefore, that investment in the oil industry remains one of the republic's main priorities. President Shaimiev stated:

> Thanks to the use of new technologies and a resilient fiscal policy, in the period of reforms we managed to increase oil output by two million tonnes a year. Let me

remind you that before that, the republic's oil output was decreasing year after year over a period of nineteen years, and even the year 1996 was not overly productive. Despite this fact, our oil companies entered the world capital market, and their quotation initially exceeded $100.[7] I can offer one more example here. Within the framework of the new conditions of produce division accepted in Russia, from our own Romashkino oil field alone we shall, over the next sixteen years, get six times more oil, than under the previous tax regime. That is why we regard the oil industry as a priority.

Indeed, one of the most visible aspects of Tatarstan's sovereignty, is its sovereignty over its oil resources. These resources are not as vast as they were in 1944, partly because of the hurricane extraction policies of the Soviet era which resulted in the extraction of some 2.6 billion tonnes. Another misfortune of Soviet policy was that the extraction methods were often barbaric, pumping water and paraffin into the wells increased the output, but such methods resulted in the near destruction of such extraordinarily rich oil fields as Romashkino. Still, Tatarstan's proven oil reserves are about 25 million tonnes per annum for thirty years, and each tonne of crude oil yields an average of 40 cubic metres of natural gas. Today, it is estimated that Tatarstan oil production will be at the level of 30–31 million tonnes annually up to 2020. In 1996, the American auditing company Miller & Lents, estimated the proven reserves of the Tatneft company at 841.1 million tonnes, which at a stable rate of production ensures its work for another thirty-five years.[8]

Tatarstan's government has retained a controlling stake in the major republican oil company Tatneft, in which the federal Russian government has no share at all. Tatarstan is also the site of the former Soviet Union's largest estimated reserves of bituminous or heavy oil. This has in effect to be melted during drilling and so far the cost has proven prohibitive. But if new technology were to become available, the potential is colossal. Tatneft has several joint ventures with Western companies, aiming to transfer advanced technology and institute environmental controls. The largest of these joint ventures is with the French company Total. The others are with Global Natural Resources in Houston and Germany's Mineraloil.[9] In 1994, Tatarstan received the largest Eximbank credit of US$270 million for the rehabilitation of its old oil wells. In fact, the recent increase in oil output would be much smaller, had the Tatarstan leadership not introduced a policy of privatization of the more difficult wells. This policy has proved quite successful, and the oil output has been increased through the means of private, mainly domestic Tatar capital. In 2005, the Tatneft company, which has extracted over 25 million tonnes of oil out of the annual republican oil output of 30.5 million tonnes, won the most prestigious Russian competition for the 'Best industrial enterprises of Russia' in the nomination of 'The Most financially effective enterprise' of the energy sector. Remarkably, 11 million tonnes of oil in the republic were extracted because of the new technologies introduced in Tatarstan as well as because of the growing effectiveness of 'low-capacity' wells privatized by Tatarstan in the early years of transition.

Still, President Shaimiev is well aware that the future lies not in the extraction of crude oil, but rather in the further development of Tatarstan's petrochemical industry and therefore a significant effort is being made to attract foreign investors to the planned expansion of the oil-refining sector of the economy. Tatarstan has already signed agreements and created joint ventures with Ukraine, Moscow and Nizhny Novgorod and has received further proposals from financial-industrial groups from the CIS and abroad. In the context of the Tatar-Ukrainian international financial-industrial company, Ukrtatnafta, Tatarstan gained access to the only refinery in the CIS able to process high-sulphur oil. But the republic itself possesses a highly developed petrochemical industry viewed and structured as a single vertically-integrated industrial complex with such plants as Nizhnekamskneftekhim, the largest petrochemical plant in Europe situated in Nizhnekamsk with 40% of world production capacity of some of its products. Suffice it to say here that Tatarstan's petrochemical complex delivers 40% of the Russian output of polythene, 25% of synthetic rubber, 32% of heavy trucks, 28% passenger and 15% of agricultural tyres, 44% of pipes and pipe details of thermoplastic materials. Accordingly, the share of the Tatarstan petrochemical industry in the world markets reaches up to 25% for several kinds of petrochemical products. Today, this huge enterprise is integrated into a complex known as Tatneftekhiminvest, in which the government of Tatarstan holds a 51% stake, Tatneft – 13% stake, Nizhnekamskneftekhim and Kazanorgsyntex – 7,3% each, Nizhnekamskshina – 4.3%, Tattransgaz – 3%, Tatnefteproduct – 2.3%. In 2005, due to the thoughtful management and strategic innovations, the net profits of the holding grew 10.7 times as compared with 2003, and all of this income was re-invested into the fund for the further development of the holding.

The development of the Tatarstan petrochemical industry declared by the president to be a priority in the industrial progress of the republic pays off handsomely – due to its sound performance the gross regional product in 2005 in Tatarstan exceeded 500 billion roubles, which is approximately 6.5% higher than in 2004. The strategic vision of the Tatarstan government in 2005 was instrumental in the establishment of the Benzene (Petroleum) Plant in Nizhnekamsk (the project of the TAIF company), which is supposed to provide for up to two per cent of industrial growth in the republic. It was the first plant of its kind built in Russia for the last seventeen years. Despite the incredibly cold winter of 2006, the plant started to deliver petrol of A-80 and AI-95 brands to the Tatnefteproduct trading company at the end of February, and on 3 March the plant began supplying Tatarstan with the most widely used AI-92 brand of petrol. Today, Tatarstan provides for all its motor fuel petrol consumption, and in the present economic climate it is one of the brightest examples of Tatarstan's 'can-do' culture.

The new facilities of the Kazanorgsyntez plant reconstructed at the cost of three billion US dollars will also add to the Tatarstan industrial output, as well as a new complex of oil-refineries built in Nizhnekamsk by the Tatneft company in order to treat Tatarstan's oil which is rich in sulphur and carbons. President Shaimiev highlights especially the importance of the production of high-quality motor fuel to make up for imminent shortfalls due to the ever rising world oil prices.

This book cannot hope to describe all of Tatarstan's accomplishments as far as industrial development over the last fifteen years is concerned, despite the struggle with the consequences of the catastrophic slump in Russian output following the adventurous policies of the 'Russian reformers'. One of the most outstanding characteristics of the Tatarstan way of reform as opposed to that of Russia in general is, in the words and deeds of the president, their consistency and the recognition of what was happening on the ground. I remember how at the height of the 1998 financial crisis, which in all seriousness threatened to push Russia back into the abyss of effective economic non-existence, the president said to me:

> Look at us, in Tatarstan. We did everything our own way, our pace was slower, and we are much closer to the objectives of the IMF, than are many other regions of the Russian Federation. At the same time, there were mistakes on the part of our creditors, whom I do not want to accuse, as nobody should bite the hand that feeds them, and on the part of President Yeltsin and his government. It was they who built the pyramid of the T-bills with Western creditors calmly watching and often participating in this game. The money Russia borrowed effectively returned to the West and was again borrowed at another draconian rate. Was it not evident that these vast sums of money came and went without any benefits to industry, to its renovation and restructuring? Russia and Tatarstan still possess leading technological assets. I do not recall, though, that the IMF demanded investment in this technology with a view to supporting the industrial sector in Russia. It is, again, not to attribute blame, but all these crucial questions should have been addressed, and they were not. Everybody just speculated and everybody eventually lost – a crisis which was aggravated by the adverse economic conditions worldwide.
>
> For my part, I frequently objected to this state of affairs, always speaking of the need to support the domestic producers. The IMF talks constantly about collecting taxes. Well and good, but you cannot milk a hungry cow: nobody has yet succeeded in such an undertaking. I appreciate that our creditors may not be interested in the development of our technologies and industry as a whole. Of course, it would be unnatural for them: by developing our industrial sector, we would trade less in raw materials and, with our mighty Russian potential, will offer strong competition on the world markets. Even if this is the case, we should still find our own ways to define our priorities and develop our industry: this is the only way forward. The people of Russia always had their own way, albeit through enormous adversities and troubles. The nation which was able to send a man into space is still capable of dragging itself out of trouble. There is still some pride left. All deformities in the Russian development could not be blamed on the people: they are the direct consequences of domestic and foreign politics.
>
> And what about the gifts of foresight they say you have? I then asked. Foresight, forecast, these are funny words. As if someone really sees the future. I would say that any foresight comes out of an acute sense of reality. You can forecast based on your experience, if you have that. Premonition or not, but events have shown that Tatarstan's way was the right one, beginning with privatization. How could you have started to sell your property, when the annual inflation was running at 1,000 per cent? We admittedly started this process of voucher privatization at the same time as Russia, but we opened a personal share account for every citizen of our republic and declared a moratorium on share trading. We said, 'You cannot, until the right time comes, dispose of your property, because we first have to understand what a share market is, what a share is, how do we go about this whole business?' We said, 'Let the hyperinflation subside and we shall cancel the moratorium', and that was it.
>
> Russia went in a different direction by totally abolishing state controls in 1992.

The results were tragic: so many people became penniless – without shares and their savings eaten up by inflation. We chose to let the state control go gradually, whereas Russia abolished them at once, and instead of a free market found themselves with a free-for-all bazaar. Now they are trying to re-think the whole process and strengthen governmental control. We, for our part, now have a chance to loosen it. And then, it is a mistake to think of Russia as a weak emerging country. It is true, our industry is deformed by the military industrial complex, but our potential is still great, whether in the technological field, or in a highly educated workforce. We should look for our own ways out. For instance, so many people attacked us for our preferential attitude towards the agricultural sector. But when, just yesterday, I chaired the sitting of the Tatarstan government to assess the damage of the crisis and to look for ways of overcoming it, we saw that Tatarstan will get through these hard times much more easily than any other region, because we are self-reliant on food. In Tatarstan, we managed to preserve our own food factories, which work using our own agricultural produce. So, today, when banking operations with hard currency are stopped, we do not depend on imports. We have to attend to other matters – how to ensure the fairness of prices, what the government can do to help people afford the basic foodstuffs: milk, eggs, meat and so forth. We have a lot to do, but we did not lose our own capacity to produce food. Even Moscow today has got into the import-related trap, but we are practically free of this headache. Moscow imported up to 90 per cent of its food, and we were importing barely 35 per cent, and in some areas, none. Is this a kind of a foresight, or a simple pragmatic adherence to reality? Also, during all these years we never used foreign credit for consumption, not a dollar of it. Everything went into industrial investment, first of all, of course, into our oil and petrochemical industry.[10]

In the near future Tatarstan will increase her investment in her petrochemical complex 2.5 fold, which will for the first time exceed her investment in the oil industry. Despite federal neglect, the republic will press forward with her aircraft, auto and machine-building industry looking for innovative ways of structuring, financing and marketing her industrial output. All of this has to be viewed not only against the unique position of Tatarstan *vis-à-vis* the Russian Federation, but also in the context of the realized 'Tatarstan model', which aspires to always solve economic and social problems in their complex unity and always looking forward to the strategic destination of the republic not only as a Russian, but as a world entity in our increasingly globalized world.

Today, the multifaceted industries of Tatarstan progress at a sustainable and well-planned pace trying to achieve the possible and still dreaming about the seemingly impossible. But again, everything, which is already achieved by Tatarstan under the leadership on President Shaimiev in the most adverse circumstances of her peculiar market transition was deemed impossible only a few years ago. Yet, as President Shaimiev says, 'we can do it'. And, looking at the impressive achievements of Tatarstan in the industrial and agricultural sector, which were all but dead in 1991–92, not only citizens of Tatarstan, but of all Russia can repeat after the Tatar president: 'Yes, we can.'

NOTES

1. Figures based on the interview of the Head of the Territorial Department of the Federal Statistical Service in Tatarstan Valery Kondilov, newspaper 'The Republic of Tatarstan', 31.01.2006.

2. Such analysis can be found in my earlier books *The Model of Tatarstan under President Mintimer Shaimiev*, Curzon Press Ltd, London, and St Martin's Press, NY, 1999, and 'Президент Минтимер Шаймиев и модель Татарстана (President Mintimer Shaimiev and the Model of Tatarstan)', Curzon Press – Blitz, St. Petersburg, 2000.
3. See, for instance, Albert L. Weinstein, 'Selected Works. Soviet Economy in the 1920s', Book 1, Moscow, Nauka, 2000.
4. 'Kommersant-Daily', 16 August 1995.
5. Data supplied by the *Expert* magazine, Russia, No. 11, 23 March 1998, p. 58.
6. G. Faizullina, D. Grishankov, 'On the way to Chrysler', the *Expert*, No. 11, 23 March 1998, p. 57.
7. This interview to the *Business People* magazine (*op. cit.*) was given in summer 1997, before the oil prices slumped all over the world.
8. *Business People, op. cit.*, p. 60.
9. 'The Republic of Tatarstan', GM, *op. cit.*, p. 18.
10. See more about the 1998 crisis in R. Bukharaev, *The Model of Tatarstan Under Presdient Shaimiev*, Curzon Press Ltd, London and St. Martins Press, New York, 1999.

CHAPTER 7

MOTHER TONGUE

> My mother tongue! Your kind support
> Has helped my life to run its course;
> And since my childhood you have borne
> My hopes, my joys and my remorse.
>
> My mother tongue! In you I prayed
> Beseeching God to save my soul.
> Forgiveness for my parents too
> I sought through you. You made me whole.
>
> Gabdullah Tukai (1886–1913)

The president of Tatarstan is a Tatar, as will be his successor, unless the successor, of any other ethnicity, is equally fluent in the Tatar and Russian languages. This emphatic provision in the republic's constitution has less to do with the nature of Tatar national feeling, than with the fact that the common mother tongue of the Tatar nation scattered throughout Russia and the rest of the world is fundamental to its national unity and is its main hope for the future as a nation and people.

The history of the Tatar language and its development is also one of the best kept secrets of Russian inter-ethnic history. Belonging to the Turco-Altaic family of languages, Tatar originated thousands of years ago, but only became known to the world with the rise of Turkic ethnicities during the period of the Arab caliphate (eighth to the tenth centuries) and subsequently during the time of the famous Golden Horde (thirteenth to the fifteenth centuries), when it effectively became the language of choice of the entire region of Eurasia, on a par with the Arabic and Persian languages. The rise and progress of this language of state management, trade and crafts, highly developed agriculture and a significant corpus of literature in the thirteenth to the fourteenth centuries did not stop after the collapse of the Golden Horde as a single state and became a lasting legacy not only of the Kazan, Astrakhan and the Crimean khanates, which appeared in its place, but also the diplomatic language of a rising unified Russia. The Russian princes, the great dukes of Muscovy and the tsars of Russia from the fifteenth to the seventeenth centuries, all spoke this tongue, the vocabulary of which substantially enriched dictionaries of politics, economics, education, military architecture and civic bureaucracy of the Russian state.

After the fall of the Kazan khanate this 600-year-old language did not die out, but, in fact, survived in the Tatar 'village culture' and was carried by emigrating and enterprising Tatars to the borders of China and Japan. It never completely lost its urban character due to the fact that it was the only tongue in the emerging Russian empire which served the needs of both economic and political communication with the Muslim East and the South of Russia. It thereby retained its value as a language of international trade and diplomacy well into the nineteenth century, prompting Professor K. Fuks, for example, to note that 'this nation [of Tatars], conquered two hundred years ago and now scattered among the Russians, was able to preserve its customs, morals and national pride in a most surprising way, just as if they lived separately'. Interestingly, the survival and progress of the Tatar tongue had less to do with the Tatar system of education, because in the Tatar madrassas, or schools, some of which became veritable beacons of learning throughout Russia, the language was not taught specifically on a par with Arabic, Farsi and later Russian, since it was considered *the natural one* (mother tongue). Yet, its history is intricately linked to the business of book publishing, which started in Kazan with the opening of Kazan University in 1804, the second oldest university in Russia, whose foundations were the First Kazan Gymnasium. In this centre of education, which in November 2004 celebrated its bicentenary marked by significant state investment for refurbishment and new building, the teaching of the Tatar language began in 1769 – a tradition that later grew into the university's world-famous Oriental School. In 1855, the Faculty of Oriental Languages was transferred from Kazan to St Petersburg, but Oriental studies, which exist in Kazan even today, were continued by scholars from the Faculties of History and Philology. The history of Kazan University forever remembers the names of its famous orientalists, including W. Radloff, I. Berezin, V. Grigoriev, N. Katanov, H. Frehn, A. Kazembek and I. Gottwald, let alone the names of the Tatar scholars I. Halfin, S. Mardzhani and K. Nasyri who taught at the university, or participated in the work of its famous Society for Archaeology, History and Ethnography. In 1853, the Arabic, Tatar and Turkish languages were taught at the university by the Society's outstanding pedagogue and orientalist H. Faezkhanov who in 1862, after his transfer to St Petersburg University, wrote his 'Brief Grammar of the Tatar Language'. His untimely death in 1866 was a huge loss not only for Tatar, but for all-Russia culture.

With the opening of Kazan University Press in 1804, the Tatar written literature and scholarship spanning over 800 years[1] received a new impetus. The Emperor Paul I was the first to permit the publication of Tatar secular books in the Arabic script, but only the committed efforts of Tatar educators with the assistance of some university scholars managed to turn this permission into reality. The university press, in fact, could make ends meet only because of the Tatar commissions that were paid. As the outstanding Tatar scholar A. Karimullin wrote in his book 'The Tatar Book in Post-Reform Russia':

> As early as in 1845, the professor of Kazan University as well as the censor of Tatar books, A. K. Kazembek, wrote that 'the publishing of the *Quran* and other Asian books brought in constant revenue to the university press, without which it could hardly have existed'.

The number of Tatar books published by the university press in the second half of the nineteenth century totals some 1415 volumes, and the combined print run of 1170 of them totals 9,399,010 copies, i.e. an average print run of any one book was almost 8000 copies, or ten times more that the average print run of the books published by the university itself, or those commissioned by other publishers ... The main commissioner of this press was one Shamsutdin Husainov, a peasant from the village of Lower Kursa of the Kazan district, who started his publishing activities in the 1870s. At the university press, he published annually almost 500,000 copies of books costing up to 6000 roubles. He also placed commissions with other Kazan printing presses. The great majority of Tatar folklore and literary works saw the light of day thanks to this one publisher. It was also he who published five out of six volumes of the *One Thousand and One Nights*, translated by F. Khalidi, as well as a number of Tatar calendars. He also published books of religious content. Kayum Nasyri also published his books through the university press, as did Tatar educators, scholars and writers such as G. Makhmudov, G. Vagabov, G. Faezkhanov, R. Amirkhanov, A. H. Maksudi and S. Tagirov. The energetic publishers at the university press were also booksellers – for example, the petty bourgeois Fatkhulla Bikbaev Kataev, his son Abdulkarim Kataev, the honorary citizen Galimzyan Muhametzyanov and others.

In the year following the opening of Kazan Public Library in 1865, thirty-four Tatar books were published by various presses in Kazan. In all, during the second half of the nineteenth century, some 3300 Tatar books with a combined print run totalling 26,864,000 copies were published. Some years saw the annual production of Tatar books reaching two million copies. These were books not only of religious and folklore character, but also dictionaries, self-tuition manuals and textbooks of Tatar, Russian, Arabic, French, Turkish, Persian, as well as philosophical works of the great thinkers of East and West. Kazan of the nineteenth and the early twentieth centuries was, in fact, one of the largest book-publishing centres in the world. The works of Tatar authors published in Kazan in Arabic, Turkish and Persian, were widely distributed throughout Central Asia and appeared in India, Chinese Turkestan, Turkey, Persia, Afghanistan and in the Middle East. In the twentieth century Kazan continued its role as the book-publishing centre for the USSR republics: here books and textbooks in many of the languages of Eurasia were published – the Chuvash, Mari, Kyrghyz, Kazakh and Turkmen languages among them. Thanks to Tatar translations, Russian and Western-European literature and philosophical thought became available to the Turkic-speaking nations. At the same time, permission to open Tatar public libraries was only given to Kazan Tatars in 1905–07, which also saw the arrival, long-awaited, of the Tatar periodical media which immediately burgeoned into tens of newspapers and magazines published in Kazan and other centres where there were considerable Tatar populations, including Moscow and St Petersburg.

When any Tatar, be he the President of the Republic or an aspiring student, starts talking of his mother tongue, he or she inevitably mentions the greatest poet of the Tatar nation – the inimitable Gabdulla Tukai (1886–1913) who, like the great majority of Tatars in the beginning of the twentieth century, never was a student at Kazan University. He, just like many notable Tatars of the nineteenth and the early twentieth centuries, received his education in a village madrassa and 'among the people'. Tukai was a poetic genius and an 'eternal orphan' doomed in his short life to all the bitterness of homelessness and human misunderstanding. His fate reflects the best qualities of the Tatar people: directness, truthfulness, selflessness, generosity and grandeur of soul. His heartfelt poems written in a living, clear and moving tongue are permeated with notions of profound solitude and an elevated sadness. Nobody has stated the idea of the sacredness of the mother tongue and native culture better than Tukai, projecting the idea of the necessity of national freedom for the spiritual and material wellbeing of a people in order to be a force for good. It is therefore no coincidence that Tukai (who, more than any other Tatar of his time, understood the hopes and wishes of his nation and most vociferously called for the revitalization of the ancient Tatar civilization, statehood and culture) had most fully represented in his verses the national and state ideal of Kazan and Tatarstan, the essence of which is *a free development of Tatar people in a free Russia*, where the word 'freedom' is the key word:

> Here we were born, grew up, and here we shall meet the death hour,
> Fate itself has bound us to this Russian land.
> Be gone, you low creatures, you cannot confuse our sacred dreams!
> We all aspire to the universal goal – we all want a free Russia.

It is striking how Tukai's verses, published in Kazan in 1907, are still relevant in today's Internet age! Many of Tukai's poems became folk songs. He also created a new literary language that was closer to the people, and in his tragic verses and long satirical poems, as in an honest mirror, he showed the people their true nature and their true destiny. Having achieved so much in his short life, Tukai died of TB at the age of only twenty-seven. The literary art of Tukai became a summit of not only a thousand years of Tatar written literature, but also of world poetry, thanks to his prolific translations into his Tatar mother tongue. Like so many geniuses, Tukai was only fully appreciated after his untimely death. His monuments stand near the bank of the Kaban Lake and alongside the Kazan Opera Theatre, and each year, on the anniversary of his birthday, 26 April, Poetry Days are held at the foot of each of these monuments. In 2006, the celebration of Tukai's birthday was especially momentous, as it was the 120th anniversary of the great poet. Because of that, and also because of the centenary of the birth of another famous Tatar poet, Musa Jalil (1906–44) and the centenary of the Tatar professional theatre, the very first professional theatre in the entire Islamic world, President Shaimiev and the government of Tatarstan declared 2006 to be the year of Arts and Culture celebrated not just in the Republic itself, but all over Russia and abroad, amongst the Tatar émigré communities.

Given the sacredness of Tukai's legacy to all Tatars, it was only right that 26 April should be declared the Day of the Mother Tongue, which was introduced by Tatarstan's government in 1992. Importantly, this day is celebrated not just by Tatars, but by all ethnicities living in the republic, for whom this day is also a celebration of their own respective mother tongues. Today, in multi-ethnic Tatarstan, there are 1,400 ethnic schools, out of which 1,187 are Tatar schools teaching Tatar as an obligatory subject, 145 Chuvash schools, forty-five Udmurt schools, twenty-two Mari schools and four schools for Mordvin children.

However, it must be remembered that although the pre-revolutionary trend of the sustained development of the Tatar language, education and culture continued into the early Soviet years – boosted by the sheer power of Tatar intellectual strength in literature and the sciences – in the 1950s the development was effectively halted by the removal of the Tatar tongue as a compulsory subject from urban school curriculum. By 1958, in the whole of Kazan there remained only three secondary schools teaching in Tatar and seventeen schools with mixed Tatar-Russian education, which meant that 83 per cent of Tatar children studied in Russian schools. Thus, people like me were denied education in their mother tongue, the very survival of which in Tatarstan's urban areas became problematic. I, for one, had to learn my mother tongue on my own, helped by my translation and historical research activities, but not every urban Tatar was so lucky, especially those in higher education. Not surprisingly, this situation with regard to the Tatar language gave rise to the *de facto* appearance of the 'village elite' in the Tatar government at the end of 1980s, as it was only in the villages that Tatar education continued uninterrupted. Tatar children graduating from rural secondary schools, however, had either to join the Tatar Language and History Faculties of Kazan University and Kazan Pedagogical Institute (also turned into a university today), or save their mother tongue for home activities and receive higher education in Russian.

Thus, the Soviet years generated an enormous challenge for the very survival of the Tatar tongue; no wonder, therefore, that its present-day existence and future became pressing concerns for President Shaimiev and the Tatar intellectual elite immediately following the Declaration of State Sovereignty in 1990. In an atmosphere pervaded by the domination of the Russian language in all spheres of life, it was, and continues to be, an uphill struggle. In parallel with increasing governmental attention to Tatar kindergarten, secondary and higher education, President Shaimiev and the Tatarstan government have provided a system of subsidies for Tatar book publishing and media in the Tatar language. In addition, there are various material incentives for learning the Tatar language, for example, kindergarten teachers receive a 15% salary bonus, if they are proficient in the Tatar state language. Unfortunately, but perhaps not surprisingly, such measures aimed at the survival and development of the Tatar language met with disapproval from the Russian media and the Russian State Duma, where they were branded as nationalistic and separatist. Not everyone in the West approved of them either:

> In Tatarstan, where the number of ethnic Russians and ethnic Tatars is about equal, there are few Russians in the administration. In the Tatar capital Kazan, the local council approved a measure to pay employees an extra 15% if they spoke Tatar. It is not that Tatarstan, or Moscow, want to break from the Russian Federation. Rather the local elites want to enjoy all the advantages of living in a large, potentially powerful country – without the constitutional responsibilities.[2]

The author of this statement, James Meek, – intentionally or fortuitously – chose not to mention the fact that the Tatarstan constitution provides for a whole spectrum of ethnic measures, which safeguard not only the rights of the ethnic Russians, but also those of other ethnic minorities of the republic, including Chuvash, Mari, Udmurt, Jewish and many others – not least the Assirrians who number only 150 people in the entire country. The responsibility it places on the 'local elite' in providing all these ethnicities with ethnic schooling and finances for the development of their respective languages and cultures is, in fact, immense, given the present state of economic affairs even in such a relatively prosperous country as Tatarstan. As far as the payment of the additional fifteen per cent is concerned, this measure, which also caused uproar in the Russia media, is available only for kindergarten, primary and secondary schoolteachers. It was undertaken in the context of Tatar, along with Russian, being one of the two official languages of the republic, and the fact that it had been neglected for so long, and thus required special measures to prevent its further decline.

Putting Tatar on the same footing as Russian, as a state language, immediately removed the tension which was beginning to develop among the peoples of Tatarstan in 1990. Furthermore, justice demands that we acknowledge the fact that the development of the indigenous Tatar culture and language had been stifled over the course of centuries culminating in the ideological pressure of the Soviet era. Therefore, the priority development of the Tatar mother tongue and Tatar culture became, from the outset, one of the president's main concerns. As he himself has said:

> Language is the soul of the people. Loss of language would mean a loss of the national soul. We need a kind of equality, which will allow us, firstly, to improve the standing of the Tatar language. Such an approach would not be a violation of the principle of equality, merely a restoration of historical fairness. But, one has to approach it without haste or forceful measures. We should not make a condition: Learn the language, otherwise we shall sack you! It might only frustrate people and discredit the whole idea. At the same time, it is essential to create the proper conditions for those wanting to master the Tatar tongue – we have to open new primary and secondary schools with their curriculum in the Tatar language; to introduce the mother tongue in kindergartens and in clerical work; to publish textbooks, prepare basic structures and so forth. You cannot accomplish this in one go. It is a lengthy job requiring decades for its accomplishment.[3]

Would the authors of the articles such as the one quoted above from the *Guardian* care to note that the same programme is actually being implemented for all the languages in multi-ethnic Tatarstan? Of course, it is easier to use clichés like 'local elite' and 'iron grip on power', than try to explain to the foreign reader the deep complexity of the issue in question, not to mention its strategic ideological importance. But there is no need to enter into any further polemics. President Shaimiev has made the position clear in the following statement:

> On the first day we proclaimed statehood, we declared that our sovereignty was not ethnic in nature. No one can reproach us for a lack of respect regarding the interests of other nations, or human dignity in the past or present. This proceeds naturally from our ethnic principles. The Republic's multi-ethnic population has always looked to the future with optimism, because it appraises friendship and likes to work. Today, it is represented by at least 100 nationalities. Tatars and Russians constitute the majority. We also have Chuvashes, Ukrainians, Mordovians, Bashkirs, Maris, Jews, Germans and some other nationalities, some of whom have set up their own cultural centres. There are German and Jewish cultural clubs, the

'Oguz' Azerbaijanian society, the 'Kazakhstan' society and the Chuvash and Mari centres. The Chuvashes recently began publishing their own newspaper, *Suvar*. There are Tatar ethnic groups and a few Slavonic societies in the republic. The constitution of Tatarstan guarantees equal rights to all citizens, regardless of their nationality. Tatar and Russian are both state languages, we guarantee the preservation and development of other languages . . . Some people consider such notions as dignity, honour and friendship as relics of the past. I disagree. There always have been and always will be intrinsic humanitarian values; one's native land, honour, human dignity and cooperation have always been sacred for us. These are the principles we are prepared to collaborate on with all interested parties.[4]

It is against this background that we should understand the furore surrounding the official part of Kazan's millennium celebrations in August 2005, when the President of Russia Vladimir Putin read the first part of his official address in Tatar, marking the first time since the end of the sixteenth century that any Russian head of state had publicly paid tribute to this tongue – once the principal diplomatic language of Eurasia:

> I would like to emphasize a few things, and for this reason I will dare to utter some words in the Tatar language: In the thousand-year-old destiny of Kazan the most important stages of the Russian history – [applause] and this is not all that I can say in Tatar – and the destiny of our Fatherland are reflected like in a mirror. Here we can discern objective problems as well as merits of the indeed unique Russian statehood, which is centuries-old, multi-ethnic and multi-confessional. It would not be an exaggeration, if I say that Kazan has played a truly inimitable historical role in the formation of the united Russian nation, in the making of the united and cohesive people of Russia. It is necessary to mention here that we related with understanding to the organization of this jubilee, keeping in mind the significance of Kazan for Russia . . .[5]

Considering the history of Tatarstan and her native tongue, especially the last four centuries of it, this five-minute-long televised speech in Tatar was accepted as something much more than just a sensationalist goodwill gesture. For many people in the wider audience it presented a moment of truth, which, along with many other social and economic revelations of the historical metamorphosis of Kazan, prompted them to evaluate the events in a completely new light. During the later sitting of the Tatar World Congress dedicated to the Kazan millennium, President Shaimiev specifically referred to this event, which was an open recognition of the role played by the Tatar culture and state-building skills in the history of Russian statehood.

President Shaimiev, as the leader of Tatarstan, is naturally proud of one of his major achievements, and that is the existing inter-ethnic and inter-religious accord in his country. In the early 1990s, when bloody inter-ethnic conflicts were commonplace in many former parts of the USSR and Yugoslavia, the firmly established ethnic stability in Tatarstan with her ethnically and religiously mixed population became the show-case for the world and the base for the 'Hague Initiative' for the resolution of such conflicts jointly promoted in January 1995 in the Hague by the President of Tatarstan, Harvard University and the Carnegie Foundation. Tatarstan always argued that Russia at large lacks clearly formulated politics for its multiple nationalities, but, at the same time, developed her own policies in this regard. In the words of President Shaimiev, such policies can be summed up in one word: *internationalism*. The utmost respect for the ethnic traditions of all ethnicities populating Tatarstan and equal attention to their cultural needs lies at the centre of Tatarstan's nationalities politics, and these are not mere words: in the country even the electoral ballots are printed in six local languages, and every ethnicity has its own media outlets and cultural establishments, such as clubs, national folk ensembles, etc. In pursuing her distinct nationalities policy, Tatarstan in 1993 adopted her own law 'On Ethnic Cultural Autonomies in the Republic of Tatarstan' further amended in 2005. True to this law defining Tatarstan's national politics, government support is available to the ethnic minorities in publishing books, periodicals, and audio and video materials. The Republic now has over fifty ethnic communities united under the auspices of the Association of Ethnic Cultural Organizations, the headquarters and ethnic headquarters of which occupy the House of Friendship in Kazan. The distinctive feature of the nationalities policy in the 'Tatarstan model' is that the officially formed ethnic organizations can communicate their needs to government in a democratic way 'from below' and are not dictated or mentored 'from above', since it is assumed they know much better than anyone else what their own needs and requirements are.

President Shaimiev himself actively participates in all major events and festivals of the republic's ethnic minorities, be it the Jewish Hanuka, or any other ethnic or religious festival. It would require another book to take an in-depth look into Tatarstan's minority issues. Given the fact that President Shaimiev hails from one of the most ethnically 'pure' Aktanysh regions of Tatarstan with a 92% Tatar component in the population structure, his commitment to a multi-ethnic society is all the more significant. It is not surprising, therefore, that Kazan is often visited by representatives of European and world organizations, including the leaders of all-Russia ethnic and religious minorities, dealing with the rights of minorities. Tatarstan has many things to show in this respect of inter-ethnic accord and religious tolerance. As an example, true to the tradition that saw the publishing of the first ever Chuvash newspaper in Kazan a full hundred years ago, today the republic supports publication of five Chuvash newspapers and also radio programmes in the Chuvash language. Tatarstan also makes available the school textbooks in Chuvash in the context of supporting education in the mother tongues of her major minorities. Is it any surprise that the experts from the neighbouring Republic of Udmurtia came to Tatarstan in order to learn how to restore the teaching of their own mother tongue in schools and, also, for the textbooks and methodical literature? Nor was it any coincidence that President Shaimiev was one of the leading figures in political resolution of the Chechen conflict and his credo in this respect was at the time as clear as it was unyielding: 'Why do we look for enemies? All kinds of strong expressions are being used in Russia against our own people which, in many respects, was forced to take to arms. Sometimes it is said that "that side" is becoming weaker, but what do we mean by "that side"? They are all our people.' Such an approach to the nationalities issue on the part of the Federal centre troubles Tatarstan even today. In March 2006, the State Council of Tatarstan voiced its disapproval of the draft federal law 'On the Foundations of the State Nationalities Policy of the Russian Federation' arguing that this draft contradicts the multi-ethnic nature of Russia, as it effectively declares the dominating position of the ethnic Russian people over all the other ethnicities of Russia. This argument was based on the irrefutable fact that Tatarstan never demanded exclusive rights of Tatars *vis-à-vis* other ethnicities of the Republic, of which ethnic Russians constitute forty-eight per cent of the entire population. The need to develop Tatar culture and bring it up to par with Russian culture does exist in Tatarstan, but even then such a need is only being highlighted and not promoted as a priority over cultural needs of non-Tatar citizens of the republic.

One of the main indicators of inter-ethnic accord in Tatarstan is, of course, the number of inter-ethnic marriages, which constitute one third of all marriages in the country. I once asked the president, how he would describe Tatarstan society? 'For me,' he said, 'it is a mixed family.' Two things emanate from this simple sentence: firstly, the very Tatar idea that one has to take care of one's family whatever the difficulties that life might present and any human complications within that family that might occur; and, secondly, the simple-heartedness of this natural answer reveals that President Shaimiev does not even think that such an answer could elicit the recurring opposing media accusations that he allegedly runs Tatarstan in the interests of his own family and kin. Such notions did not even enter the mind of the president during his answer, and, indeed, his pride in making Tatarstan the country of inter-ethnic harmony is totally justified, even if you can never satisfy everyone in human society.

Interestingly, the tradition of inter-ethnic marriage bonds goes back much further than the Soviet period in the republic's history, despite the fact that the pre-1917 history of Tatars can be viewed as strictly Islamic. In the present atmosphere of deep apprehension and distrust towards Islam widely felt in Europe, the USA and, to some extent, Russia herself, the example of the Tatar nation in this respect is all the more instructive.

THE STORY OF TATAR ISLAM IN RUSSIA

Let us recollect that for two centuries Islam, which formed the basis of Tatar national culture, was effectively banned in Russia, and the people professing it were subjected to immense spiritual and physical burdens, double taxation, soldiering and a complete denial of civil rights. Knowing this history of centuries-long persecution, the tolerant and all-embracing nature of the 'Tatarstan model' becomes even more remarkable. Surviving and at the same time preserving one's cultural origins and mother tongue under such adverse circumstances was nothing short of an amazing achievement containing a strong spiritual dimension: the Tatar nation preserved itself as an ethnic and cultural reality, despite the fact that this nation with its thousand-year-old written literature was forbidden to publish its own newspapers and magazines until 1905. Immediately following the conquest of 1552 all mosques in the Kazan Kremlin were demolished, but such systematic destruction later spread to the whole of the former Kazan Khanate, as the mosques in the Tatar villages and suburban settlements continued to be built despite all the prosecutions and persecutions. For the sake of fairness, it is necessary to say that in the decree of Ivan the Terrible given to the first archbishop of Kazan Gury in 1555, the 'first baptizer' of Kazan and his assistants were told to christen the land without resorting to compulsion and violence, but the Sofia chronicle tells us that Ivan the Terrible, even before the capture of Kazan, was not distinguished by any special meekness in or lack of force in converting a Muslim people into Christians, even if it concerned his allies:

> In the same year of 7043 [1535] the Grand Duke Ivan Vasilyevich of all Rus' became displeased with the Tatars of the Tsar Shah Ali, and as there were in Novgorod eighty or more of them, he threw them into prison, where they, because of their filthy faith, all died in five days; also in Pskov seventy of them soon died. One of them, however, chose to be baptized with his wife and with children; formerly called Hasan, he received in baptism the name of Mikhail.

After the fall of the Kazan khanate the great majority of Kazan Tatars remained faithful to their Muslim religion, and, according to the testimony of the second Novgorod chronicle, no sooner had the Russian tsar delivered his imperial pastoral exhortation in 1555, than religious violence became more the rule than the exception as far as the Kazan Tatars were concerned.

> In the year of 7060 [1552] . . . the Kazan, and, later, other Tatars were brought from Moscow to Novgorod, and given to the archbishop, and certain merchants for feeding, and their number, in all, was sixty; and in the same year they built in the city three prisons and put the Tatars in them . . . In the year of 7063 [1555] . . . In the same winter, on 1 January, on Tuesday, the dyaks (civil servants) allocated to the monasteries those Tatars who were in prison, but wanted to be baptized and those who did not want to be baptized were thrown, by the dyaks, into the river.

The Kazan Orthodox prelate Germogen, following the path of St Gury the Baptizer, also experienced difficulties with the conversion of Tatars into Russian Orthodoxy through meekness only, although the business of the Orthodox education of the gentiles was helped by genuine miracles.

On 23 June 1579, there was a terrible fire in Kazan, after which the city-dwellers had to rebuild their houses. It was then that the ten-year-old daughter of the head of the Streltsy troops Danila Onuchin, Matrena, had a prophetic dream: in this dream she was visited by Our Lady (Mary, the mother of Jesus) who revealed to her that there on the site of the burned-down house of the Onuchins a miraculous icon was hidden. Despite being ridiculed by the adults, Matrena managed to find this miraculous icon in the ashes of the great fire. With the arrival of the Kazan archbishop Jeremiah for the appropriation of the icon, the miraculous image of the Kazan Mother of God was transferred to the church of Nikola of Tula, and even on the way the miraculous healing of cripples took place on the church parvis (enclosed area in front of the church). Later, this icon became one of the main miraculous icons of all Russia – it was its presence among the Kazan home guard, it is thought, which bestowed victory over the impostor to the forces of Cosma Minin and Prince Pozharsky, and thus rescued Moscow and Russia during the Time of Troubles. From then on, this icon became the most venerable icon of Russia: the victory over the armies of Napoleon in 1812 is also thought to have been facilitated by it, and the Kazansky cathedral in St Petersburg was erected in memory of this famous victory.

Kazan marked the appropriation of the icon by building, in the autumn of 1579, the temple of the Holy Virgin, and, later, the Kazan Maiden Monastery, of which Matrena Onuchina herself became the first nun. In 1595, a stone church was built on the site of the wooden church, whereas the main church of the Maiden monastery was built in 1797, and, as the expert on Kazan, Professor K. Fuks remarked, at the beginning of the nineteenth century the monastery church came to be 'one of the best buildings of Kazan'. On the night of 29 June 1904, the icon of the Kazan Mother of God was stolen because of its precious icon setting and for a long time was considered to have perished, which misfortune, however, never stopped the flow of pilgrims to the place of its appropriation.

The history of the miraculous image of the Kazan Mother of God entered a new chapter at the end of the twentieth century, when the Tatarstan authorities, the President of the Republic M. Shaimiev and the Mayor of Kazan K. Iskhakov, initiated the process of bringing the icon home to Kazan in the knowledge that this holy relic, after lengthy wanderings across Europe and America, had come to rest in the personal chambers of Pope John Paul II in the Vatican. After several years of persistent negotiations the icon was finally returned to Russia in August 2004, and Kazan received it back on the eve of its famous Millennium. Today, the icon of Our Lady of Kazan rests in the place of its appropriation – in the newly restored church of the Maiden Monastery of Kazan. This is only one example of the careful attention that is given to the needs and beliefs of the republic's Orthodox Christians, where churches are being built or restored to believers on a par with mosques.

Christian churches were nothing new to Kazan even before the Russian conquest, because of the liberal tradition of the Kazan khanate which had been hallowed by religion and the khan's decrees, not only from the Muslims of Volga Bulgaria, but also from the khans of the Golden Horde famous for their practice of religious tolerance. As it is well known, the Golden Horde khans, true to their Islamic beliefs, safeguarded the sanctity of Orthodox and Catholic churches and monasteries under their protection under the pain of death; furthermore, the churches were never burdened with any taxes whatsoever, which brought about a veritable flourishing of the Orthodox culture in Russia.[6]

There never was such a thing as Tatar-Russian animosity among the two great nations. The conquest of Kazan was officially motivated by the need to rescue the Russian captives in the Kazan khanate. Yet, according to documentary evidence, many Russian captives were in no hurry to return to a Russia enslaved by Ivan the Terrible, and at the end of the sixteenth century still lived in the country of their former detention. The anonymous author of 'The Kazan Chronicler', expressing his dismay at this, says that even after the Kazan-Moscow treaty of 1551: 'Many of them who had grown old in captivity and changed their faith, have remained, not wishing to be converted back to Christianity and finally losing all hope for being saved, and they have rejected the light of the true belief, and fallen in love with darkness.' This situation along with the fact that the conquered Kazan khanate became the place of exile for many German and Baltic prisoners of war in the second half of the sixteenth century, formed the nucleus of today's multiethnic structure of Tatarstan. As the Kazan metropolitan Germogen complained in his letter to the Tsar Fedor Ioannovich in 1593 that 'many Russian captives and non-captives live with the Tatars, and also with the Cheremises and the Chuvashs, and drink with them and eat from the same utensils, and marry there...' The Metropolitan also complained to the tsar that the newly baptised Tatars 'do not accept the teaching, and do not reject the Tatar customs, and live in great fearlessness, and have finally left the *(Christian)* faith, and are very saddened by their earlier apostasy ... Other Tatars not only do not want to be baptized into the Christian faith, and not only swear at it, but more – in the forty years after the capture of Kazan there were no mosques in the Tatar settlement, but nowadays ... they started to build mosques very near to the trading quarters.' The royal answer to this complaint prompted a new wave of religious persecutions in Kazan. First of all, the tsar ordered the newly baptized Tatars to be separated from all others so that they 'do not convert back to their Tatar faith from the Christian faith, and do not mix either with Tatars or Germans, and do not eat and drink from the same utensils with them, and do not hold non-Christian Tatars and Cheremises, and Chuvashs, and German captives close to themselves, and those newly baptized who had children with non-Christian Tatar women or German captive women should baptize their children, and, in similar fashion, they should aspire to baptize all Tatars, and Cheremises, and Chuvashs, and German and Lithuanian prisoners in their service'.

This imperial decree is illuminating not only because, in it, we are informed about the multi-ethnic structure of Kazan's population and settlements at the end of the sixteenth century, but we also can appreciate the fact that peoples of various nationalities and confessions lived together quite peacefully and concluded inter-ethnic marriages in Kazan. This gives us some idea of how far back Kazan's tradition of inter-ethnic marriages goes, which even today account for one third of all marriages registered in the city. However, continuing with the letter of the Tsar Fedor Ioannovich, we come to the really disturbing part of its contents. I quote:

> And as to those newly baptized who would not be steadfast in the Christian belief and would not start to heed the instructions of the metropolitan and holy fathers, you should give the order to suppress them, and put them in prison and beat them, and put them in irons and chain them, ... all of this in order to bring all the newly baptized into the Christian faith, and to break them from the Tatar faith and to make them fear ... And as the Metropolitan wrote to us about the Tatar mosques, that the Tatars started to build many mosques in the Tatar settlement, whilst from the fall of Kazan up to now no one dared to erect Tatar mosques in Kazan, and as there are decrees of our father, the Tsar and Grand Duke of blessed memory, Ivan Vasilyevich of all Rus', and our own decrees that any building of mosques in Kazan is not allowed and that happened due to your negligence and your mistake, because the harm was made and nobody wrote to us about that, whereas at the time of our former boyars, commanders and dyaks the Tatar mosques were not there from the fall of the Tatars up to your time, you should give the order to demolish all Tatar mosques and convey to the Tatars the prohibition to build them in the future, so that those Tatar mosques could be finally exterminated. And, also, the Metropolitan Germogen wrote to us that many Russian captives and non-captives live with the

Tatars, the Cheremises and the Chuvashs, and drink with them and eat from the same utensils, and marry there; and that many Russian people, old and young, live with the Germans in the settlements serving them voluntarily and for money, and these people had thus forsaken the Christian faith and turned near the Tatars into the Tatar, and near the Germans into the Roman Catholic and Lutheran faiths, you should order the Russians to serve the Tatars and the Germans neither voluntarily, nor for money.

The process of the building and destruction of the mosques, that is to say, the entire system of the Tatar way of life and education continued through to the middle of the eighteenth century. In the 1649 'Codex' of the tsar Alexei Mihailovich, the Muslims were effectively outlawed, with the right of the state to dispossess them of their land possessions, on the grounds of their religious beliefs. And, of course, the very notion of religious tolerance was non-existent in the first formal Russian 'Codex', which (Chapter XXII, clause 24) states:

> And if a Muslim would by any means – through violence or deceit – force a Russian person to accept the Muslim faith, and would circumcize him according to his Muslim faith, and it will become known for certain, then that Muslim is to be, after the investigation of the matter, put to death – burnt by fire without any mercy.

In 1681, Alexei Mihailovich issued a decree 'to seize the estates and lands with the peasants and solitary men from the Murzes (nobles) and Tatars of the Lower Volga cities, and from the wives of those Murzes and Tatars, and from their widows, and their adolescents, and their maidens, to the benefit of himself, the great sovereign'.

The so-called enlightened eighteenth century, which began with the reign of Peter I, did not bring any relief to the Kazan Tatars – in fact, it was exactly the opposite. By the 1682 decree of tsars John and Peter, the order was given 'to take away to the treasury half of the estates of unbaptized Murzes and Tatars, leaving them the other half'. This decree continued the policies of the time of Alexei Mihailovich, when in 1675, under the decree of the tsar, 'the Tatar ancestral lands and estates taken from them and allocated among the Russians and the Newly Baptized for their conversion into the Orthodox faith shall remain with the present owners and shall not be returned to the Tatar landlords'. And last but not least, in 1713, Peter II issued a decree, repeated in its generality in 1715, by which even the hereditary aristocracy of the former Kazan khanate lost the right of freedom of conscience under the threat of alienation of their estates:

> The great sovereign has enjoined to convey to the Muslims of the Islamic faith in the Kazan and Azov provinces, possessing estates and ancestral lands, in which they employ peasants, servants and craftsmen of the Orthodox Christian faith, his, the great sovereign's, decree that they, Muslims, should finally be baptized in half a year ... And should they not be baptized in half a year, then those estates and ancestral lands of theirs, with all people and peasants, should be taken from them and given in benefit to him, the great sovereign, and not given back to anyone without a special decree.

Peter's successors continued the same policies, and from time to time these policies did indeed reach the point of irrationality, as was the case in the middle of the eighteenth century with the establishment in Kazan of the so-called 'Offices for the Newly Baptized' under the leadership of archbishop Lucas Konashevich. In his time, religious persecution and forced conversions were promoted on such a scale that long after him Tatar mothers would frighten their children with his name. As a result of these policies by 1744, hundreds of mosques in the Kazan and Siberian provinces were destroyed:

> In the account sent from Kazan province about those mosques it is shown that in Kazan and in the Kazan district the number of Tatar mosques was 536, of which number 418 are demolished; and 118 still stand, and about all those it is declared that some of them were built even before the subjugation of Kazan under Russian control, and others 200 or more years ago.

In response to such cultural devastation elected representatives of the so-called Service, or Yasak, Tatars attempted to appeal to the Governing Senate with the request for 'reconstruction of the demolished Tatar mosques' in which it was said that:

> If all the mosques of them, the Tatars, were to be demolished, from that, for them, the Tatars, nothing but the offence to their law would follow; and the disclosure of that might reach such places in other countries, where the people of the Greek faith live among the Mohammedans, and where the Lord's churches are built, and, from that, some persecution of these people might result; and, also, the Tatars of the Mohammedan law in Russia are brought to oaths according to their own laws in their mosques.

Certainly, such a continuing onslaught on the very essence of the spiritual and cultural life of the Kazan Tatars drove them to take part in many peasant revolts during the seventeenth and eighteenth centuries, including, of course, the largest revolts under the leadership of Stepan Razin and Emelian Pugachev. Only at the end of the eighteenth century, in the wake of the Pugachev revolt, were some of the restrictions concerning religion, education, crafts and trade removed from the Tatar people, allowing Tatar culture to return gradually to its enchanted capital.

Spiritual compulsion, aggravated by economic pressures and the denial of Tatar rights to property ownership, pursuaded the Tatar aristocracy, which already had had blood ties with the Russian nobility for two centuries, to accept baptism in order to preserve their privileges. Thus, many Russian aristocratic families were born: the echoes of Tatar descent can be plainly heard in the sound of such famous crème de la crème Russians as N. Karamzin, G. Derzhavin, A. Radishchev, K. Ryleyev, A. Chaadaev, S. Rachmaninov, D. Mendeleyev, A. Kuprin and A. Skriabin. So, for centuries, contrary to the state policy of alienation of Tatar culture, the ancient Bulgar-Kazan culture not only cooperated, but from time to time even merged with traditional Russian culture. The saddest outcome, however, of the persecution of Tatar culture and religion is that only a quarter of the Kazan Tatar nation now lives in the territory of the Republic of Tatarstan and the rest is scattered all over Russia and as far as the USA, Japan and Australia. In the 1990s, this fact caused Tatarstan to bring about the formation of the World Congress of Tatars, the members of which would come over to Kazan from around the world and the former USSR every five years to consider their culture's past, present and future. All of them look to Kazan as the beacon of national revival, and this is fully understood by the president, even if he says soberly that the economic capacity of Tatarstan, for all her willingness and continuing support, is simply unable to maintain Tatar culture and education throughout Russia, let alone the 'far abroad'. But then, the Tatar education historically went on without any help from the Russian authorities, based on charitable donations from wealthy Tatars. Here I must quote the enlightened comment by Alexandre Bennigsen and Chantal Lemercier-Quelquejay:

> At the beginning of the twentieth century, in response to the extraordinary effort made by the people as a whole, led by the bourgeoisie, the cultural level of some Muslim groups, particularly the Volga Tatars, had risen to a remarkable degree. The Muslim cities of Russia, and particularly Kazan, had taken on the character of genuine intellectual centres, capable of rivalling Constantinople, Cairo and Beirut. Their influence crossed the Tatar frontiers, making itself felt in all the Muslim territories of the Russian empire and even beyond ... Very soon, the reform movement passed beyond the confines of religion, language and education, and began to have a profound effect on all other aspects of life ... Throughout the Muslim world, thinkers were searching for the best way of recovering the power of the first centuries of Islam, of producing a political renaissance by providing Muslim society with foundations better suited to the modern age.[7]

As opposed to the present-day fundamentalist madrassas in many parts of the Muslim world, the Tatar madrassas were well equipped to teach not just theology, but also natural sciences and humanities. One of them, built at the end of the eighteenth century, housed the most important madrassa in Russia, the 'Muhammadiya', where over the years many outstanding representatives of Tatar culture studied. These included the founder of the Tatar theatre, the dramatist G. Kamal, the writer and the best friend of G. Tukai, F. Amirkhan, the dramatist and actor K. Tinchurin, one of the very first Tatar musical composers S. Gabyashi who composed the first Tatar opera *Saniya* and the scores for many performances of the Tatar theatre. The director of the madrassa was a remarkable scholar and religious activist, as well as being one of the reformers of the Tatar educational system, G. Barudi. It is to him, as well to other Tatar reformers like the great Islamic reformer Musa Bigiev, that Tatarstan owes its tolerant and enlightened view of Islam, which, rather then being an obstacle, became even at the beginning of the twentieth century the Tatar nation's engine of its social and economic development.

Among other things first introduced by Tatars to the Islamic world, was such unheard-off art as the art of the professional theatre. In December 2006, the Tatar Academic Drama Theatre in Kazan celebrated its 100th anniversary. In his review in *The Stage*, of the troupe's UK tour, British theatre critic Nicolas Awde wrote:

> The Islamic world's first modern professional theatre company is celebrating the 100th anniversary of its first performance in 1906. And next year will mark the centenary of Sakhibjamal Gizatullina-Volzhskaya joining its ranks to become the world's first professional Muslim actress in a troupe equally adept at Chekhov as a homegrown Tatar classic. Named after the pioneering playwright of the period, the

Galiaskar Kamal State Academic Theatre is based in Kazan.... In fact, many of the first performances were within the walls of the local madrassas, or religious schools – which in Kazan taught the Quran along with secular subjects such as chemistry and physics on par with colleges in Moscow.[8]

Besides the professional theatre, which started with amateur performances in the Kazan 'Mukhammadiya' madrassa, Tatar Islamic culture in the 1920s and 1930s pioneered such arts as professional music, painting and even the art of 'colour music' – the brainchild of Dr Bulat Galeev, grandson of the head of the 'Mukhammadiya' madrassa G. Barudi, first seen in Kazan in the early 1960s.

The greatest personalities of Tatar Islam belonged to the Naksbandiyya stream of Sufism,[9] and in my forthcoming book *Islam and Science in Russia*, I argue that the dynamic investigative philosophy of this Islamic world outlook boosted by the historical Tatar quest for learning later, when Islam was again all but banned in the Soviet era, enabled a significant Tatar participation in dynamic scientific research (the first Tatar lady mathematician, S. Shakulova, for example, graduated from Sorbonne University as early as in 1913). But, as a matter of fact, during the atheistic Soviet years Islam became, for Tatars, more of a cultural tradition, than a professed faith. Islam became dissolved in family traditions of the reverence for the elders, especially respect for females, above all the mothers and grandmothers of the family, together with social tolerance and the need for learning, and it is in this sense that we can say that President Shaimiev is indeed a Muslim. In the relatively recent atmosphere of angst with regard to Islam, President Shaimiev is paying particular attention to the problems of Muslim believers in the republic and is often asked about his views on the present situation. He always rightfully argues that, historically, Tatars adhere to a 'more tolerant form of Islam better suited to the co-existence of people of different ethnicities and religions' than some radical versions of the faith in various countries of the world. He points out that the reform movement of Jadidism completely transformed Tatar Islam, opening it to the outside world and releasing the huge humanistic and social potential that the rightly understood faith of Islam has to its credit. Tatarstan as an open country is, of course, vulnerable to outside influences, but the president and the republic's religious leaders clarified the fact early on that help from the Islamic world always comes with strings attached. Such realization was especially crucial at the beginning of the economic and social transition of the early 1990s, when Tatarstan did not have her own system of religious education and had to make do with Imams educated abroad. The influences they brought with them were not always conducive to normal religious life and ran contrary to the tolerant and inquisitive nature of the historical form of Islam found in Tatarstan. The conflict in Chechnya further added to the danger of Islamic radicalization and, indeed, in the republic there were some instances of quasi-Islamic radical cells being formed. President Shaimiev is fully aware of the danger of such developments, but he would not be the person he is, if he did not seek an answer to the threat:

> There was, indeed, an incident in the Naberezhnye Chelny, from where some guys got to the training camp of Hattab in Chechnya. Can you imagine – those were the boys who graduated from our secondary schools? In a very short time they became fanatics – it shows how seriously those training camps work with their attendants. But we, as they say, have nipped this phenomenon in the bud. In such cases, when

something hurts the people of our republic, we can show formidable character. Yet, the heart of the matter lies not just in religious fanaticism. We wanted to delve deeper into the problem and realized that at the beginning of the Perestroika period Tatarstan possessed twenty-three mosques. Now, we have over a thousand mosques. Every rich person can afford to build a mosque. Now, there are a lot of mosques in the republic, but very few Imams for them. Until recently, we had no facilities to teach them. But we cannot wait for religious emissaries to come from abroad. We know quite well, who comes from where, what kind of struggle they are engaged in, when trying to take our mosques under their influence. And so, despite the fact that we are a secular republic, we decided to open colleges for clergy. Thus, in 2000, we opened the Russian Islamic University in Kazan. If there are believers, we have to help them. Democracy brings with it justified freedoms, the freedom of religion, for one. Consequently, a democratic state should approach this issue in a stately manner, which we do, unlike the Russian federal centre, which does not give enough attention to such problems.[10]

Interestingly, radical nationalistic and religious elements in the Tatar society come mostly from outside the republic. The town of Naberezhnye Chelny, the home of the giant KamAZ factory, is especially notable in this respect, because the workforce for the construction and running of the plant came from all over Russia and the former USSR. Tatar migration from the former Republics of the disintegrated USSR also exacerbates the problem, but Tatarstan's President and the government pay constant attention to the challenge of providing them with work in proper social conditions, so that one can say that even in the challenging times of today, the problem of Islamic radicalism in well under control in Tatarstan, and that this control is mostly effected by the democratic means of establishing inter-ethnic accord and peaceful co-existence of various faiths and ethnicities. Quite naturally, Tatarstan's considerable experience in this context is known to UNESCO, the Council of Europe and other leading world organizations. In February 2006, the completely renovated Kazan Rathaus welcomed the International Seminar on 'Dialogue, Tolerance, Education: the joint activities of the Council of Europe and religious confessions' held under the auspices of the Council of Europe Human Rights Commissioner Alvaro Gil-Robles who came to Kazan with his recently elected successor Thomas Hammarberg, the former head of 'Amnesty International'. This important meeting brought together many religious dignitaries, among which there were representatives from the Roman Catholic, Orthodox and many Christian Churches, Islamic countries and organizations, Jewish centres from Russia and around the world. It was then that the outgoing Human Rights Commissioner of the Council of Europe noted that everywhere in Tatarstan he saw 'the spirit of tolerance' and proceeded to say:

> This encouraged me very much on my previous visits; therefore, I rather wanted to return here in order to complete the cycle of conferences on religion and human rights on this soil. What exists here and what is considered the norm here, should become the rule everywhere – in Europe and the world: this respect for everyone's uniqueness.

In the opinion of Thomas Hammarberg, the situation regarding human rights in Russia has changed substantially in recent years, although there is still a lot to be done in this regard. There is no doubt about it; indeed, one has only to compare what was and what is, not forgetting that we see Russia and Tatarstan in transition, where no human value can be imposed from above, but rather convincingly encouraged to develop and even fought for. In the words of President Shaimiev on the same conference: 'Today, Russian society which has chosen the way of democratic development, is more than ever in need of educational support and, also, help in promoting human rights.' However, the president never agreed with some Western notions that it is Islam that impedes development of democratic and human rights in countries that are in transition. The entire history of religious enlightenment in the context of Islamic educational reform in Tatarstan disproves this notion. When asked, does Islam help him as a secular leader and a man, President Shaimiev replied:

> Islam is a very flexible religion, especially the Tatar version of it. There are Islamic norms which say that one has to abstain from alcohol, one has to toil for a living and respect one's elders. Islam encourages social and entrepreneurial activities. And, by the way – about the inter-confessional tolerance ... In the Quran, there are Surahs that establish the virtues of Christianity and Judaism along with those of Islam. And, what is more, the true Islam demands that a man be educated. As the Prophet would say, there are various paths to Paradise, yet the shortest path is through education. Now judge for yourself, does it help me, or not?

We shall consider education in Tatarstan in the next chapter, but we cannot conclude the present one on the Tatar mother tongue without mentioning the 'Salyat' intellectual movement, which unites, via the Internet, students and teachers of Tatarstan schools and colleges who for the last eight years participated in the activities of the summer educational camps of the same name. The children attending these camps are gifted Tatar children, the winners of various republican and all-Russia competitions in mathematics, physics, the Tatar language and other subjects who are also willing to learn or progress in their knowledge of the Tatar mother tongue as well as pursue a deeper knowledge of the natural sciences, especially theoretical and practical computer studies. The camps bring together up to 500 gifted children and are organized each year in various locations – from the historical sites of Bilyarsk and Bolgar-on-the-Volga in Tatarstan to the Black Sea.

This initiative was started in 1993 by a group of young scholars from Kazan University and the joint laboratory of the Academy of Sciences of Tatarstan and Kazan University who addressed the question of 'Problems of Artificial Intellect' under the scientific guidance of Dr D. Suleimanov and the founder of Kazan school of theoretical computer sciences, R. G. Bukharaev, who wanted to prepare specialists in computer technologies and computer linguistics from the outset of secondary school. As with many other educational initiatives in Tatarstan, this one was sponsored by the government, the Academy of Sciences, the special 'Salyat' foundation and many commercial and private sponsors. The above-mentioned activity aimed at the development of young gifted children in the spirit of modern technologies in their own mother tongue, is only one facet of the attention paid in the republic to the huge task of computerization and the further modernization of the republic's educational, economic, social and political life. Suffice it to say that Tatarstan's government has long since modernized its IT requirements and the agreement with Microsoft on entering the Tatar tongue in its list of computerized tongues is yet another indicator of how carefully the republic's leaders and scholars think about the future of the Tatar language in today's increasingly globalized world.

Here, we should also address the row, which erupted between Tatarstan and the Russian State Duma, on the reintroduction of the modified Latin script for the Tatar language abolished by the Soviet authorities in 1939 in favour of the modified Cyrillic one. Previously, in 1922, the Latin script was introduced instead of the Arabic one which was considered outdated, even if this was the script, in which Tatars wrote and read for the thousand years of their history since the acceptance of Islam as their faith in AD 922. So, twice in one century, the great cultural legacy was taken away from the people, and that suited the Soviet authorities quite well, as much of the 'ideologically heretical' literature of the 1920s and 1930s became unavailable for the general reader and was kept in the archives for specialists only.

At the beginning of the twenty-first century, when demands of the Internet and the need to supply, with its help, the contents of Tatar books and periodicals to Tatars scattered all over Russia and the world have once again called for the reintroduction of the Latin script, the mere news of it causing a great fuss in the Russian media and among Russian federal law-makers. It was argued that by introducing the Latin script Kazan wanted to isolate itself from the rest of Russia. Despite the fact that the choice of written script is a prerogative of Tatarstan falling within her own sphere of competence, the federal Duma with the help of a panicky Russian media insisted on putting the issue on hold. It was all the more hilarious insofar as the Tatar Cyrillic script is just as illegible to the Russian deputies as Latin would be; but they are still comforted by the Cyrillic appearance of the present script of the Tatar tongue. At the same time, those who cry the loudest about the lack of all-Russian patriotism in Tatarstan on the grounds of the proposal to introduce the Latin script for the Tatar language, would be well advised to remember one fact from history. In 2006, Tatarstan and all-Russia celebrated the centenary of the birth of another great Tatar poet, the hero of the the Second World War, Musa Jalil, who was guillotined by the Nazis in 1944 in Berlin for his anti-fascist resistance activities in the German prison camps for Muslim prisoners of war. The most patriotic poems about Russia, the 'Moabit Notebooks' of Musa Jalil written in Nazi captivity, were, however, written in the Tatar Latin and Tatar Arabic scripts and those scripts did not preclude the poet from not only being a patriot of his country, but from sacrificing his own life in her name.

There is only one comment left to be added to this chapter for Western readers. As the author of this book and as a Russian citizen, I can feel and see the ambiguity of the Western reaction to the celebrations of the 60th anniversary of the Russian victory in the Second World War, during which the name of Musa Jalil was also frequently mentioned. I can appreciate that, for the West, the results of this war are only seen in the light of the post-war division of Europe and the beginning of the Cold War announced by Churchill in his famous Fulton speech. But, for Russia and Tatarstan, which lost 350,000 of its people out of more than 20 million lost by the USSR, that anniversary was not an anniversary of the beginning of the Cold War. Incidentally, the Second World War is called the Great Patriotic War in Russia, which will never forget her enormous sacrifices, so highly spoken of by Churchill in the same speech, and of which pro-Russian content only the mention of the Iron Curtain has remained in the West. There is something inherently uniting for the Russian multi-ethnic people in the memory of all the sacrifices and sufferings of the Great Patriotic War, synonymous with which are still existent values such as 'native land, home, fatherland', even if those values now sound too lofty and even hollow for a sceptical post-modern Western mind. But, in the mind of the Russian people, these traditional values live on and will not be let go of lightly. If one is still sceptical about it, consider the fact that, in the mountains of the island of Gran Canaria of all places, the 600 Russian residents who have permanently lived and worked there since the 1990s came together to celebrate the 60th anniversary of the Russian V-Day and some of them even managed to procure old Russian uniforms and war-time forage caps for that occasion. If this is not convincing in the context of what V-Day still means for any person of Russian background, I will rest my case in the sad realization that the West just does not want to see anything from the Russian, let alone Tatar, perspective and therefore any fear of any 'clash of civilizations' is entirely of its own making.

The main driving motto of President Shaimiev – 'Social Accord in the Name of Creation (of good)', which brought about the atmosphere of inter-ethnic and inter-religious harmony in Tatarstan, is based as much on the democratic values of tolerance and peaceful coexistence, as on the inherent unity of the entire Russian nation as regards the enormous trials and sacrifices of its common history. And it is with this motto and with all her other traditional values, proved valid by the ancient and recent history of the republic, that Tatarstan faces the outside world and aims to participate in the yet inconsistent, but imminent process of its globalization.

NOTES

1. See, *The Historical Anthology of Kazan Tatar Verse* edited and translated by D. Matthews and R. Bukharaev, Curzon Press Ltd, London, 2000, and *The Poetry of the Golden Horde* first compiled and translated into Russian by R. Bukharaev (Natalis-Ripol Classic, Moscow, 2005).
2. 'Ethnicity comes between Mother Russia and her sisters', *Guardian*, 14 March 1998.
3. R. Mustafin and A. Khasanov, *Mintimer Shamiev, the First President of Tatarstan*, Kazan, 1995, p. 77.
4. *Passport to Tatarstan*, Special issue, 1993
5. President V. Putin, 'The Address at the Ceremonial Gathering Dedicated to the Millennium of Kazan', Kazan, The Opera and Ballet Theatre, 26 August 2005.
6. See more in R. Bukharaev, *Islam in Russia: the Four Seasons*, Curzon Press Ltd, London and St. Martins Press, New York, 2000; R. Bukharaev, 'Poetry of the Golden Horde', in Russian, op, cit; R. Bukharaev, 'Saga of Kazan', op. cit.
7. See, Alexandre Bennigsen and Chantal Lemercier-Quelquejay, *Islam in the Soviet Union*, Pall Mall Press, London, 1967.
8. *The Stage Weekly*, London, 23 February 2006.
9. See, R. Bukharaev, 'Sufism in Russia', in the book *Sufism in Europe and North America* edited by D. Westerlund, Routledge-Curzon, Taylor and Francis, 2003.
10. 'Nezavisimaya Gazeta', 27 February 2001.

CHAPTER 8

TATARSTAN IN THE GLOBAL WORLD

If America wants globalization to function, she should not shy away from behaving on the world scene as the almighty superpower, which she really is. The invisible hand of the market never acts without the invisible fist. MacDonald's cannot prosper without MacDonald-Douglas, the maker of the F-15. And that invisible fist, which assures the security of Silicon Valley, is called the army, fleet and air force of the USA.[1]

Globalization . . . meets its limits; globalization is never attainable . . . In contrast to neo-liberal assumptions that more market means less state, market economizations produce an enormous demand for legal regulations . . . In the transitional economies of Eastern and Central Europe we hear the call for order, for contractual and legal security so that private 'investors' can make their decisions under conditions of calculable 'risk' . . . The pure disembedded market is thus a mirage.[2]

In 2006, Russia restored her GDP to the 1991 level, and the role of Tatarstan – a country in transition faced with immense difficulties of an economic and political nature – in this process of industrial and agricultural resurrection was exceptional by any standards. But in all truth, the main contribution of the republic to the all-Russia revival consisted in strengthening the unity of the Russian Federation, despite all the talk of Tatarstan being the *raison d'être* for the imminent disintegration of Russia in the early 1990s. It is worth mentioning that it was specifically Tatarstan and Daghestan, the most ancient Muslim countries in the federation, that eventually saved Russia from the looming break-up; the former with her innovative federalist and nationalities policies; and the latter by firmly standing up to the radical pseudo-Islamic forces which, in 1999, recklessly invaded Daghestan from territory in Chechnya. Considering these facts, any suspicions that Russia's Muslim republics presented a threat to her integrity and stability would seem far-fetched, and yet, the overall atmosphere concerning Islam around the world inevitably, perhaps, also finds its way into Russia.

'Some of your suspicions are sinful', urges the Holy Quran. Even if Islam as a faith, let alone ideology, plays only a limited cultural role in the structure of the Tatarstan model, its essence as essentially ethnic may still create doubts about the relevance of such a nation-state model to the process of globalization as understood by its architects. Probably, the most complex and difficult task of today's globalization is not its formation as an open world market, but how to achieve cultural cohesion. Tatarstan is prepared to articulate and argue the universal relevance of having fifteen years' experience of convincing Russia in the validity and soundness of her position. But there are still problems of mutual understanding which reflect similar problems on a much larger, world scale. Any meaningful dialogue aimed at facilitating mutual understanding has to allow for attempts to empathize with the driving life philosophy of non-Western nations and see the world from their perspective. Sadly, the understanding gap between East and West has not diminished, but, paradoxically, has actually grown wider with the arrival of the age of global communications. This mismatch, however, is due not to a different understanding of human values, as is sometimes argued, but to the significance of these values. For instance, when early in his presidency President Shaimiev coined the phrase, which became the motto and the essence of his approach to the nationalities issue in his republic, everyone in Tatarstan and Russia could easily relate to it. At the same time, I, as the author of this book, have trouble with the exact translation into English of this phrase that states and defines President Shaimiev's credo in the age of globalization: literally, 'Social Accord In the Name of Creation'; what does it mean? The word *sozidanie*, meaning 'creation or making' in the Russian language has a somewhat different connotation from that of English. Apart from the meaning of 'making things', its connotation also implies that the things made should possess not just material, but also some spiritual value. This word from the Orthodox religious vocabulary has long since had nothing to do with religion, but the very soulfulness of the Russian language adds this spiritual dimension to the task of doing and producing things in this world, as if it simultaneously implies the question what are the things made for – just for consumption and profit, or also for making the world a better place in the 'spiritual' sense.

In short, there are countries in the world where traditional human values are still held sacred, and one should not be surprised that the key concern of Tatarstan's president regarding globalization is not the fear of competition. 'We are used to competition', he says. 'Economic globalization is, after all, just the appearance of another, global market and we will find our own place in it.' No, his chief worry is about the culture of misinterpretation that is increasingly felt all over the world. This culture, which yet may undo all the positive achievements of globalization, was once more emphasized in early 2006 following the great outcry among Muslims regarding the Danish cartoons which depicted the Holy Prophet Muhammad, God forbid, as a terrorist. President Shaimiev is not a devout Muslim, and even if he were, he, in the true time-tested Tatar fashion, would not protest publicly, but, as a political leader, he was obliged to make his attitude known to the outside world. 'The situation is becoming so heated', he said, 'that we cannot do without a full-scale evaluation of what has happened in order to reach some agreement between the states and the religious confessions that will eventually lead to a dialogue between civilizations. Such events, and it is not important which religion we have in mind, are attempts to undermine the fundamentals of the faith and a blow to people's moral foundations.' As already noted, Islam permeates the entire Tatar culture in respect of the reverence to one's parents and tolerance of other people's beliefs, traditions and customs. Sadly, however, my own efforts to explain to my British colleagues the gravity of this insult to every Muslim in the world fell on deaf ears. Vainly, I tried to describe my feelings, saying that in any free society one would not allow one's parents to be publicly insulted for the sake of freedom of speech and would not desecrate graves, even if the offender should go unpunished. I was left with my grievances in complete solitude. As I said, Tatar Muslims were civilized enough not to stage any silly protests, being faithful to the ancient Tatar proverb: 'Even if your mouth is full of blood, do not spit it out in public.' President Shaimiev himself has strongly condemned all violent responses to the affair on the part of radical Muslims, but still questioned the position of some European countries:

> In these countries Muslims are being urged to be patient, and at the same time their newspapers proceed to insult the feelings of the believers, publishing the caricatures over and over again. This, however unjustifiably, gave grounds for some extremist organizations in Muslim countries to stage attacks on Danish embassies and cause violent demonstrations, which have already led to the death of many people.

Being a responsible politician answerable for inter-ethnic and inter-religious peace in his own country, President Shaimiev is always against fuelling all kinds of instability in as much as 'all these issues can be resolved calmly and, by doing so, facilitate better understanding between people of various ethnicities and religious confessions'.[3] Instead of trying to understand the complexity of the Islamic world and support the healthy reformist forces in Islam in order to defuse the situation, the West just fuels its irrational fears and anxieties, seeing the Islamic world as one big powder keg waiting to explode.[4]

I am not in any way privy to the discussions that take place in President Shaimiev's political kitchen and, like many people, see only the end product of his political thinking. He is a formidable, skilled and experienced politician, very often with a reassuring smile on his face, and one seldom sees him struggling with uncertainty. In my rare face-to-face meetings with him during the last fifteen years, only twice has he seemed baffled and questioned the very sanity of Russian federal policies: once in 1996, during the give-away of Russian oil and mineral resources to a crony group of commercial bankers in the so-called auction privatization, which created the oligarchic system now dominating the country, and, secondly, in spring 1999, before President Yeltsin's resignation, when he seemed really perplexed with the course Russia was taking. Off the record, he just exclaimed on both occasions something like: 'Who can tell me what on earth is going on?'! It was a manifestation of real anxiety on his part, which I remember very well, so out of character it was for this man who presumably always saw the light at the end of a tunnel. His mounting concern about the course world events are taking now reminded me of those two incidents, and I then understood how seriously the president evaluates the hidden dangers of the globalization process. It is all the more serious for multi-ethnic Russia that in the current stand-off between the West and the Islamic world the latter are seen and treated only as a faceless mass of people despite all the emphasis that Western liberal tradition places on the rights and personal uniqueness of the individual. This disparity in attitude and the tendency to deal with 'Muslims' as a faceless entity is also entering the Russian psyche as well to dangerous levels, giving rise to the ugliest displays of Russian ethnic nationalism bordering on chauvinism, even if it is only a fraction of the Russian people who manifest such an attitude.

In the above context, President Shaimiev once again pointed out that all the existing problems of an inter-ethnic and inter-confessional nature are highlighted in Russia only when some unpleasant or tragic incidents occur that are not defused beforehand, as was always the case in Tatarstan even in the most trying periods of recent history. The entire inter-ethnic policy of Tatarstan is aimed at resolving potential problems before they gain any momentum, which means constant attention to people's religious and cultural needs. In short, it needs understanding and plurality, which is so scarce in the sphere of actual globalization today, whether we speak about the agony of dogmatic beliefs in the Islamic world, which makes people resort to violence in the absence of any valid arguments in response to mounting economic and cultural pressures, or about the neo-conservative 'we can do no wrong' ideology, which, instead of defusing, is fuelling the discontents of globalization to the point of explosion. In this situation President Shaimiev, as the voice of the overwhelming majority of the people of Tatarstan and Russia, has this to say: 'By showing patience and tolerance, we can reach a dialogue. It is impossible to achieve otherwise, as it is impossible to subdue the values of different nations and religions in a violent way, trying to enforce one and the same uniform model.'

Not many people in the outside world yet understand what is at stake here, and what harm the present tide of ideological globalization insistent on uniform conformity to its Western vision may cause to the very idea of worldwide democracy. My generation of Russians still remembers the Soviet Communist ideology and, for all its willingness to learn how universal democratic interests should work in the modern world, was sometimes better placed to distinguish those from other, not so universal, interests. Indeed, the general problem of any 'domineering' ideology is that any deviation from it is considered an offence to its 'all-embracing' notions of 'truth'. Ideology is, of course, devised by theorists (not infrequently aware of certain pressing corporate concerns), but it is pushed forward, often at any cost, by pragmatic forces which promote and resolve through it their own private interests, even if those are disguised as the universal concerns of all humanity.

Globalization in the contemporary world is a fact, even if in many aspects a less comforting one than was academically forecast. There is no hiding from it. Every country and every region in the world will have to find its place in the emerging order of things and inevitably change in the process. But why are more and more people asking: is globalization indeed a democratic process, or something else under the guise of liberal democracy?

There are many pressing questions about the less attractive tendencies that have emerged in the globalization process. First and foremost is, how can globalization, advancing under the banner of democracy, be effected by completely undemocratic means? The ideological and financial sponsors of the globalization process, the IMF and the World Bank, both unelected bodies with 51% US Treasury capital, devise economic recipes and dictate their application to sovereign countries whilst being democratically accountable to no one on the world scene. Reading the books and interviews of the Nobel prize-winner Joseph Stiglitz, once the chief economist of the World Bank, one appreciates his concerns that, firstly, the IMF-World Bank plans, 'devised in secrecy and driven by absolutist ideology, never open for discourse or dissent ... undermine democracy'. Secondly, 'they don't work'.[5] It would seem natural that any global scheme in the name of democracy has itself to be democratic to succeed. Yet, to be democratic would mean to heed regional voices and concerns and act in accordance with them. This, however, has yet to happen in the globalization process; rather, we are witnessing the exact opposite.

Another question is about the pace of necessary changes, which, however, may be evolutionary or revolutionary and may be effected from inside or from outside. The common sense of evolution dictates that all changes should be effected gradually and by the imperatives of the inner momentum of growth, because that is how evolution has always worked. The pace of these changes may be slower than some would like, but they will be irreversible and built into the fabric of the economy and society of a particular country. Alas, we all live in a revolutionary world, where dominant ideologies are once again considered sacrosanct and untouchable. What is even worse, this revolution, which breaks through sovereign boundaries, is driven not so much by charitable well-wishers, as by the unbelievable amounts of liquid speculative money always on the lookout for a one-night stand instead of a home.

Therefore, the globalization processes we see today are raising many more questions than they are providing answers. In the Introduction I made clear my attitude to the vivisection methods of changing the world according to the bossy Western academic and think-tank theories of today. The greatest of them all postulates that, first of all, the world of the victorious democratic market economy requires the immediate establishment of a Western-type democracy in all parts of the planet as the preordained requirement of Western-style economic prosperity for all. Despite all the cold calculations, which plainly show that the planet cannot sustain the level of Western consumption for all countries, the axiom, until recently, seemed so obvious that its promotion did not stop at the biggest and maddest blunder of invading Iraq without any after-thought of what would happen, if the theory were not to work and the people on the ground were to have other ideas. This mistake, if it can be called that in all its gravity, may still prove utterly destructive not just for the country of Iraq, but for the entire ideology that brought it about against the will of the UN, in other words, against the very notion of democracy at the world level. It is not I who first said that undemocratic methods cannot serve democratic goals. 'Violence breeds violence' – this axiom has been proven right time and again throughout human history, before the latter was declared to be 'ended'. But the misunderstanding and abandonment of this principle in the overall ideology of globalization may yet prove much costlier that anyone could have predicted. As any ideology pushed beyond the boundaries of common sense, it may well harm the very foundations on which it has grown. The predictable exit of the coalition forces from Iraq sooner or later may still prove more significant than just the problem of saving the face of the USA and Britain. Just as the exit of Soviet forces from Afghanistan brought about the collapse of Soviet ideology, there and then foreseen by Z. Bzhezinsky, the eventual exit from Iraq may prove fatal to the entire process of 'democratization through pressure'. The world outlook of globalization gurus is already changing, and the signs of that are becoming increasingly frequent. Even such architects of the Iraq war and towering philosophers of 'Western-style' globalization such as Francis Fukuyama now see in the events not so much 'the end of history', but the end of the 'one-size-fits-all' model of making the world happy by the application of political and economic pressure and military force. Is it just incidental that in his 'insider' criticisms of the global neo-conservative model Fukuyama now links the ideology of transforming the world by force and compulsion to that of the Communist ideologues? He even compares the architects of the Iraq war to Leninists who 'believed that history can be pushed along with the right application of power and will. Leninism was a tragedy in its Bolshevik version, and it has returned as farce when practised by the United States.'[6] One could argue that what happened is more than just farce, because it not only changed the perception of essential freedoms in the very country that pioneered them, but also sowed more seeds of deep scepticism in British democracy, after it transpired that the common-sense protest of the overwhelming majority of British people against the Iraq adventure never translated itself into a democratic imperative and the country went to war despite the popular will of her citizens. In the reaction of leading observers to the present Iraq debate one can feel the inevitability of a major correction of the present-day globalization ideology and of its return to the common-sense roots of democracy as the will of the people, and not the will of those 'who know best'. 'We must keep firmly in mind that democracies can fail.' This simple statement by American political analyst Anatol Lieven may yet become a bitter eye-opener for many of those who, in whatever they do in reality, recant the seemingly all-powerful mantra of democracy, the essence of which, as Lieven states:

> ... in truth, only applies to Western democracy during a few balmy decades after 1945. Those decades were closely associated with a period of unprecedented and seemingly unending economic prosperity unlimited by ecological, demographic or resource constraints; and also with a European generation that had been so terrified by the experiences of Nazism, Stalinism and the Second World war that they possessed deep internal barriers to political extremism. Neither of these factors were inherent to democracy – even to Western democracy – but were historically contingent, and may well now be coming to an end. For that matter, even during those decades the picture of democracy as a defender of civil liberties and human rights did not apply to the colonial or neo-colonial wars waged by France and America in Vietnam, France in Algeria and Britain in Kenya, any more than it does to the United States-led campaign in Iraq and Afghanistan today.[7]

I hope that the above will not sow doubts about the author's, or about Russian, or Tatar, commitment to democracy. Democracy in its ideal form of 'power for the people and by the people' will always be attractive if only because it is a sound common-sense political arrangement, if and when it is aimed at freeing human potential without destroying the base of traditional values, on which this potential rests in the first place. In my comments above, I only wanted (for a change) to agree with post-Iraq Francis Fukuyama who recently confessed:

> By definition, outsiders can't 'impose' democracy on a country that doesn't want it; demand for democracy and reform must be domestic. Democracy promotion is therefore a long-term and opportunistic process that has to await the gradual ripening of political and economic conditions to be effective.[8]

How long and how much human suffering will it take on the part of the West to subscribe to this rational truth that has long been obvious to any non-Western country 'in transition'? The plain truth is that you cannot have all you want immediately regardless of how badly you want it. All fruits must ripen at their own pace, and this is the natural law applicable to the evolution of human societies as well. And yet, the recently published 'Blueprint for Russia'[9] featuring 'prominent figures from Russian *progressive* politics, as well as leading specialists and policy advisers from around the world', while broadly approving Russian economic policies, cast doubt on the creative potential of the political landscape in Russia judged by the same final measurements of the imaginary 'universal democracy'. Russia, indeed, has a lot of room for democratic improvements, yet to bemoan the fact that today's Russia has deviated from the path of her 'free-for-all' oligarchic democracy of the 1990s and slowly turned her face to the real demands of her then utterly impoverished, deceived and despised people, is a little too much for the 'progressive' politics of Russian contributors like M. Kasyanov and G. Yavlinsky – the latter, unlike his seasoned 'reformist' colleague, never practising his ever-ready advice in the real world. Just compare today's Russia with the old USSR and it will become evident how far the country has progressed on the road to democracy, despite all the thorns and pitfalls facing it along this road. The recent correction in Russian political direction is therefore not, as it is sometimes argued, a U-turn from democracy, but rather a temporary, if necessary, measure aimed at strengthening the functions of the state, which became all but non-existent in the 1990s. The immensity of this process, it seems, fails to register with those observers who now chastise Russia for the absence of completely independent TV-channels in the country. Well, the 'independent' channels that existed in the 1990s were financed by the Russian oligarchs in support of their own particular interests and by all the means at their disposal advocated the *status quo*, of which the author Stephen Cohen, for instance, writes:

> Since 1991, Russia's realities have included the worst peacetime industrial depression of the twentieth century; the degradation of agriculture and livestock herds, even worse in some respects than occurred during Stalin's catastrophic collectivization of the peasantry in the early 1930s; unprecedented dependence on imported goods (foremost is food and medicine); the promotion of one or two Potemkin cities amid the impoverishment or near-impoverishment of some 75% or more of the nation; more new orphans than resulted from Russia's almost 30 million casualties in World War II; and the transformation of a superpower into a beggar state existing on foreign loans and plagued, according to the local press, by 'hunger, cold and poverty, and whose remote regions 'await the approaching winter with horror'. All this, scholars and journalists have called reform, remarkable progress, and a success story.[10]

In all truth, one should wonder not at the strengthening of the role of the state by Putin's government, but rather at the relative mildness with which it is being done. Faced with a similar question of the survival of the entire nation, what would Western democracies do? Maybe, they could then bring themselves to look at what is happening in Russia from the Russian perspective, and not just from their own. The much smaller catastrophe of 9/11 brought about a total rethinking of the essence of civil liberties not only in the USA, but also in Britain, the mother of all democracies. In the circumstances facing Russia today, it seems appropriate that the all-Russia TV-channels concentrate more on the evident successes of transition, than on its failures, thus inspiring people to participate in building the country's present and future, and not disillusioning them to the point of committing suicide, as was the case previously. The oligarchic TV channels of the 1990s, in their post-modern contempt of history and anything held sacred by the Russian nation, never found a minute to inspire and encourage the people they intellectually despised for their alleged 'slave psychology', thus destroying the remnants of national pride and traditional values. The latter, however, were in the first place instrumental in building the highly industrialized superpower state, which, at the time, all but turned into the private property of a few smart swindlers. Yes, today's Russia will not be ordered about, but this is, after all, the only way to command some respect in the contemporary world. As for its market economy credentials, instead of the seven oligarchs of the mid-1990s, Russia now has thirty-three dollar billionaires[11] and this colossal private wealth is, as Luise Croll of *Forbes* magazine says, 'the result of speedily growing, profitable Russian markets'.

So then, why is Russia, which, in understanding her national interests, does not interfere in world affairs and concentrates instead on its inner growth and development, so threatening to some people in the West? It is, I presume, the consequence of not fitting into someone else's worldview, but this is indeed another matter and has nothing to do with objective evaluation of Russia's policies.

Parroting the recent American slogan 'Who is not with us, is against us', the former 'Chicago boy' G. Yavlinsky is at one with M. Kasyanov in saying:

> For Russia, there are only two possible paths. We can become part of the core of the world capitalist economy – the European path – or we can look for a spot on the periphery. There is no third, special Russian way. Understandably, some fear the European path will mean a loss of sovereignty. Yet, the only alternative is the sidelines and other limits on sovereignty, limits that would be informal but significant.[12]

In trying to be nice to the already fatally wounded 'one-size-fits-all' ideology, the eternal political hopeful G. Yavlinsky does not say that where there cannot be a special Russian way, there still can exist a specific 'Russian model' of democratic market economy in the same vein as the very successful Japanese and German models, both based on national features and feelings. This new 'Russian model', however, in many of its economic aspects reminds us of President Shaimiev and his government's 'Tatarstan model', tested by fifteen years of sustained, consistent and logical transition of the republic to her chosen destination.

There are times when even a developed market economy is in dire need of state support (I avoid mentioning colossal agricultural subsidies, as well as those for fuel prices, in the USA and European Union). It is only recently that the Russian government recognized this necessity after years of utter neglect. For years, Russia was calling for direct investment into her ailing economy and infrastructure, but it never materialized. Who then can blame the Russian state that it now takes upon itself to invest into the country's fixed capital to fill the abysmal gap that foreign investors failed to fill when it was so badly needed? The introduction of the state regulation is a common-sense imperative today, and, in doing that, the all-Russia government increasingly looks at the experience of Tatarstan in combining market and state regulation tools in balancing and fine-tuning her economy in the process of transition.

Again, it is the matter of the right perspective. In 2006, we learned that the Russian Prime Minister Mikhail Fradkov recommended that his government should analyse and learn from the so-called system of indicative planning existing in Tatarstan since 1994. In 1997, Tatarstan adopted her 'Concept of State Regulation of Economy', which since 2000 is used in the republic as the basis of her economic planning. In the words of the Economy Minister of Tatarstan, ethnic Russian Boris Pavlov, this concept 'allows us to achieve sustainable dynamics of growth according to the macroeconomic indicators, so according to all components of the integral gauge of "the quality of life" in the republic'. This gauge of the quality of life is the sum of twelve basic indicators monitoring average wages, housing conditions, social infrastructure, unemployment, energy and communications, provision of roads and some others. Logistically, state regulation according to this gauge is achieved through the definition of priority economic objectives and by the creation of economic stimuli and incentives for private companies, which agree to act in accordance with the recommendations of the government. Such planning, reminiscent of Franklin Roosevelt's New Deal, is being exercised at four main levels of the Tatarstan economy: macroeconomic at the republican level, territorial at the regional level, microeconomic at the enterprises level and on the so-called 'meso-level' in the structure of meta-corporations uniting private enterprises and those with a controlling governmental stake. One such meta-corporation, for example, is the oil-mining conglomerate 'Tatneft' together with the privatized petrochemical enterprises and government structures designed for the trading of petrochemicals and fuel.

From the standpoint of developed market economies, such an arrangement will seem outdated, as it was discarded by major world economies at the end of the 1970s. But, in the context of economic transition, the important thing is that such indicative planning *was used* in the West to achieve what it has now. In the early stage of market relations, its 'invisible hand' is still too weak to provide for public social security worthy of the name, and this was abundantly proved by the Russian 'shock therapy' experience. Again, such state-regulating arrangements are viewed by President Shaimiev as only a temporary measure in the process of creating the right conditions for real market competition able to satisfy ever more sophisticated demands of the population. Today, such conditions are being gradually and consistently facilitated, whilst the state law safeguards the enterprises and population of the republic from the chaotic movements and social dramas like the one that occurred in 1998, when Russia was, in effect, forced to change her course of reforms because of the excesses of the globalization of financial markets.[13] The self-reliance and 'import-substitution' policies of President Shaimiev may seem anathema to those active supporters of globalization driven by the need to sell their own goods and services, but they proved crucially right at the time of the world financial crisis of 1998, which all but undid the achievements of market reforms in Russia and starved her of hard currency needed to sustain imports at pre-crisis levels. Then, it became obvious to everyone who still wanted Russia not only to survive, but to prosper, that the peculiarities of the Russian economic situation in view of the harshness of her climate, the vastness of her terrain and the urgency of her regional development priorities today require a special attitude, not unlike that of Western market democracies at the time of recovery after the Second World War. The debate, however, is still raging, even if, after eight years of relatively stable development and ever rising oil prices, it cannot do much to force Russia to revert to her erstwhile path advocated by the sirens of complete deregulation which would lead to economic and social disaster. It remains to be seen, of course, to what extent the future membership of Russia in the WTO will affect her sovereign economic decisions.

As far as Tatarstan is concerned, she steadily readies herself for participation in the global economy without great anxiety, but with the remarkable foresight and constancy so peculiar to the Tatarstan model. The republic's role as a world market player is, in the first place, assured by its oil and petrochemical industries, but, as we said, Tatarstan looks much farther into the future than the period of reliance on her known oil reserves, which, at today's rate of extraction, will last for thirty-odd years. Her preparation for the global economy has several aspects, including the formation of the legal and practical base of her foreign trade activities as well as building the ever expanding network of her economic links to the outside world. In this context, in which the state role in building a foreign customer base for the large state industries cannot be overestimated, the issue of foreign investment into the republic's economy also plays an important role. In the 1990s, Tatarstan held the third place after Moscow and St Petersburg in attracting foreign inward investment, although very little of it was in the form of the most urgently needed direct investment into state enterprises. The financial crisis of 1998 dealt a blow to this process, yet in recent years the situation has steadily improved. As President Shaimiev said in an interview to the 'Tatarstan' magazine after the celebration of Kazan's Millennium:

> Through our policies, through our jubilee we have sent a message to the whole world – namely, there is political stability in the republic, which we over the years have built up and, most importantly, safeguarded. Now everyone sees that! The most well-known companies have come to Tatarstan – IKEA, Ramstore, Metro, Crossroads and others. By doing so, they gave a signal to all investors: here they enjoy stability – one can and must invest here. As you see, big business has come to our republic and here there are many visible and invisible positive sides for Tatarstan. I believe, this process will continue in the future.

Indeed, since 1998, the volume of foreign investment has steadily increased. In 2000, the flow of foreign capital into the republic grew sixfold as compared with 1999, and the share of direct investment constituted 37.5% of all foreign investment and increased twofold in comparison with 1999. This trend continued in 2001, when foreign investment grew 4.6 times and constituted 650.9 million US dollars. In 2003, foreign investment in Tatarstan was $176.1 million, in 2004 – $596.14 million, and the share of direct investment into state-controlled enterprises grew progressively, assured by solid safeguards and obvious advantages of state legislation covering the rights of foreign investors. International rating agencies positively reacted to the improvements in Tatarstan's investment climate, which in 2005 posted the biggest growth of investment in her fixed capital of 21.4 % as compared with 2004. Standard and Poor's in September 2005 raised the long-term credit rating of Tatarstan from B-stable to B-positive. Moody's Investor Service rated the hard currency credit-worthiness of Tatarstan as Ba1–stable (raised from Ba3–stable) and Fitch, in May 2005, defined Tatarstan's rating as BB-stable. The European derivatives of large Tatarstan corporations like Svyazinvestneftekhim, Nizhnekamskneftekhim, KamAZ and the Ak Bars bank attracted $625 million into the state economy in 2005.

In the not-so-distant past, attempts at participation in the global economy were not always successful for Tatarstan enterprises. One of the most eloquent cases, shedding light on some less pleasant aspects of globalization, was the only 'truly global' work distribution venture in Tatarstan – the assembly of Chevrolet Blazer cars in the town of Elabuga under an agreement signed in 1995 with General Motors. Seemingly, in this case Tatarstan was viewed as yet another 'source of cheap uneducated labour'. The components of the car came from Brazil, and Tatarstan workers were required to assemble them with a simple screwdriver. The whole enterprise failed not because of some inability of the people of Tatarstan, but because the assembled cars proved less than perfect for the ever more demanding Russian market and there was a storm of complaints about the road performance of this particular model. The 1998 default, which was a direct consequence of Russian openness to the global financial markets, put an end to the whole enterprise, because the Russian market had in its wake demanded cheaper and better cars. The entire venture collapsed, because it was based on the assumption that the Tatarstan and Russian markets could and would swallow anything. It appeared, however, that the Russian market became increasingly sophisticated and, with this global venture, Tatarstan learned another lesson in economics the hard way: there is no globalization without direct investment, which Tatarstan's enterprises are now attracting due to the political stability and good performance of Tatarstan's economy.

One has to say that, on the part of Tatarstan, the unfortunate venture with General Motors was not a life-saving arrangement, but rather an honest effort to revive the earlier project of constructing, in the vicinity of Elabuga, the Elaz light tractor plant, which was one of the last ambitious ventures of the Soviet period.

The town of Elabuga, which will celebrate its own millennium in 2007, was famous for being the birthplace and long-time home of the great Russian painter I. Shishkin (1832–98) whose canvases now fetch huge sums at London art auctions. Elabuga is also known for being the last refuge of the great Russian poetess Marina Tsvetaeva (1892–1941) who is buried here. There are many other dignitaries of Russian history from many walks of life who also lived and worked here, but the ancient town once again came under the spotlight, when in 1984 the Soviet authorities decided to build nearby a complex of plants for the production of light universal tractors as well as their diesel engines and fuel equipment. A vast amount of money was invested from 1984 to 1988, when, in the growing economic uncertainty of *perestroika*, it was decided to transform the tractor plant under construction into a consumer car plant, which took the name of ELAZ. The story of the rescue and development of the ELAZ site with the huge capital already invested in it and crying out for development, is yet another example of the economic assiduity of the Tatarstan government as well as another sign of the continuity of Tatarstan history. As happened with the KamAZ heavy truck-building plant, Tatarstan had very little say in the Soviet decision-making process with regard to the ELAZ project, before the entire burden of problems connected with it fell on her shoulders. It would have been a terrible waste to leave the plan undeveloped, and here came the agreement with General Motors which raised so many bright hopes. The first 'Chevrolet-Blazer' jeep was assembled at the end of 1996, but, as already mentioned, the venture never really took off. In 1999, however, ELAZ opened a new production line for the Opel-Vectra car model, which proved more successful for the Russian market. In 2005, in fierce competition with other Russian regions, Tatarstan secured for the Elabuga industrial development programme the official federal status of a free economic zone, which, it is hoped, will boost car, truck and bus-making, engine-making, petrochemical, oil-refinery and innovative machine-building and instrument-making plants on its territory.

The status of the free economic zone with its tax and customs advantages is already encouraging more foreign investment into the Elabuga economic district: one-third of the thirty functioning enterprises here have a foreign stake in them. In March 2006, for example, President Shaimiev met in Kazan with the president of the Italian De'Longhi Group, Giuseppe De'Longhi. His company, a world leader in production of heaters and mobile air-conditioners, now owns an oil-radiator plant in the Elabuga zone and looks forward to broadening the scope of its Tatarstan enterprise. As Mr De'Longhi said after meeting President Shaimiev, his company will produce goods with the aim of beating strong competition for similar goods produced in China and S. Korea, while retaining their high European quality. In the last five years, the Elabuga industrial zone has received investment totalling 2 billion roubles, and in 2005 it produced 5.7 billion roubles worth of industrial goods. Steady development of its infrastructure will continue until 2009, including construction of a housing complex for 3,200 flats, where about 10,000 employees of the free economic zone enterprises will be able to live near their place of work.

But for ever more successful efforts in establishing and maintaining global economic links, Tatarstan fully understands that the real cutting edge in the process of globalization lies in the sphere of technical innovations and IT. In 2003, Tatarstan saw the start of synthetic oils production – the first of its kind in Russia. In the plan for the 'Programme of Development of the Oil, Gas and Petrochemical Complex in Tatarstan', eighty large and middle-sized projects are envisaged at a cost of $5.7 billion. Out of those, the Nizhnekamsk Tyre Plant is already producing highly effective 'Pirelli' tyres and Nizhnekamsk

Petrochemical giant has introduced new technologies in its own lines of production. The republic in strategic partnership with the Russian Academy of Sciences, has adopted its own programme of activity in the field of innovation, to which end the creation and successful operation of the 'Idea', 'Kama Master', Idea South East' Techno Parks also serve, developing and testing innovative projects for their introduction into the state economy.

Tatarstan has also created the Investment Venture Fund supporting small and medium-size enterprises, which help to introduce innovative technologies to all spheres of the Tatarstan economy. In 2006, President Shaimiev announced the creation of yet another Venture Fund aimed at supporting small enterprises working in IT spheres. In 2005, the republic held its first competition for 'The Best 50 Innovative Ideas', in which more than 3,000 scientific workers of Tatarstan took part. Twenty-three winners of this competition in 2006 received five gold and seven silver medals at the VI Moscow Salon of Investment and Innovation.

The president and the government of Tatarstan pay special attention to the development of IT in their country, being fully aware of its crucial importance in the age of globalization. Info-communication activities in Tatarstan develop along two main lines – informatization and telecommunications. Activity in these spheres envelopes practically all aspects of life in Tatarstan – business, education and government. No other region of Russia has a similar large-scale programme of computerization and Internetization of village schools, as Tatarstan. In 2006, Tatarstan almost completed the task of school computerization within its territory connecting every state school to the World Wide Web at a cost of 485 million roubles from the republic's budget and 108 million roubles from the federal budget. Today, there is one computer for every twenty-six students in the republic, which is one of the best computerization results in Russia. Every year, Tatarstan introduces new lines of telecommunications with a capacity exceeding 100,000 numbers. The republic also launched its own satellite 'New Age' channel and steadily develops its mobile communication networks. And yet, the Tatarstan government is not satisfied with the pace of IT development, especially in the executive branches of Tatarstan power. The Prime Minister, Rustam Minnikhanov, in March 2006, demanded more rapid informatization in the spheres of health service, education and culture. As well as making the work of government more efficient, informatization also helps to make it more transparent. However, the creation of a system of electronic documentation covering the 'Eletronic Government' project was planned to be fully completed by January 2007. The complex 'Electronic Tatarstan' programme is a part of the strategic 'Programme of Social and Economic Development of the Republic' for 2005–2010. It is aimed at the creation and integration of state electronic networks in all spheres of life as part of the effort of forming an information-oriented society in Tatarstan and more tightly connecting the citizens of the republic with their government.

In justifying the difficulties occurring in the transition process, President Shaimiev has every right to emphasize in his answers to journalists: 'It is our wish – to be first in everything.' Yet, when asked, what is, in his opinion, the main achievement of the transition process, the President says:

I would say it is that we have achieved a change in attitude towards the Tatar people. It has become positive. This, however, was not accomplished by our wish alone. This is the result of our creative, meticulous, sometimes invisible efforts. Tatarstan, happily, has achieved that in a very short time. You may recall, what the attitude towards Tatars was in the Soviet and post-Soviet eras: generation after generation, schoolchildren were taught history, which completely distorted the origin and development of the Tatar nation. In recent years, we have won the respect of the rest of the world.

Indeed, sometimes it is difficult to follow the pace of Tatarstan's development even on the part of the most interested observers. In 2003, British scholar Leo McCann published a book entitled *Economic Development in Tatarstan*[14] as his contribution to the on-going debate on globalization and 'global' capitalism. His book is based on first-hand 'eye-opening' experiences in Tatarstan and on a significant number of interviews conducted among representatives of various social and economic strata in the republic. In his book, McCann tactfully and thus convincingly argues against superficial and detached clichés squeezing a colossal variety of cultures with their particular economic and political circumstances into a Procrustean bed of the singular neo-liberal view of globalization. In this respect, his work must also be viewed in the context of present-day debates between uniformist 'globalizators' and those who maintain that indigenous social-economic structures and historic paths of development have a much greater role to play in defining the economic future of various regions.

Tatarstan is, as the author says, 'rarely mentioned in the Western press, other than to raise occasional fears about the extent of the powers of regional bosses or to report on rare political developments ... The global stage is of limited relevance to the action taking place in Tatarstan.' The economic analysis carried out by McCann is not overly favourable to the local political establishment. Of the elite networks in Tatarstan he says, 'Tatar networks remain largely based on the former *nomenclatura* links that emerged to manage the distinctly *old* economy of the command-administrative system.'[15] From these, and similar, statements it is, however, not clear, why Tatarstan's capitalist transition is relatively successful, not only in terms of market metamorphosis, but also with regard to 'the good of the people'. With peculiar British scepticism towards politicians as a class of their own, McCann for all his insights into the workings of 'Tatar capitalism' does not seem to suppose that a paced market transition in post-Soviet circumstances necessarily involves a paced political transition as well. This may also sound like anathema to the apologists of 'immediate democracy' and total deregulation, but the local experience of Tatarstan shows that, without the state's grip on the transition process expressed in the strong will and influence of the president, the 'invisible hand' of the wild Russian market (with some help from outside) would quickly rob the republic of all its valuable assets and leave her at the mercy of a tiny group of powerful players having no national interests at their heart. As the Russian observers often remark:

> As yet, all attempts by the Russian oligarchs to penetrate these republics [Tatarstan and the neighbouring Bashkortostan] have failed. Most probably, during the next presidential elections in those republics the federal centre and oligarchic structures

will undertake new attempts to break local political and energy monopolies, passing the power into the hands of their protégé.[16]

What was painfully put in place over the last fifteen years, can thus be undone in days, and nobody expects either better economic management, or 'the public good' from the structures only driven by greed in the best 'liberal economy' fashion.

If anything, the experience of Tatarstan shows that political reins in a country such as Russia can be relaxed only gradually, because in the process of transition only the state can secure the interests of the overwhelming 'not-so-well-to-do' majority of the population against the interests of a rich few. 'The epoch of President Shaimiev' in Tatarstan's capitalist transition is indeed an epoch of political transition from a command-style economy towards a democratic market. His present policies and his legacy are therefore to be judged not only against his presumed intentions and the assessments of outsiders, but against the validity and fulfilment of the objectives he has set. In an atmosphere of almost total lack of social trust in Russia, any statements given by people driven by social frustration, business interests or political ambitions should be taken with a pinch of salt, or sugar, for that matter. This distrust, among other reasons, also emphasizes the phenomenon of 'familial networks', whether or not they in reality exist as a nepotistic obstacle to the fairer development of a democratic market economy in the region. One may have the right to accuse Tatarstan of the existence of such networks only after having scrutinized each instance on its merits, but to do so fleetingly in the full belief that any non-Western country is intrinsically corrupt, would be at least unfair. Of course, in the initial turmoil of Russian transition, it was often risky and even naïve to rely on anyone 'from outside', especially in the Yeltsin years, when so many swindlers appeared from nowhere, making all the right noises about democracy and waving their brand-new IDs as 'presidential advisers'. Whether we like it or not, the reality of political and economic life is that people surrounding the decision-makers should be trusted. In the long-established democracies, this trust is placed in civil servants who are, ideally, removed from party politics and the current policy-making process. In a whirlwind market transition, such trust, however, had to be placed in time-tested, professional officials, some of whom may even have had familial links in a comparatively small republic. In itself, it may not always be the menace it is portrayed to be, as it is never pictured as such in Western democracies with their dynasties of presidents and governors. Indeed, corruption starts when familial reliance turns into nepotism, so that family members are allowed to remain in the business establishment despite their absolute uselessness. For all unsubstantiated charges of 'corruption' in the Tatarstan government, no one could ever say that this or that person holds his post only by the virtue of being somebody's relative, while being entirely ineffective in discharging his responsibilities.

One cannot argue that it is President Shaimiev's vision of transition that had firmly put hitherto all but unknown Tatarstan on the map of foreign scholars and the media. In spite of British doubts as to the intentions of powerful Russian politicians, even the BBC diplomatic correspondent Bridget Kendall had to admit that 'President Shaimiev knows the wisdom of keeping the broad mass of the population happy.'[17] American researcher Helen Faller after her own field study in Tatarstan has also observed that 'indeed, Tatarstan's political, social, and relative economic stability may perhaps provide a model for the kind of federalism that may sustain Russia'.

As we said, Tatarstan serves as an example, if not *the* pattern, of the most recent economic developments in post-Communist Russia, which, under President Vladimir Putin, increasingly seems to follow Tatarstan's once singular and non-conformist economic and social path. This is, however, not a coincidence, but a direct consequence of Tatarstan's insistence on democratic federalism based on the assumption that, at the federal or global level, democracy should grow upwards from the grass roots and not be imposed from above.

As a statesman having the national interests of his country at heart, President Shaimiev also believes that true globalization has to grow from 'the grass roots upwards', and not be foisted upon various regions from above by the Western theorists of 'shock therapy' and 'one-fits-all' economic formats. Tatarstan, as the president says, is not against 'healthy globalization', but all her experience of recent years suggests that she will not be easily satisfied by the economic role written for her either by the all too familiar Russian 'Big Brother', or a strange 'Big Uncle' from overseas. For instance, the present-day 'localization' of Tatarstan's economy has its roots not only in the Soviet past, but also in the fact that after proclaiming itself sovereign in 1990, the republic took steps to lessen its dependence on the centrally regulated framework of the all-Russia economy with its emphasis on 'rush privatization' and the total neglect of the military-complex enterprises representing about 70% of Russian industry. Under the circumstances, it was a wise thing to do, because in 1991-92 the republican leaders seriously visualized a scenario of a total economic blockade by the Moscow centre, and therefore carefully assessed all strategic advantages and disadvantages of the state economy in order for the republic to survive, if need be, on her own. The political vector has since changed, but the overall strategies of relying on one's own economic potential are still there, especially since in the initial euphoria of the victorious 'End of History' the West made so many mistakes in trying to enforce its vision on the rest on the world, which substantially harmed its hitherto 'fair image'.

This policy of self-reliance as part of the much wider policy of openness to the outside world can be discerned not only in Tatarstan's oil business, but also in the functioning of her petrochemical and petroleum enterprises and her agricultural sector. The fact that Tatarstan fully satisfies local demand in basic foodstuffs is no small thing for Russia, especially against the background of other regions, which, during the 1998 default, had to import their food for hard cash. The establishment of the state oil refinery also shows this strategic trend to reduce Tatarstan's dependence on the mood swings of the Russian federation.

Leo McCann writes about the perceived failure of Tatarstan to be a part of the wider global network, which is, however, 'neither her fault, nor a well thought-over option'. Most encouragingly, many assessments in his work are rapidly becoming outdated, and life itself shows that more pessimistic scenarios based on Western understandings are not always valid for such 'unpredictable' countries as Tatarstan and Russia at large. In recent years, however, this unpredictability always turned positive, even if Tatarstan's successes cannot always be calculated according to Western expectations.

In her policies of self-reliance dictated by the entire history of the Tatar nation, Tatarstan does indeed sometimes seem like a 'localized' region with little relevance to the world of globalization. In this respect, the fact that the fifth MacDonalds outlet in Tatarstan recently opened in the state oil capital, the town of Almetyevsk, is no more an argument for globalization, than smuggled trendy jeans were in the former Soviet Union. At the same time, the Nizhnekamsk Petrochemical Works and other petrochemical industries of Tatarstan still supply a fair share of the world market for synthetic rubber and other petrochemicals, as in the days of the USSR, and as such are of course an integral part of the global network. But Leo McCann also rightly observes:

> The establishment of Russian forms of capitalism may well prove stronger than people expected. The trappings of Westernization (brands, management technology) hardly constitute a serious expansion of Western organizational forms eastward. Despite the uniqueness of Russian or Tatar social systems, there are also major economic reasons why 'global capitalism' should not be at all concerned with Tatarstan. Western firms are interested in Tatarstan oil reserves, but show little interest in other sectors. In the case of oil they are only interested in exporting Tatar oil, not really (so far) in investing in infrastructure to find more of it ... Despite the rhetoric of globalization, and the spread of Western managerial and business concepts into Russian economic actors' discourse, why would a Western transnational corporation bother to invest in Russian industry, if it could make profits from other less-risky ventures in more-developed regions?[18]

If the rosy dream of 'global' capitalism is, principally, the free flow of capital in order to revitalize the world economy, then this 'global' capitalism, in all truth, did next to nothing to achieve this goal in Russia. And indeed, common sense says that no one in his right mind will create a competitor. The disillusionment of all Russian regions, including Tatarstan, in the once promised 'Samaritan help of the West' was due to the lack of any meaningful direct investment in her strategic enterprises. As this 'help' was not forthcoming when it was badly needed, Tatarstan had to manage on her own to satisfy, first of all, her own consumer markets and the social requirements of her own workforce and wider population. Luckily, this policy proved successful, and the tide is turning with more and more foreign investment coming into the republic which now has a proven track record for its political stability and economic worth.

Leo McCann's conclusion is therefore rather relevant in the present globalization debate, as he says, 'the Tatar story contributes to a growing body of literature that emphasizes the importance and persistence of local varieties of capitalism'.[19] And, 'the localized and highly politicized Tatar economy does indeed appear to be a stable and relatively successful variety of capitalism, and we can expect it to retain its key features for some time to come'.[20] In 2006, this prediction already looks overly cautious, even if we judge the state of the Tatarstan economy by the increasing volume of foreign investment only and overlook the fact that the same amount of money in Tatarstan goes much further than in the West. Unbelievably, the overall amount of investment into the state economy over the last fifteen years, which not only has restored all its sectors to 1991 levels, but also provided for the major overhaul and rebuilding of Kazan and other cities and towns, including the launch of the Kazan Metro and construction of three vital bridges across the Volga, the Kama and the Kazanka Rivers, is, in fact, less than the amount which went in the same period towards keeping the London Underground in its present, far from perfect, state. So, when we note that in 2005 Tatarstan received $843.5 million of foreign investment from nine countries including the USA, the UK, Germany, Italy, Turkey and Luxemburg, of which $214 million is in the form of FDI, we should keep in mind the creative capacity of these funds.

Tatarstan's potential for FDI was once more demonstrated in March 2006 at the major annual MIPIM real estate exhibition and investment forum in Cannes, France, where Tatarstan presented over forty investment projects in the areas of residential housing and infrastructure, trade centres, hotel, sport and fitness, entertainment complexes, transport infrastructure, techno parks and so forth. Among others, the State Housing Foundation under the auspices of the Presidency of Tatarstan presented its Social Mortgage Programme, which will be one of Tatarstan's new social policy priorities in the coming years. The Russian Economic Development Minister, German Gref, at the opening of the Tatarstan exhibition referred to Kazan as 'a European city, the most beautiful in all Russia after Moscow', but also, importantly, 'the most rapidly developing city in Russia'. 'Tatarstan is a region, about which the Russian federal government can confidently say – you may invest here, your investment will be safeguarded and will flourish.'

As for President Shaimiev, who also participated in the MIPIM investment forum, he told foreign investors about various new construction projects in Kazan and added:

> The President of Russia put forward the task of doubling the all-Russia GDP by 2010. We, In Tatarstan, have set for ourselves an even bigger task – we aspire towards *effective* doubling of our GDP. The Tatarstan economy is a mirror reflection of the all-Russia economy. Already seven years ago we set out our perspective of 'Tatarstan without oil'. In the conditions of the stabilization of oil extraction we are able to increase the GDP more quickly. The republic is intensively developing its petrochemical sector, and it is not just our whim, but dictated by facts on the ground. Many of the projects in this area are already accomplished, but new projects continue to emerge. In the petrochemical sphere we have no products with less than 19–20% of profitability. We are not looking for 'some investment' only. We need investment, which would come together with qualitatively new technologies in the production of goods and services. We are creating all the necessary conditions so that investors can come to us and stay for good. Any other approach is uncompetitive. What you see in Tatarstan, is not just a business-project. It is what we have already done.

In 2007, Tatarstan will be presented at the MIPIM in Cannes with her own independent exhibition, so the question for investors is not whether it is clever to invest in the time-tested economic performance of Tatarstan, but who will be clever enough to get there in good time to reap the best rewards of their investment. It is also because the development of Tatarstan is based not just on political stability and the sound management of an already growing economy, but also on the continuing historical quest for learning and education, which permeates all spheres of life. It was no coincidence that, among other engagements in Cannes, President Shaimiev visited the leading European Sophia Antipolis educational centre and Techno park, when it was agreed that young scholars and experts from Tatarstan would be studying in this famous business-school as well.

Education is indeed one of the first priorities of Tatarstan's vision of her democratic market future, and it is being facilitated in the republic through technological, scientific and management studies, as well as in the important sphere of a learning democracy. This is, however, the topic of our next, concluding chapter.

NOTES

1. Unnamed American official speaking before the bombing of Belgrade in 1998.
2. Altvater, E., and Mahnkopf, B., (1997) 'The World Market Unbound', in Scott, A. (ed.), *The Limits of Globalization*, Routledge, London.
3. M. Shaimiev: We Need A Dialogue of Civilizations', newspaper 'Vremya I Dengi (Time and Money)', Kazan, 16 February 2006.
4. To be fair, there are organizations in the Western world that honestly try to bridge the gap of understanding with the Muslim world. Among others, are the Bradley Foundations and the John Templeton Foundation in the USA.
5. 'G. Palast, 'IMF's four steps to damnation', *The Observer*, 29 April 2001.
6. Alex Massie, 'Neocon architect says: 'Pull It Down', *The Scotsman*, 21 February 2006.
7. A. Lieven, 'Democratic Failure: Festering Lilies Smell Worse Than Weeds', 27 October 2005, OpenDemocracy Internet site www.opendemocracy.net.
8. *The Scotsman*, op.cit.
9. Foreign Policy Centre, London, published in the context of the FPC 'Future of Russia' project, August 2005, www.frc.org.uk/publications.
10. S. Cohen, *Failed Crusade: America and the Tragedy of Post-Communist Russia*, Norton, New York, 2001.
11. The *Forbes* list, March 2006.
12. G. Yavlinsky, 'A Road Map For Reform', in the *Blueprint for Russia*, op.cit.
13. See, R. Bukharaev, *The Model of Tatarstan under President Mintimer Shaimiev*, ibid.
14. Ibid.
15. Ibid, p.43.
16. V. Lysenko, 'Governors and Business: Marriage of Convenience?', *Russia and Contemporary World*, issue 2, (39), 2003, Moscow.
17. 'Inside Putin's Russia: State within a state', BBC World Service, 29 December 2003.
18. Leo McCann, op. cit, pp. 140–141.
19. Ibid, p.19.
20. Ibid, preface, xi.

CHAPTER 9

THE NATIONAL IDEA

◳

There is an idea, which is not without its advocates, that a vigorous Executive is inconsistent with the genius of republican government. The enlightened well-wishers to this species of government must at least hope that the supposition is destitute of foundation; since they can never admit its truth, without at the same time admitting the condemnation of their own principles. Energy in the Executive is a leading character in the definition of good government.

James Madison, American President, The Federalist Papers[1]

No man has a right to fix the boundary of the march of a nation; no man has a right to say to his country – thus far shalt you go and no further.

Charles Stewart Parnell (1846–1891), Irish national leader

When, in the immediate wake of the celebrations of Kazan's millennium I asked President Shaimiev, why he was so confident in the future of his country, he suddenly told me about his visit to Malaysia, one of his many visits abroad during his long presidential tenure. He told me how, looking out of the window of the office of the then Malaysian Prime Minister Mahathir Muhammad, he told him how he was impressed by the towering landscape of the business quarters of Kuala Lumpur and expressed a wish that the Tatarstan economy could develop as rapidly as the 'Asian tiger' economies of that pre-1998 era. Interestingly, Mahathir Muhammad turned to him and said, 'And I would dearly like to have the same level of public education and the educated, qualified workforce, you have in Tatarstan and Russia.'

Indeed, the well-educated workforce is one of the major assets of Tatarstan in the age of globalization. This, however, is one of the healthier legacies of the Soviet period, which, in Tatarstan's policy of continuity of the best features of her history, needed a lot of attention and investment at the time of transition. Kazan was one of the most developed centres of education and scientific exploration in the entire USSR, a position which was heavily boosted during the Second World War. During the war, along with many strategic USSR enterprises, one-third of all scientific institutes and well-known scholars of the USSR Academy of Sciences, along with its presidium, came to Kazan led by the vice-presidents of the Academy, the academicians O. Y. Schmidt and E. A. Chudakov. Jointly with Kazan scientists, the evacuated scholars did work of colossal defensive importance, and this highly creative atmosphere and rapid scientific development prompted the opening, in 1945, of the Kazan branch of the USSR Academy of Sciences headed, from 1945 to 1965, by the outstanding chemist, academician A. E. Arbuzov. During the war, 300 important scientific results were obtained at Kazan University, about 380 at the Institute of Chemistry and Technology, and 100 in all at the Institute for the Professional Development of Physicians and the Institute of Microbiology. During the war, at Kazan University a discovery was made of truly worldwide significance: in 1944, E. A. Zavoysky discovered the phenomenon of paramagnetic resonance. In Kazan high schools their scientific and educational activity never ceased: in the war years approximately six thousand expert mathematicians, physicists, chemists, weather forecasters, geologists, biologists, teachers, doctors and many other experts of the highest skill graduated from the university and other educational institutions.

After the war, the momentum of Tatarstan's educational and scientific activities only increased, propelled by the start of the full-scale extraction of oil and the overall scientific boom in the USSR with its pioneering outer space programme. In Kazan, there were then eleven higher educational establishments and three branches of various central institutes, in which, at the end of the 1970s, 50,000 students of more than forty nationalities studied. Teaching in high schools was led by about 5,000 professors and teachers, among whom there were 250 doctors of sciences and 2,500 candidates of sciences.

Today, besides Kazan University, which celebrated its famous bicentenary in November 2004, there are thirty high schools and twenty-three educational institutions in Kazan alone, in which 120,000 students now study. Up to 10,000 young men and women graduate from the high schools of Kazan annually. And this educational and scientific development also rests on historical tradition and is, therefore, highly maintained and purposeful.

We can easily appreciate that well-developed skills in chemistry were essential in the establishment of the petrochemical complex of Tatarstan, but this was far from all among scientific achievements of the republic in view of its unique 'can-do' culture. When President Shaimiev, in respect of the immense tasks lying ahead, says 'we can do it', pointing to past achievements of the Tatarstan model, sceptics may ask – and what about the rocket science, can you do that as well? Well, Tatarstan has been doing it since the very beginning of the Russian space exploration programme. Kazan Aviation Institute, turned today into Kazan Technical University, was and remains one of the main scholarly bases for the all-Russia Space Exploration Programme in developing the engines for Russian launch rockets, which continue to give Russia a unique edge in world space exploration. There are many other scientific education centres in Tatarstan, covering all the principal spheres of the contemporary economy and fundamental research beginning with the Institute of Construction and the Economic Institute to the Agricultural Institute, from which President Shaimiev graduated in 1959. The crown of Kazan's educational glory is, however, the renowned Kazan University, founded in 1804, which celebrated its bicentennary in 2004.

The main building of the university, with its three classical porticoes along the whole façade, was built under the supervision of its great rector, the father of a new and revolutionary type of geometry, Nikolai Lobachevsky in 1822. In 1832–41, all other university buildings were constructed to a design by the architect M. Korinfsky: the Anatomical Theatre, the Chemical Laboratory, the Physics Cabinet, the Observatory and the Library. Interestingly, the university complex finally got its complete classical aspect only for its bicentenary, when its long-planned left wing was built and Kazan University at last acquired its finished appearance as intended by its architect in the nineteenth century. This is yet one more paradox of Tatarstan. During the period of transition, she managed to complete the project, for which the city could not obtain any funding in 1904, when the centenary of Kazan University was celebrated. In the two centuries of its existence, Kazan University has made a huge contribution to the development of Russian natural sciences and the humanities. Here, besides N. Lobachevsky, mathematicians V. Imshenitsky, A. Popov and I. Gromeka, the great chemists N. Zinin, A. Butlerov and K. Klaus, the historians K. Fuks and A. Schapov, the physicians E. Aristov and P. Lesgaft, the astronomer I. Simonov and many others worked and taught. The university has nurtured an entire pleiad of outstanding scholars in all fields of science, among which were the physicists E. Zovoisky and S. Altschuler, the chemists B. Arbuzov and G. Kamai, and the mathematicians N. Chetaev and N. Chebotarev. The scientific and educational activity of the university provided the fertile ground on which the brilliant Kazan school of scholarly research later developed. It is to the faculties of the university that the largest Kazan scientific and educational institutions trace their origin.

As far as its students are concerned, in the list of the former students of the University we read the names of the writers Leo Tolstoi, S. Aksakov, A. Melnikov-Pechersky, the composer A. Balakirev and, certainly, V. I. Lenin who, not unlike Leo Tolstoi, was only fleetingly glimpsed in the history of the university, which cannot be said of course about the history of Russia and the entire world.

Today, the university continues its large-scale educational and research work. Its faculty of Physics and Mathematics branched out into three separate faculties: the Physical, Mechanical, Mathematical and Applied mathematics; other faculties are also being re-organized to meet current demands. The world importance of Kazan University was recognized also by UNESCO, which entered its bicentenary in its calendar of major cultural events in 2004.

As we have said, Kazan University became a mother-school for all other educational, scientific and research institutions in Tatarstan, of which the Kazan Medical Institute occupies a special place not only in the history of Tatarstan science, but also in the view of 'the good of the people', which is, as I have tried to demonstrate in this book, the only true indicator of any politics. In the sphere of national welfare, its developed and affordable health service is especially important. In the time of transition, when the all-Russia health service worsened dramatically for lack of appropriate funding, Tatarstan never failed to take this sphere of public good into account. The health service is one of Tatarstan's national projects: in 2005, five new hospitals and four clinics were built and the wages of doctors and nurses, as well as the allocation of funds for food and medication in hospitals were increased twice, the growth of funding reaching 299 million roubles. In 2005, some 415 physicians and 334 general practitioners were educated in Tatarstan. Tatarstan also introduced the institute of GPs, to which end forty-three polyclinics were transformed into centres of general medical practice and state GPs received 1,200 special kits of medical instruments and over a thousand computers. As a result, twice as many people now have annual medical check-ups as before, and the number of medical emergencies has decreased by 9.7%. In 2006, Tatarstan was planning to increase GP wages by 25% and allocate 200 million roubles for the medical equipment of polyclinics. Importantly, GP centres are being introduced and equipped not just in urban, but increasingly in Tatarstan's rural areas.

In Tatarstan, a number of ground-breaking achievements in modern medicine are being introduced, especially in the spheres of heart surgery and neurosurgery, transplant surgery, oncology, onco-haematology and others. The republic has its own bank of stem cells and the first patients are being treated by cell technologies in the State Clinic Hospital. At the same time, the share of private medical facilities in the Tatarstan health service grew in 2005 by 8.5%, with the participation of foreign companies like 'Euromedic International' and 'Rocada Med'. In his 2006 Annual Address, President Shaimiev said that the republican health service needs deep systemic changes in order to continue its development, and one of those changes already introduced is additional medical insurance, which allowed the population to receive free of charge 2.3 times more medicines than in 2004. In view of the near-catastrophic situation of the mortality rate in Russia, Tatarstan's attention to the medical problems of her population cannot be overestimated, and, for 2006, the republic's budget envisages the growth of free medication subsidies by 36.9%.

But Tatarstan also builds new as well as modernizing existing large medical facilities. The building of the largest inter-regional clinical centre, worth two billion roubles, is nearing its completion. This centre will be able to perform over 10,000 sophisticated heart, vascular and brain operations, for which patients currently apply to the all-Russia and foreign medical institutions. The republic has also allocated over one billion roubles for the modernization of the State Centre of Oncology and the State Centre of Ophthalmology. Special attention, as one would expect, is paid to children's health. The State Children's Hospital, which has been ranked as the best in Russia for the last three years, performed 200 heart operations and 148 brain operations in 2005 alone. For the last twelve years, in the Department of Onco-Haematology of this hospital the rate of survival of children with certain types of leukaemia constitutes 93% and, in some cases, 100%. Importantly, the developments in the health sphere do not concentrate on the capital, but on the entire republic: in 2005, modern medical facilities were also opened in provincial towns such as Leninogorsk with its new antenatal clinic and surgical and intensive-care units.

The ever-improving performance of the Tatarstan economy makes things possible in both health and educational spheres. But, for all the importance of money, money is by no means everything, if the attitude of the people working in these spheres is not motivated by greater vision. Of course, the investment in health and education in Tatarstan is not as yet at the level of the developed countries. But the question is not how much you actually spend, but what results you get for all that spending. In the UK, for example, journalists still complain that although education spending has risen to 67 billion GBP, 'nearly 40 per cent of five-year olds struggle to write their own name. More than a third of six-year-olds are unsure of the alphabet. By the age of eleven, one in four children leaves primary school without having mastered the three Rs. And a report this month found that many students arriving at university are 'so illiterate they cannot even write a sentence'.[2] Is that the destination Russia and Tatarstan are supposed to reach after abandoning their own, currently cash-starved, comprehensive system?

This makes it all the more shocking that Russia is being so hard-pressed to 'modernize' her education and health services in the fashion of the developed countries. The market is dictating its rules and attitudes, of course, but in the present situation, when the general public cannot afford expensive treatment and schooling, the best option would still be to vary state and private facilities. It is especially important in education and, for Tatarstan, its destination in the educational sphere is today described by the vision of creating a base network of qualitatively new, innovative schools – 'the schools of the future' – in every region of the republic and for this Tatarstan has budgeted, in the coming two years, 767 million roubles from the federal funds and 570 million roubles of her own funds allocated for purchasing laboratory equipment and software, the modernization of school classes and the further training of highly-qualified teachers. In a market economy, one cannot always plan the training of certain kinds of specialists. Recently, Russia saw an overproduction of lawyers and economists at the expense of technical staff for mechanical engineering, and this gap is being filled in Tatarstan by special colleges funded by state enterprises which educate and prepare their own qualified and expert workforce. As for state education, 2006–7 planning envisages the creation of a lycée network for 10–11-grade students, which will play the role of resource centres concentrating on the newest educational and information technologies. Tatarstan youth, therefore, can choose their professional life path while still at school, fitted to their talents, aspirations and capacity for learning. With regard to the latter, Tatarstan pays increased attention to children with impaired hearing, eyesight and other physical deficiencies, installing the necessary equipment in state schools and boarding schools. In 2005, out of fifteen special boarding schools in Tatarstan, seven were equipped with appropriate technical facilities and thirty children having to learn at home received home computers. In 2005, Tatarstan allocated 8.5 million roubles for creating facilities for the virtual education of such children. Overall, Tatarstan holds the second place in Russia after Moscow in building and renovating educational facilities through the national 'Education' project envisaging the stimulation of innovative comprehensive schools and professional colleges, support of the best teachers, the introduction of new educational technologies, the encouragement of talented youth and the development of professional army training.

Revolutionary changes in the Russian state system from Socialism to the democratic market economy heavily impressed themselves in the educational system as well. With the change in state ideology, history was, as ever, the first subject to suffer. However, for the first time in Russian history, schoolchildren and university students not only learn sciences and professional skills, but also democracy and this is, perhaps, the most important single achievement of all in the Russian and Tatarstan educational systems. As a result, the democratic future seems assured and the trend is helped by international cooperation: the student seminars, such as 'Russia–EU Relations: Sociological and Political Perspective' at Kazan University in March 2006, are very frequent events. This brings us to the very notion of democracy in present-day Tatarstan, which could be a case study for the entire Russian federation in this aspect of her daily life as well.

The backbone of Tatarstan's democracy is, in my view, the notion that the electorate, which three times brought the president to power with a healthy majority, seems to subscribe to his conviction that 'the people of Tatarstan see the path of reform as their own'. The policies of the president at the beginning of market transition, which, for all their unavoidable pain, helped the people to adapt to new circumstances and rules of life, were continued with remarkable step-by-step consistency, when no next step was undertaken before the results of the previous one had sunk into the fabric of Tatarstan's social and economic life. No observer would argue with the fact that President Shaimiev always won his terms in office with the general approval of the Tatarstan electorate and, when the federal rules changed, his re-appointment by the Russian president, pending approval by the State Council of Tatarstan, was generally accepted as a completely natural decision in the view of the visionary economic tasks that were initiated by President Shaimiev and had to be accomplished by him.

As in many other respects, we must be careful not to gauge the achievements and shortcomings of Tatarstan's democracy by the patterns of Western democracy, which, after all, took a thousand years to develop. Today, the state of a democracy is rather often judged by its outer appearances – the fact, for example, of holding regular elections and regular changes of leading political figures. But such judgement rarely takes into account the state of the presumed popular readiness to make informed choices, and this readiness is heavily dependent on many factors in all transitional countries, especially in times of historical upheavals and overall political and economic instability. It is considered that democracy in itself will always bring the desired results, but the 2006 example of the landslide victory of Hamas in the Palestinian Authority at least puts a question mark over this assumption. In the later days of the USSR, popular democracy brought about not so much a working parliament with a clear vision of where the country should go, as just a talking-shop for people to let off steam regarding their frustration with the old order of things. Democracy, it seems natural, ought to be based on a sustained vision of the general direction towards 'the good of the people', yet people with little or no experience of democracy are, as a rule, too gullible to distinguish between short-term slogans and sustained vision.

In Tatarstan, parliamentary democracy evolved in a somewhat different way from Russia at large, if only because the republican parliament (later transformed into the State Council), despite differences in opinion, always shared the common objective of upholding the limited sovereignty of Tatarstan *vis-à-vis* the Russian federal centre. This common task put Tatarstan's democracy on a firm footing at the very beginning of the transition process, and, to all intents and purposes, there is democracy in Tatarstan, especially if we judge it by the stark contrast with what existed before 1990. At the same time, democracy in Tatarstan is still wanting in as much as the people themselves are still learning how to live in a democracy. Interestingly, those complaining about deficiencies in Tatarstan's democracy usually belong to those parties and movements which regularly lose elections, having little or no popular base. People in Tatarstan, like their counterparts in the West, still vote with their pockets, which, however, become deeper by the day. Such economic changes are accompanied by the process of younger post-Communist generations steadily growing into political maturity by learning democracy and living in it.

In established democracies any change of government never involves a complete change of direction, as happens in transitional countries. Even if such change happens, as in the UK during the Thatcher era, it was intrinsically prepared by the latent public demand for modernization and change, and not in the manner of abrupt revolutions brought about by euphoric street democracy and lacking any firm foundations for the actual fulfilment of public demands, except fiery slogans and all the right noises so reassuring to the West. This reassurance, however, can be short-lived precisely because real democracy comes from the people, and not from the change of the pro-Western or anti-Western elite. Nationalistic slogans directed towards neighbours and smooth-talking addressed to the West may sustain such quasi-democratic arrangements for the time being, but developments on the ground will rectify things sooner or later. There is no democracy which denies people their daily bread, and this is precisely what we see in some countries after their much-hailed colour revolutions.

The establishment of real democracy takes time, as economic development opens people's eyes to things other than daily survival. Democracy in Russia will necessarily come of age, even if, as in may other aspects of globalization, there is an unstoppable urge to introduce its full-fledged version in a matter of days, as if this were possible. In order to have democracy, you first have to restore people's self-confidence in the political and economic spheres, and this is what Tatarstan is aiming at by means of the political and economic steps she undertakes on her path of transition. Some argue that regular elections in Russia did not bring the required results inasmuch as they did not immediately bring Western-type democracy into the country. But the fact of the matter is that these elections still reflected the people's choice in their present socio-economic conditions and, if anything, these conditions are to blame for the fact that populist demagogues can often win over visionary politicians in transitional countries. For all the pressure that is exerted to introduce, by whatever means, the 'one-size-fits-all' democracy to the entire world irrespective of the cultural and intellectual traditions of the people, one always recalls the famous saying of the Russian Empress Katherine the Great who dearly wanted to make Russia more like her tiny native German princedom. She was absolutely sure that 'Africans are the very same Russian *muzhiks* (peasants), only black'. But for all the deficiencies, which the West sees in present-day Russian democracy, Russia and especially Tatarstan can still teach the West a thing or two about the real benefits of multiculturalism, which effectively became a byword for failure in Western democracies. This also should be kept in mind when judging the state of democracy in Russia and, as world events show, this is no small thing for democratic peace and stability.

In contrast with the many countries in transition, Tatarstan was fortunate enough to have a visionary president committed to democracy and economic transformation from the very beginning of transition, but, as has been noted throughout this book, this good fortune was preordained by the entire course of the very instructive Tatar history. Despite laments that President Shaimiev could have relinquished the reins of power some years ago and thus become an icon of the Tatarstan movement of self-determination, his remarkable presidential performance in the twenty-first century, including the immense economic and political achievements of the Kazan millennium, completely defied his fiercest critics. The presence of Mintimer Shaimiev on the Russian political scene was always natural, if we judge his political life by the widespread respect he commands in Tatarstan, Russia and abroad. In January 2007, the president will be seventy and some remember that he once said he would not want Tatarstan to have a president over seventy years of age. After he was reappointed as president in 2005, one of his critics who is also his erstwhile press-secretary, had this to say:

> Knowing Mintimer Shaimiev, I can suppose that he indeed did not want to fight for the continuation of his presidential term, but wanted to talk with Putin about his successor. Putin, as it seems, was not ready for such a conversation and proposed to Shaimiev not to hurry and govern the republic for some time more ...'[3]

Political scientist Larisa Usmanova who did her doctorate in Japan and was able to observe the state of things in Tatarstan from afar, also said in 2005:

> If the question of power change in Tatarstan would arise today, who could honestly be worthy of it? Alas, to date we don't see any political figure *potentially* equal to Shaimiev, and we cannot even talk about a really equal figure. It is good and bad at the same time. Shaimiev did not do what he was supposed to do – prepare a pleiad of bright and responsible representatives of the elite, which after any power change would still work in accord and togetherness. So, the words of the president that in the last months his problem was how not to run for presidency, are absolutely honest. Today, he could not have gone for retirement with a clear conscience that he had done all he could for a smooth succession of power.[4]

I do not think that Larisa Usmanova is right inasmuch as she, like many other observers, deems President Shaimiev irreplaceable. For, above all, he himself does not think so, always stating that:

> ... in the coming years, the power in Tatarstan will be democratically transferred to the people who today directly serve the republic and work in the interest of her population. And we today have plenty of those. We have a very good team – a young and energetic government, which knows what it does, a stable parliament and well-prepared heads of administration of cities and regions.[5]

At the same time, it is obvious that:

> ... as analysts emphasize, the keys to Tatarstan stability are in the hands of Shaimiev – both in the sphere of balancing political forces in Tatarstan, especially in the field of inter-ethnic relations, and in the economic sphere, above all in the oil-and-gas sector. When asked by his colleagues about a new term, Shaimiev himself answered that 'I have no problem with running for the office. I have the problem of how not to run for it'. In accordance with the changed legislation, he was able to go for a

fourth term. But he said many times that he would not do that, for he does not want to see an aged president at the helm of republican power, even if he is not complaining about his health. The only person who was staunchly against his re-appointment was his wife Sakina. 'There is indeed a strong opposition', the President says smiling, 'But to date I am able to negotiate with this opposition, or rather find a common language.'[6]

President Vladimir Putin's choice can be easily understood in the context of Tatarstan's continuing political and inter-ethnic stability, as well as ground-breaking economic progress. He might also repeat the words of the Vice-Speaker of the Russian State Duma Oleg Morozov, who once famously reproached federal attempts to put unnecessary pressure on Tatarstan in an attempt to strip her of her hard-earned regional rights, 'There is a Tatar proverb which says that one should not scratch where it is not itching. Russia is not itching as far as Tatarstan is concerned. Thus, do not scratch!'[7]

However, the question of succession in Tatarstan is much deeper than a simple informed public choice between possible successors. It brings up the vital issue of how to introduce a viable mechanism of democratic accountability into the fabric of Tatarstan's democracy at the grass roots – a task that President Shaimiev has been dealing with since the dawn of democracy in Tatarstan.

He understands full well that the really important thing is not to skilfully bring about the change of the ruling elite for a more accommodating one following a cleverly orchestrated 'colour revolution', but to give the people the real means to influence the political process. This, again, as Tatarstan in the person of her president has always argued, can only be done from the grass roots upwards, and, in this regard, the introduction of local self-government, likewise at municipal level, is vital for the present-day Russian Federation. At this level, people are indeed better able to hold the elected official to account for all their needs, which is much harder with higher elected bodies.

The approach of Tatarstan to the introduction of the Federal Law on Local Self-Government is also very characteristic and clearly shows the process of bringing about real democracy within the republic. When this law was adopted by the Russian State Duma some years ago, the Russian regions were, as is traditional in Russia, hard pushed to introduce full-scale local government immediately, although some succumbed to this pressure from Moscow, whose idea then was to diminish the power of local regional bosses by squeezing them between the federal power and the power of local self-government in their respective regions. The result was rather cheerless and once again served to disillusion Russian people as to the very notion of democracy on any level. Why? Simply because the law described the rights and responsibilities of local government without providing any material base for their actual functioning. What can a local government do without funds of its own? Of course, it just serves as another example of the good intentions which pave the road to hell. Instead of providing a base for local democracy growing upwards and making this growth ever more transparent, the destitute local and municipal governments had to beg for cash in front of their respective republican and district authorities, and, of course, such economic dependency entailed political dependency as well.

In those years, Tatarstan flatly refused to introduce local and municipal self-government along existing lines and, as it happens, had to withstand another storm of accusations of undemocratic behaviour. Even if the launch of local self-government without any economic base went against common sense (how many such attempts Tatarstan and her president had to oppose in recent years, one is left to wonder), President Shaimiev was blamed squarely for stopping the development of democracy at local republic levels. He, however, then insisted on the soundness of his position, arguing that society was not ready for the implementation of the law on self-government in its then form and that Tatarstan first needed to lay sound economic and legal foundations for its proper functioning.

So it was done, and when in October 2005 Tatarstan adopted her law on self-government in accordance with the much improved federal law, President Shaimiev justifiably said that of all the Russian regions, Tatarstan was the one most ready to implement the self-government law at all lower levels of state power. 'The funding of each municipal polity is well budgeted in Tatarstan', the president said, 'without that, the local government could not become a master of its own territory'. Of course, in Tatarstan, as in any Russian region, there are municipal structures requiring subsidies, but, as the president said, 'There will be problems, of course, but the power of the people is the basis for democracy, and without proper local self-government we cannot progress along the path of democratization of our society. I believe, that, economically and politically, Tatarstan is now ready for it.'[8]

As regards the economic and political development of the Tatarstan model, President Shaimiev expressively says: 'We in Tatarstan take a long time to harness the horse, but after that without fail reach our destination.' In the same vein, President Shaimiev previously argued against holding republican elections along party lines, for which he was angrily criticized by local nationalists and 'shock therapy reform' adherents alike. He then reasonably said that the stratification of society along party lines in the absence of stable political parties had not yet taken place, and before that, any elections will fall pray to the 'parties-for-the-day' under their most tempting, but unrealizable populist slogans. Today, the situation has changed in this respect as well, due to the consistent party-building policy of Tatarstan, where not only all-Russia parties are now participating in the elections on the basis of their party lists, but also the leading republican 'Tatarstan – New Century' party, the programme of which reflects the destination of the Tatarstan model in both domestic development and at the federal level.

The state of democracy in Tatarstan can also be judged by the level of press criticism and public debate concerning the transition period. The Tatarstan press, especially such papers as 'The Evening Kazan' and 'MK in Tatarstan' are quite irreverent, even if their criticism always reflects the respect President Shaimiev still commands among the people. The state media acts in accordance with the famous saying of American President James Madison who said that 'all men having power ought to be mistrusted'. But then, all considered, is it not the public trust that puts men in power in a democracy? This reverse side of the coin often escapes political critics, but that is in the nature of democratic discourse. The old proverb says 'one does not change horses in mid-stream'. For all the validity of this common-sense observation, its application in politics is, of course, dangerous, as it may provide an excuse to a leader holding on to power at all costs. Still, the validity of this wisdom is quite obvious when it comes to fulfilling one's vision in unprecedented circumstances of economic and political transition, when everything has to be grasped, thought over and enacted in all its complex entirety not only in the economic sphere, but also in the sphere of providing and maintaining political, inter-ethnic and inter-religious stability.

President Shaimiev always had plenty to show for the length of his presidential tenure. Therefore, in times of transition, one is inclined to think that the process of democratization ought not always to mirror the demands of democratic puritans, but rather judge a leader on the merits of his vision and actual achievements in realizing this vision. In this light, the length of President Shaimiev's stay in power will be judged by his performance in the previous presidential tenures and by the weight of his political authority that made President Putin re-appoint him as the president of Tatarstan in 2005.

When one thinks of his work, one suddenly remembers the words of the head of the US Federal Reserve, Alan Greenspan, at the time of his retirement: 'I only just realized that I was on twenty-four-hour call for the last eighteen years.' President Shaimiev can also be believed, when in one of his interviews to the opposition 'Evening Kazan' newspaper he said: 'As a president, I had no easy years in power.' The sheer scale of his achievements briefly outlined in this book bears witness to these words, and for all their impertinence, even the ever-inquisitive all-Russia newspapers never questioned the weight and well-earned authority of President Shaimiev.

We have already cited Lev Ovrutsky, one of Tatarstan's most outspoken journalists who, together with the political scientist Dr Midhat Mukhametshin are regular sources for Western 'value-free' researches like those of Leo McCann and Linda Røysi. In the book expounding his view on the political realities in Tatarstan, he writes:

> Generally, President Shaimiev is very rarely taken ill, and even his catching cold is frequently of diplomatic character. It is widely believed that the tough schedule which he rigorously follows is even more difficult for his relatively younger co-workers. As any honest clerk, he comes to work at half past nine and leaves it at half past seven (excluding Saturday, when he hurries home for family lunch). But, Mr Shaimiev, when leaving his office takes along a pile of documents. Such a life-style cannot be called healthy, even if Mr Shaimiev does not smoke and, being a non-Russian person, does not indulge in the traditional Russian weakness.[9] At the same time, one of the important factors, partly off-setting his physical and nervous strains, is his fitness culture. Two or three times a week – tennis, rowing, skiing. There are legends that once a presidential bodyguard could not keep up with the president on a skiing track, after which Asgat Safarov, the present-day Minister of Interior and then the head of presidential security, gave all staff strict orders to improve their physical fitness.[10]

In the famously irreverent daily 'Moskovskyi Comsomolets', answering a question about his workload, President Shaimiev said:

> I always maintained that a person of weak character should not enter politics. Life is tough – every morning they put on my table a record of all that happened

yesterday, and it seldom makes pleasant reading. Or, for instance, a parent whose child is dying, comes to see me, because in Tatarstan the child cannot be treated – only abroad. Such cases unsettle me. I recently formulated a new goal – all progressive foreign methods of medical treatment should also be available in Tatarstan. As in cases of child leukaemia. Fingers crossed, today we treat that at the level of European doctors.

When asked: 'Do you love being in power?', he replied:

I have not got this disease. For my entire life, I was in positions of power, I was a Director at twenty-five. During the *perestroika* years, plenty of people surfaced who thought that they were able to govern, and many of them indeed reached positions of power. But they overreached themselves. They thought they could, but they could not; the people did not believe them. As for myself, I think the people view me in such a way: the president spoke, so it will be done. They know me, and I know this life from its grassroots. When I come to visit the regions, they are, of course, preparing for that, but I immediately see, what's just for show and what's not. My slogan is – all people are our people. Nobody came here from a different planet.[11]

The president is indeed a wise man: he always knew that he had to work with what he had, and although it was not little, he never had ideal conditions. He always knew when the situation was ripe for action, and only then pursued it to its end in full knowledge of all relevant factors. In that, he presents a stark contrast and a welcome example to some political leaders of the former USSR who tried to deal in slogans while waiting for a miracle to happen. In his faithfulness to historical continuity, including the better features of the Soviet past, he understands that one cannot suddenly change the direction of the historical destination of one's country, and any such abrupt change will bring about undesired and, most importantly, unforeseen consequences so painful to the people on the ground. In this respect, the cost of the much-hailed 'colour revolutions' in Georgia, Kyrgyzstan and even Ukraine turned out to be greater uncertainty regarding the country's future, despite all the right noises about freedom and democracy. The leaders who come to power in street demonstrations, as Machiavelli might have said, 'make their journey as if they had wings; their problems start when they alight. This is the case with men who either buy their way into power or are granted it through the favour of somebody else'.[12]

The bright picture of the victorious democracy in such countries cannot stand any honest scrutiny either economically, or politically, as far as 'the good of the people' is concerned. But, unfortunately, people in the West see only what they want to see or, rather, what they are shown, which makes it even harder to bridge an ever widening gap of understanding between Russia and the West. This is not to say that Western ideals are not valid, they are, but they cannot be made to work in the atmosphere of massive delusion encouraged by the seemingly pro-Western mass media. At the same time, lone voices in the world start to question the wisdom of pushing Russia into a corner, despite her evident willingness to cooperate with the West in all serious matters of world politics. Mikhail Gorbachev, the father of Russian democracy, on the occasion of his recent seventy-fifth birthday again said:

In almost all my speeches in the West I now say: why it is that you support Russia by the word of mouth, but in reality try to keep her in a semi-suffocated state? It would seem that in the new world order and in the face of global challenges no single state, however powerful, is able to cope on its own. It is high time to join forces. And what is the reality? America starts to dictate her own understanding of democracy to the entire world, she divides Europe into new and old, shaking and juxtaposing countries against each other. Russia starts to unnerve them, because she is getting stronger and that does not suit them. They try to build a new wall around Russia – Ukraine, the Baltic states, Georgia. A kind of *cordon sanitaire*. The present-day leaders of Georgia and the Ukraine who still have to earn the right to be called leaders, follow the lead of others, and they are not independent. Attacks on Russia strain relations. But Russia should not respond to provocation given that all people want to live in a peaceful world.

British journalist Mary Dejevsky thinks that Russia should improve its PR activities in the West. Maybe, this is also necessary, but what is one to make of the following comment by Anatol Lieven, a senior fellow at the New America Foundation, when, referring to the hard-liners in the American administration, he says:

... they advocate forming anti-Moscow military alliances with Russia's neighbours and giving overt support to domestic political opponents of President Vladimir V. Putin ... Tension between the US and Russia is a gross distraction from the mortal threat posed to the world by Islamist terrorism. Why at this critical moment of history, would Washington pick unnecessary fights with Russia, a country that certainly has differences with the US, but that threatens neither American lives nor vital US interests?

Some proposed US policies towards Russia seem deliberately provocative. The US should certainly support Georgian and Ukrainian democracy, but is it really in US interests to back the Georgians in their ethnic civil wars against Russian-backed separatists? And why is it in the interest of the US to take Ukraine into NATO, long before that country has become a stable free-market democracy and when a great many Ukrainians strongly oppose such a move and continue to favour an alliance with Russia? Encouraging conflicts on Russia's borders is especially unwise and immoral given that, because of the war in Iraq, the US does not actually have troops available to back up any security commitments it might wish to offer countries that break with Moscow. Of course, the West is right to oppose Moscow on some questions, such as Russia's backing of attempts to rig the last Ukrainian election. But on other issues, there is either room for compromise or reason to question Washington's assumptions.

If my arguments about the necessity of the paced transition to market economy and real public democracy, both of which cannot be learned in a day or even a year, seem overly 'patriotic', here is what Anatol Lieven has to say on this:

After all, the 'democracy' that Putin has allegedly overthrown was, in fact, not a real democracy at all but a pseudo-democracy ruled over by corrupt and brutal oligarchical clans. During the 1990s, the administration of Boris N. Yeltsin, under the sway of the oligarchs and the liberal elites, rigged elections, repressed the opposition and launched a bloody and unnecessary war in Chechnya – all with the support of Washington. To ordinary Russians, Western-sponsored 'democracy' meant watching helplessly while 'liberal' elites looted the country and transferred vast fortunes to Western banks, to the profit of Western economies ... Because Putin is seen as having ended the post-Soviet decade of chaos, looting and national humiliation; because he has presided over rising living standards; and yes, because he has stood up to the West, he currently has the support of a large majority of Russians. By contrast, the Russian 'democrats' Washington favours have no chance whatsoever of winning a free election. Moreover, the more ardently we support them, the more unpopular they become. Excessive Western criticism of Putin, far from strengthening Russian democracy, angers ordinary Russians and risks driving them further toward chauvinistic nationalism. Yet Washington still seems to not understand the consequences of its disastrous Russia policies of the 1990s ... Of course, Russia has been largely to blame for the decline of the relationship; but exclusively to blame, for everything? This is the kind of witless propaganda expected from arrogant, ignorant, obedient Soviet apparatchiks during the Cold War – not from supposedly independent scholars in the world's greatest democracy.[13]

Against this background, this book is also a sincere attempt to generate a more positive view of Russia through the example of Tatarstan, a country that knows its destination and therefore still has a historical destiny. Its destination, as proved by all its achievements and on-going developments, is to establish a democratic market system, which will be, first and foremost, beneficial to its multi-ethnic people and will definitely take into consideration their historical values, traditions and dreams.

The historical continuity of Tatar history, reflected in all aspects of the Tatarstan model, also becomes transparent when we look at the ancient, but recently revitalized architectural ensemble of the Kazan Kremlin. Since 1992, the Kazan Kremlin has been the acting centre of the presidency of the Republic of Tatarstan. The Kazan Kremlin, which in 1994 was awarded the status of a historical, architectural and cultural museum-reserve, is also one of the world's historical monuments as well as being protected under UNESCO's architectural heritage programme (since 2000). The Kremlin was always an attraction for visitors, but today it has indeed many things to offer. One of the results of the complex restoration and archaeological research of the Kazan Kremlin was the construction on its territory of the Kul-Sharif mosque and the revitalization of the most ancient Cathedral of the Annunciation, for which purpose the major part of more than 160 million roubles was provided by the state oil company Tatneft towards the reconstruction of the Kremlin. Both projects were executed in the Kremlin simultaneously, as if drawing a line under the historical rivalry of Islam and Christianity in Kazan: both great religions have entered a new era of mutual understanding and cooperation in the name of public accord and inter-ethnic peace in Tatarstan and Russia at large.

As Tyler Nottberg of the Eisenhower Institute in Washington DC says:

The construction of Kul Sharif and the simultaneous renovation of Blagoveschensky (Annunciation) Cathedral stand as peaceful examples of the widespread tolerance and cooperation prevalent in Tatarstan. For example, mosques throughout Kazan now stand blocks away from churches, and more of them are being constructed each year. When Nurullah mosque was recently opened, the Archbishop of the Russian Orthodox Church of Kazan attended the ceremony, along with President Shaimiev. As Western influences continue to grow, the prominent coexistence of

Christian and Islamic cultures will remain part of the republic's foundation. Drawing on this tradition of coexistence could even strengthen Tatarstan as a model for the international community. Much work must be done to maintain this delicate balance, but the people of Tatarstan appear ready for the challenge.[14]

President Shaimiev is the only statesman in Russia to possess the highest orders of both the Russian Orthodox Church and the Spiritual Board of Russian Islam for his activities in establishing inter-religious peace and understanding, of which the co-existence of the Kul Sharif Mosque and the Cathedral of the Annunciation in the Kazan Kremlin is, probably, the most eloquent symbol.

The historical Governor's palace – the official residence of the President of the Republic of Tatarstan – has also undergone restoration and returned to its former majestic shape. This classical building in Pseudo-Byzantine style, constructed in the 1840s, has literally received a new life – in it, the idea of the historical continuity of the state of Tatarstan from its foundation to the present day again reveals itself: here, according to archaeological and historical data, the medieval palace of the Kazan khans once stood.

The Kremlin is the living heart of Kazan, and its ensemble continues to exist as a living organism to whose external appearance the builders and architects of the Kremlin made their own contribution over many centuries. It is only natural then that a new monument to them has arisen on the ancient square near the Cathedral of the Annunciation, which itself has gone through external and internal revitalization: restorers have repaired its iconostasis which was all but destroyed in the anti-religious 1930s. The process of revival has touched the walls and towers of the Kremlin, and also the complex of buildings of the Cadet's School, which nowadays houses the National Picture Gallery and the Hermitage Rooms.

It is in the presidential palace that Mintimer Shaimiev works and receives his many state guests and business visitors. All major foreign ambassadors come here, both after their appointment and during their trips across Russia. In early 2006, the Plenipotentiary Ambassador of the USA William Burns visited Kazan, which, in his words, amazed him with the changes that had occurred in the city since his first visit ten years earlier. 'It seems the economic situation in Tatarstan becomes better step by step,' he said, 'I am sure that there are many opportunities for American investors in Kazan, and the expansion of our economic contacts is one of our priorities.' During his visit, the Ambassador met with the graduates of American educational programmes in Tatarstan, which today number over 600. In 2006, the American Cultural Centre in Kazan, jointly established by the Embassy of the USA in Russia and the Government of Tatarstan, will mark five years of its existence. He also met with the representatives of the various religious denominations of Tatarstan, remarking afterwards that, to his knowledge, 'Kazan plays a very important role in the history of Islam in Russia. It seems to me that the entire world must follow your example and traditions of inter-religious tolerance'.

It was no accident that during the meeting with President Shaimiev in the Kazan Kremlin, the American Ambassador talked not only about the Russian and Tatarstan perspective of joining the WTO, but also mentioned other, much less positive aspects of globalization – the insensitivity and arrogant contempt towards other people's traditional values. It was in the heat of the worldwide controversy after the publication of the notorious caricatures of the Prophet of Islam (the peace and blessing of God be upon him) and the Ambassador could not avoid this subject which was disturbing the President of Tatarstan. 'The USA', he said, 'believes that the publication of the caricatures is deeply insulting, although we believe that people must express their frustration through peaceful means.' He again reiterated his view that the Tatarstan model as it represents the peaceful coexistence of Islam, Christianity, Judaism and other religions is especially valuable, inasmuch as 'Looking at the experience of Tatarstan, where people live side-by-side, understand each other and are tolerant towards each other's beliefs, we recognize that this is precisely the objective to which all countries should aspire. Precisely such a model of openness and tolerance in the long term makes the society, in which such values are rooted, stronger', he said.

This is also the belief of the President of Tatarstan and his colleagues in government. This belief, as all the other convictions of the president, comes not as a result of political studies, but as the product of life-long experience and hard practical work aimed at transforming Tatarstan from a little-known region left in historical obscurity, to a show-case of a successful market economy and a democratic society transition for all to see. Sometimes, when people reach the age of seventy, they stop to recognize the world around them and do not comprehend the changes that occur in their society. This is not the case with the President of Tatarstan, because he was at the heart of all the positive changes in his country. The metamorphosis of Tatarstan is his brain-child and his vision, and there are not many people in the world that could credit such a huge transformation to their lifetime work.

Today, Tatarstan is a nation which has not only revived its thousand-year-old historical statehood, but has also proved its worth both on the Russian federal and world levels. It has achieved social, inter-ethnic and inter-religious peace and stability on a scale unimaginable in many other countries and made its multiculturalism a working social phenomenon aimed at the good of all its ethnic groups, while at the same time resurrecting the indigenous Tatar language and culture without any detriment to any of the republic's other ethnic cultures and languages. 2006 was declared by the president to be the Year of Arts and Culture in Tatarstan celebrating the rich variety of cultures in the republic of more than a hundred different ethnic groups.

Much attention is being paid in Tatarstan to education in all its forms, and the priority is information provision and the transition of the educational sector to modern IT facilities. With the support of the Ministry of Information and Kazan University an Intranet network with a vast resource database has been created in Tatarstan. It now connects some 1806 educational institutions and is in the process of transition from the existing 'dial-up' system to broadband. Apart from Kazan University, there are thirty high schools and twenty-three educational institutions in Kazan alone. In the overall historical quest for better education, envisaging the full computerization and internet connection of schools in Tatarstan, close attention is being paid to religious education in order to preserve and increase the peaceful traditions of Tatar religious upbringing and at the same time reject religious radicalism in all its forms

– a commitment which is being reinforced at the new Russian Islamic University in Kazan. A serious contribution to the business of spiritual education has been introduced by the higher education Muslim madrassa 'Muhammadiya' and the higher education Muslim madrassa named after the 1000th anniversary of the acceptance of Islam by the Volga Bolgars. The new Tatar Humanitarian University built in Kazan plays a special role in Tatar national education in all areas of the social sciences and humanities. In March 2006, Kazan was host to a conference of over 500 teachers of Tatar language and literature from all over the world, including countries of the former USSR, Germany, USA and Australia.

This ever-growing educational base and inter-ethnic social and political stability, when people are working together in conscious unity, has made it possible to almost completely overhaul the economy of Tatarstan through thoughtful, well-paced and fair privatization and sustained investment in industrial and agricultural development and in the fixed capital of the republic. 'The strategy of Tatarstan's economic development is a "life after oil" or "life without oil",' Shaimiev said in an interview in Cannes, France, on 14 March 2006. 'This should become a model for Russia's economy.'[15] Tatarstan is seeking more investment in domestic chemical companies to boost the output of European-standard fuel, increase the output of hydrocarbons, such as propylene, used for making plastics and produce more goods made from plastics. 'Why should we import goods such as plastics? We should produce domestically and win export markets instead,' says President Shaimiev. 'The added value should stay in the republic,' adding, 'This is how we'll get rich.' Oil processing and the chemical industry account for about 8% of Tatarstan's $18 billion economy. OAO Tatneft, Russia's fifth-largest oil producer whose largest shareholder is Tatarstan, plans to build another $3.1 billion oil refinery by the end of 2008.

In 2005, the pace of economic growth in Tatarstan outpaced average growth in Russia's other regions for the third consecutive year. Record oil prices boosted Tatarstan's economy by a preliminary 6.6% in 2005, compared with 6 per cent the previous year. Besides the oil industry, Tatarstan developed effective petrochemical and mechanic engineering industries, in which automotive and aviation industries play an ever-increasing role. Tatarstan, the home of truck maker OAO KamAZ, which is to float on the London Stock Exchange, will soon be the site of a new factory built by Great Wall Automobile Holdings Co., China's biggest maker of pick-up trucks. The Chinese company may invest as much as $100 million, planning to assemble as many as 50,000 vehicles a year. The Elaz plant in the Elabuga free economic zone will also produce 7,000 tractors by 2010, thus fulfilling the purpose for which the plant was designed as long ago as the early 1980s. Tatarstan's car-making industry is increasingly sustained by Russian federal orders – in 2006, 2,000 KamAZ trucks were due to be purchased by the Russian military. The KamAZ company, saved from total bankruptcy by the prudence of the Tatarstan authorities, produced 1,760,000 trucks in the thirty years of its existence, more than half of them exported to the rest of the world. The company is now looking into expanding abroad and building subsidiaries in the Ukraine and Azerbaijan, as well as in Iran and Pakistan.

As for Tatarstan's aircraft industry, in March 2006 the government of Tatarstan signed a four-sided agreement with the Design Bureau named after

Gorbunov, the Design Bureau 'Tupolev' and the Italian 'Air Net' Group to facilitate a multifaceted programme of certification, production, sales and servicing of the Tu-214, Tu-334, Tu-324 and Tu-330 aircraft worldwide. President Shaimiev still firmly believes in the future of aircraft production in Tatarstan, which is a good sign, given his famous and creative pragmatism in economic and political matters.

Tatarstan reported foreign investments of $684 million in 2005, a 15% increase from 2004. Accumulated foreign investments had risen to $1.4 billion by the end of 2005. In 2006, Kazan became the sixth city in Russia where Hewlett-Packard opened an office as a part of Tatarstan's programme of sustained development of her IT sector. 'I visited more than 130 countries around the world', the Vice-President and Director General of Hewlett Packard, Owen Camp, said in Tatarstan: 'I can say with assurance that Tatarstan, including Kazan, develops rather intensively in the sphere of information technologies, and that is very good.'

A special good word should be put in for Tatarstan's agriculture, both in the cooperative and private farming spheres. Year on year, this agricultural sector has been achieving unbelievably good harvests, despite the geographical shortcomings of the region. Much investment in agriculture in Tatarstan has paid off handsomely, and the republic is fully self-sufficient in all basic foodstuffs. President Shaimiev has managed to prove that agriculture can be both vitally important, as well as profitable, even if the all-Russia agricultural market is still prone to wild swings. (Russian speculators earnt hundred of millions of dollars re-selling wheat and other produce to foreign markets after purchasing them in Russia for artificially low prices.) Nevertheless, the entrance of big business into Tatarstan's agricultural sphere proves that it has a large profit potential – an opportunity that has come about as a result of President Shaimiev's pragmatic insistence on his vision for the future.

The President is naturally the hero of this book, because his personal contribution to the remarkable performance of the Tatarstan model, in both the realms of ideas and their practical realization, just cannot be overestimated. Probably, it is because his political, social and economic vision is, in true Tatar Muslim fashion, that of unity – the unity of purpose, the unity of the people and the unity and conjunction of all spheres of transition aimed not only at the economic statistics, but at the actual good of the people. Thus, in his formidable drive in bringing about democratic federalism in Russia and re-shaping the republican economy along market lines, he did not forgot to provide support for the cultural, sports and fitness needs within his republic.

Beside her reputation as the model of economic and social development, Tatarstan has also become a model republic in the development of sports and the site of many international competitions and international sports festivals. But the national sports from the distant past have certainly not lost their popularity. Tatar wrestling, for example, in which force, alertness and panache are merged, is especially well developed. Traditional contests of the Tatar national festival of Sabantui (Plough Festival), which was recently added to the UNESCO world cultural heritage list, are also widely celebrated in Kazan at the beginning of summer and have also become part of the new national festival, the Day of the Republic.

There is still a lot to be done to make Tatarstan what it deserves to be. But, looking at the sustained development of this ancient country and, moreover, participating in this development, one has less and less belief in the validity of Francis Fukuyama's famous resumé:

> The end of history will be a very sad time. The struggle for recognition, the willingness to risk one's life for a purely abstract goal, the worldwide ideological struggle that called forth daring, courage, imagination, and idealism, will be replaced by economic calculation, the endless solving of technical problems, environmental concerns, and the satisfaction of sophisticated consumer demands. In the post-historical period there will be neither art nor philosophy, just the perpetual caretaking of the museum of human history.

In contrast to these nostalgic words, history, as we have seen, is very much alive in Tatarstan, still producing not only enthusiastic and many a time selfless feats of an economic and political nature, but also men and women of historical stature. Among the latter, the place of President Shaimiev is firmly assured, if only because he is a genuine representative of his hard-working, tolerant and clever people armed by their time-proven common sense, which always helped him to achieve the near impossible. In the field of politics, he proved as creative and purposeful, as his fellow Tatars Rudolf Nureyev in ballet, composer Sofia Gubaidulina in contemporary music, scientists like Roald Sagdeev in space exploration, sportsmen like the Grand Slam winner Marat Safin in world tennis and many other Tatars who are well known to the entire world, even if they are known only as 'Russians'.

The business culture of Tatarstan is indeed a 'can-do' culture, but there is much more to the essence of the Tatarstan model and its attractiveness for all of Russia. As President Shaimiev said on the eve of 2006:

> I have noticed lately one important peculiarity in my fellow people of Tatarstan. They increasingly say: 'we can', which, in Tatar, sounds like 'bez buldyrabyz'. This shortest of phrases contains the essence of people's behaviour, their sense of dignity and their capacity to do a lot. In Russia, they increasingly look for one national idea. But it appears to me that this national idea is already expressed in the two words – 'we can'. Our people are generally very educated, capable and talented. Together, we can move mountains and make our life more prosperous and happy and create for our children and grandchildren worthwhile conditions for their educational, creative and physical progress.

And indeed it appears that the recovered sense of dignity, contained in these two simple words, but earned by years of consistent efforts to make life visibly and spiritually better, can not only make Tatarstan and Russia flourish, but also, by way of example of cultural coexistence and respect for each other's traditional values, bring much good to the people of the entire world. The only thing to remember is that history is alive and we all are answerable to our posterity who, God willing, will inherit not just our drive for democracy and global prosperity, but also our efforts at understanding each other, however difficult, or even unthinkable, they may appear at the present time.

NOTES

1. The Federalist No. 10, From the New York Packet, 18 March, 1788.
2. Edward Heathcoat Amory, 'Billions Spent ... and So Little to Show for It', *Daily Mail*, 16 March 2006.
3. Irek Murtazin, 'Shaimiev's solitude', www.volgapolitinfo.ru/politics/307.
4. Larisa Usmanova, 'After Shimiev', www.tatarica.yuldash.com/society/article 214/comment361.
5. M. Shaimiev, interview on Radio Russia, 20 May 2005.
6. *Izvestia Daily*, Moscow, 14 March 2005.
7. 'Nezavisimaya Gazeta', Moscow, 25 October 2004.
8. President Mintimer Shaimiev, from the speech at the meeting of the Volga Federal District officials dedicated to the implementation of the Law of Local Self-Government', 18 October 2005.
9. Of drinking.
10. L. Ovrutsky, op.cit, p. 23.
11. 'Moscovskyi Comsomolets', 29 April 2005.
12. N. Machiavelli, *The Prince*, Penguin Books, London, 1999.
13. Anatol Lieven, *Los Angeles Times*, 20 March 2006.
14. Tyler Nottberg, 'Tatarstan and Islam's Future in Balance', The Eisenhower Institute, Washington, DC, 2006, www.eisenhowerinstitute.org
15. Bloomberg, 17 March 2006, by Halia Pavliva.

INDEX

Abramovich, Roman, 93
abyzes, 105–106
Afghanistan, 156
Almetyevsk, 49, 95, 110, 168
Altynbaev, Rafkat, 101
Amnesty International, 148
Arbuzov, A. E., 172
Armenia, 40, 45, 47
Astrakhan, 36, 132
asymmetric federalism, 66
Azerbaijan, 33–4, 40, 45, 187

Baltic states, 43, 47
Barudi, G., 146
Bashkir federal entity, 32–3
Bashkiria, 50
Bashkortostan, 165
Baumana Street, 82
Bekh, Nikolai, 125
Belarus, 47
Bell, John, 102–103
Berlin, Sir Isiah, 8
Bigiev, Musa, 146
Bikbov, Damir, 121
Bilyar, 23, 25, 35n6
Black Death, 28
Bogachov, E., 83
Bolgar-on-the Volga, 22
book publishing, 133–4
Bzhezinsky, Z., 156
Bugulma, 110
Bukharaev, R. G., 149
Bukharaev, Ravil [author]
  father, 89
  Kazan millennium celebrations, 90–1
  lecture 2003, 1–2
  pineapple juice, 89
  son's death, 7
  upbringing, 89–90
  wife Lydia, 90
Burns, William, 185–6

Carnegie Forum 1996, 42–3
Chechen, 139
Chechen Republic and Chechnya, 14, 44–5, 50, 52, 57–8, 64, 139, 147
Cheliabinsk, 52
Chernoe (Black) Lake, 82–3
Chernomyrdin, Victor, 55

Chevrolet cars, 162–4
Chistopol watch factory, 121
'Chubais approach', 111–13
Chubais, Anatoly, 111
Cities of World Heritage of Eurasia, 74
civil liberties, 159
Crimea, 132
cultural international festivals, 85–6

Daghestan, 152
Danish cartoons, 153–4, 186
Day of the Mother Tongue, 135
Declaration of State Sovereignty 1990, 37–8, 43, 46, 56
  10th anniversary, 65
democracy, definitions and theories, 3–5
democracy, demand must be domestic, 157–8
Dudaev, Dzhokhar, 57–8

Egypt, 26–7
Elabuga, 110, 162–3, 187
ELAZ, 163
evolution over revolution, 45

Fadeev, A., 88n6
Faezkhanov, H, 133
familial networks, 166
'far-abroad', 117, 118, 119, 146
Farukshin, Midhat, 101–102
federalism, 65–6
Financial Leasing Company, 123
Foreign Investment Law, 68
Fradkov, Mikhail, 160
Fuks, Karl, 103–104, 142
Fukuyama, Francis, 157–8, 189

Gaidar, Egor, 54, 55
Galeev, Rinat, 40
gasification, 115
Georgia, 45, 46, 47, 182, 183
Germogen, Metropolitan, 141, 143
globalization
  attainability, 152–3
  competition subsidized, 117
  conformity to Western vision, 155, 157
  culture of misinterpretation, 153

inner dangers, 154–5
International Monetary Fund, 155–6
pace of change, 156
World Bank, 155–6
Golden Horde, empire of the
  Black Death, 28
  influence on Russia, 25–8
  Kazan, 72
  religious tolerance, 28, 142
  Tatar language, 132
  'Tatar' name, 36–7
  trading tax, 27
'golden mean', 79
Gorbachev, Mikhail, 34, 40, 42, 47, 182–3
Great Patriotic War, 6–7, 114, 119, 150–1, 171
Great Volga Waterway conferences, 74
Great Wall Automobile Holdings Company, 187
Gubaidullina, Sofia, 189

'Hague Initiative', 138
Hairullin, Airat, 116
Hammarberg, Thomas, 148
harakatta barakat, 17
Hewlett-Packard, 188
historical myths, 18
Husainov, Shamsutdin, 134
hyperinflation, 38, 48–9, 54

Idel-Ural state, 32–3, 65
Imams, 148
International Centre for Studies of Islamic History, Art and Culture (ICSIHAC), 74
International Monetary Fund, 155–6
Investment Venture Fund, 110, 164
Iran, 187
Iraq, 11, 156–7, 183
Iskhakov, Kamil, 77, 79, 80, 83, 86, 142
Islam
  abyzes, 105–106
  'converts', 142–4
  education, 106
  effectively banned, 140

flexible religion, 149
forced baptism, 142–5
Imams, 148
Jadidism, 147
mosques demolished, 140–1, 145
Muslims as faceless entity, 155
radical cells, 147–8
religious fanaticism, 147–8
Sufism, 147
Volga Bulgaria state religion, 21, 22
Ittifak (Alliance) National Party, 49–50
Ivan the Terrible [Tsar Ivan IV], 29, 30, 35n10, 72, 102, 141

Jadidism, 147
Jalil, Musa, 135, 150

Kaban lake, 83
KamAZ heavy-truck plant, 33, 43, 118, 119, 124–6, 148, 163, 187
Karamzin, Nikolai, 22, 24, 26, 27
Kargala, 106
Karimullin, A, 133
Kazan
 Alexander Arcade, 82–3
 American Culture Centre, 185
 Baumana, 82
 Bulak channel, 90, 91
 cafés, 82
 CIS leaders meeting, 80
 conference on Kazan history, 21
 fire 1579, 141
 First Gymnasium, 133
 foundation, 21
 'Gateway to the Orient', 72
 Gentry Assembly building, 79–80
 'golden mean', 79
 hotels, 83
 House of Officers of the Kazan garrison, 79
 House of Tatar Cuisine, 82
 housing rebuilding, 76–8
 industry, 85
 inhabitants exiled, 102
 international awards and recognition, 74–5
 Kekin, House of, 94
 Maiden Monastery, 142
 Metro, 80–2, 169
 millennium celebrations, 9–10, 73–4, 90–1
 oriental capital of Russia, 71, 73
 peasant revolts, 145
 Pedagogical Institute, 136
 pedestrian shopping street, 82
 Poetry Days, 135
 Public Library, 134
 'Pyramid' centre, 94–5
 Rathaus, 79–80
 rebuilding, 73, 76–8
 religious organizations, 86
 Russian Islamic University, 148
 slums, 76, 93
 sports facilities, 83–4
 St Petersburg, 79–80
 statistics, 85

Tash Ayak, 91
Technical University, 172
University, 85, 133, 136, 172–3
University Press, 133–4
urban development, 92–4
urban metamorphosis, 73, 76–8
Kazan cap, 30
Kazan helicopter plant, 121, 123, 124
Kazan khanate
 archives, 102
 aristocratic rule, 31
 education, 103–104
 establishment, 29
 Kazan as capital, 72
 Moscow competitor, 29
 mosques demolished, 140–1, 145
Kazan Kremlin
 archaeological excavations, 20
 Cathedral of the Annunciation, 30, 90, 184–5
 heart of city, 71–2
 Kul Sharif mosque, 30, 90, 184–5
 National Picture Gallery, 79
 research and redevelopment, 184–5
 siege, 30
Kazan Mother of God icon, 141–2
Kazan [construction company], 97
Kazanka, River, 90, 169
Kazanorgsintez petrochemical plant, 95, 96, 128
Kendall, Bridget, 41
Khakimov, Raphael, 58, 59–60, 62, 63
Khazbulatov, Ruslan, 54, 55
Kierkegaard, Søren, 4, 5
Kievan Rus, 23
Kirienko, Sergei, 68
Kitezh, 19, 42
kolkhozes, 115
Kul Sharif mosque, 30, 90, 184–5
Kuly, Maula, 102, 104
Kyrgyzstan, 182

Land Code, 48, 68, 116
land reform, 48
languages
 Chuvash, 138, 139
 ethnic schools, 136–7
 Russian, 30
 Russian and Tatar co-equal, 46–7, 137
languages – Tatar
 book publishing, 133–4
 Day of the Mother Tongue, 135
 Golden Horde, empire of the, 132
 historical outline, 132
 international language of trade, 133
 Microsoft, 150
 modified Cyrillic script, 66, 150
 modified Latin script, 66, 150
 President to be fluent in Russian and Tatar languages, 69
 Putin, Vladimir, 138

removal as compulsory subject, 136
'Salyat' movement, 149
'Lashman' work, 114
Latvia, 46
Lenin, V I, 109, 113–14, 173
Leninogorsk, 174
'Liberman reform', 39
Lieven, Anatol, 183–4
Likhachev, Vasily, 59
Lobachevsky, Nikolai, 172

Machiavelli, Niccolo, 5
madrassas, 146
Maksudi, Sadri, 34
market economy, role of state, 87
Matsuura, Koitiro, 74
McCann, Leo, 165, 167–8, 181
medreses (Tatar sp.) 106
Metschera, 24
Milli Mejlis, 50
Minnikhanov, Rustam, 77, 84, 123, 164
MIPIM exhibitions, 169
Moldova, 45, 46, 47
Mongol invasion, 25, 72
Monomakh, cap of, 30
Morozov, Oleg, 179
Mukhametshin, Farit, 59, 68, 83
Muhammad, Mahathir, 171
Muhammadiya, 146–7
Muhammedyar, 102
Mukhametshin, Midhat, 181
mullahs, 106, 107
Murom, 24
Muroma, 24
Murtazin, Irek, 95
Muslim National Communism, 33
Muslim Spiritual Board, 106

Naberezhnye Chelny, 101, 147, 148
Nagorny Karabakh, 40, 45, 73
National Assembly, 50
National Communism, 33
New Tatar, 102
Nizhnekamskshina tyre plant, 95, 119, 163
Nizhnekamskneftekhim petrochemical plant, 95, 97, 119, 121, 128, 168
Nizhny Novgorod, 128
nostalgia, 78
Nottberg, Tyler, 184–5
Novo-Ogarevo process, 43–4
Nureyev, Rudolf, 189

oil
 industry, 126–8
 'life without oil', 187
 reserves of 30 years, 161
 saviour of Russian economy, 10
 synthetic, 163
 Tatneft (Tatar Oil Company), 40, 95, 121, 127, 160, 187
 taxation, 93–4
Old Ishtiryak, 102
Old Tatar, 102

INDEX

Onuchina, Matrena, 141–2
Orenburg, 106
Organization of the Cities of World Heritage, 74
Oshel, 24
Ovrutsky, Lev, 97–8, 181

Pakistan, 187
Palestine, 176
paramagnetic resonance, 172
'Party of Life', 101
Pavlov, Alexander, 123
Pavlov, Boris, 160
peasant revolts, 145
perestroika, 34, 40, 42, 54, 56, 99, 115
Perm, 50
Poetry Days, 135
post-modern approach to history, 3
Prevention of Deadly Conflicts: Strategy and Institutions, 42–3
Programme of Social Mortgage Lending, 87–8
public footpaths and pavements, 55
Putin, Vladimir
 address partly in Tatar, 138
 centralized state, 61–2, 64
 Commission for Kazan Millennium, 73–4
 conservation of the nation, 7
 democratic federalism, 167
 'if the Tatars want to achieve something ...', 64
 President Shaimiev re-appointed, 181
 pseudo-democracy, 183–4

Quran, 133

Red Orient [companies], 116–17
religious tolerance
 Golden Horde, empire of the, 28
 Tatarstan, 74, 142, 186–7
Romashkino, 127
Røysi, Linda, 99, 101, 181
Russia
 asymmetric federalism, 66
 Civil War 1918–24, 32
 Constitution 1993, 57
 corruption assumptions, 98
 credit lack, 110
 de-nationalization of economy, 92–3
 education, 175
 'evil empire', 42
 Federal Treaty, 52
 Golden Horde, empire of the, 25–6, 28
 'internal' treaties all abolished, 61
 languages, 30
 local self-government, 179
 market economy model, 159–60
 multinational state, 30
 national strategic projects, 86–7
 Parliament vs President, 54–5

possible treaty 2006, 62, 68–9
power-sharing treaty, 52–3, 58–9
privatization auctions, 111–12, 154
pseudo-democracy, 183–4
'shock therapy' economy, 6–8, 76
'shock therapy' methods, 76
social justice, 92–3
social trust, 112
transition to market capitalism, 8–9, 13
Treaty of the Mutual Delegation of State Powers, 60–1, 62, 69
voucher scheme, 112, 120
World Trade Organization (WTO), 161
Rutskoi, Aleksandr, 51

Sabantui (plough festival), 188
Safin, Marat, 189
St Petersburg, 71, 79–80
Sarai-Batu, 27
Sarai-Berke, 27, 35n8
Sayid the Elder, 106
Shagimuhammad [Mintimer Shaimiev's grandfather], 114
Shaimiev, Airat [Mintimer Shaimiev's son], 96
'Shaimiev époque', 64, 70
Shaimiev, Mintimer
 asymmetric federalism, 66
 awards for inter-religious understanding, 185
 biography, 39
 'can do' culture, 189
 credo, 151, 153
 criticism, 51
 development over confrontation, 60
 economic philosophy, 129–30
 economic reform gradually, 113
 extent of achievements, 18
 first 100 days as President, 48
 globalization from the grass roots, 167
 historical stature, 189
 National Assembly recognition, 50
 nostalgia, 78
 political credo, 34
 power, 182
 pragmatism, 9, 60, 120
 Russia resembles no other country, 63–4
 succession, 178–9
 team-work approach, 59
 transition philosophy, 76
 transition vision, 166–7
 understanding and vision, 100–1
 vision, 188
 youth, 39
Shaimiev, Mintimer – posts
 Chairman of the Supreme Soviet of Tatarstan, 44
 Chairman of the Supreme Soviet of the TASSR, 38
 Chairman of the TASSR parliament, 34

Director of rural technical assistance faculty, 115
First Secretary of the Tatar Republican Committee of the Communist Party, 40, 44
Minister for Melioration and Water Resources of the TASSR, 38–9
President of the Republic of Tatarstan, 38, 181
Prime Minister of the Republic of Tatarstan, 39–40
Vice-Premier of the Republic of Tatarstan, 39
Shaimiev, Mintimer – sayings
 'civic accord in the name of development', 47
 'reforms are worth nothing if they make the people suffer', 38, 113
 'Social Accord in the name of creation of good', 151, 153
 'soft entrance to the market', 10, 113
 'we can', 15
 'why do we look for enemies', 139
Shaimiev, Radik [Mintimer Shaimiev's son], 95, 96–7
Shaimieva, Sakina [Mintimer Shaimiev's wife], 179
Shaimiev, Sharifulla [Mintimer Shaimiev's father], 114, 115
Shakhrai, Sergei, 51–2
Shakulova, S., 147
Shigabutdinov, Albert K., 94, 95, 97
Shishkin, I., 162
Smolensk archive, 19
social justice, 92–3
Solzhenitsyn, A., 7
sovereignty shared, 62–3
sovnarkhozes, 39
statehood, 18, 30–1, 34, 42, 48
Sufism, 147
Suleimanov, D., 149
Sultan-Galeev, Mirsayid, 33, 34

Tabeev, Fikret, 33
TAIF (Tatar-American Investment and Finance Company), 94–5, 97, 128
Tamerlane (Timur), 27
Tatar Academic Drama Theatre, 146–7
Tatar Autonomous Soviet Socialist Republic, 32–4, 37–8, 72
Tatar national opposition, 61
Tatar popular movement, 49
Tatar Public Cenrte, 65
Tatar radical opposition, 49
Tatar wrestling, 188
'Tatar' name, 36–7, 72
Tatar-Bashkir Republic, 32–3
Tatarstan
 'addressed' support, 119
 agriculture 114, 115–17, 188
 aircraft industry, 187–8

attention to detail, 21
'can-do' culture, 15, 189
car industry, 126, 162–4
car ownership, 91
civil aircraft industry, 122–4
Concept of State Regulation of Economy, 160
Constitution, 53, 56–7, 62
Constitution amended 2002, 67–8
Day of the Republic, 188
Declaration of State Sovereignty 1990, 37–8, 43, 46, 56
democracy as the saviour, 47
democracy seen as people's own, 176–7
economic basis of state, 56–7
economic priorities, 118
economic weight within USSR, 43–4
education priority, 170, 171–2, 186–7
'elite theory', 98–100, 118
entrepreneurs, 109–10
farming, risky zone, 117
Federal Treaty, 52
Financial Leasing Company, 123
food self-sufficiency, 38, 115–16, 167
foreign investment, 161–2, 168–9
gasification, 115
health service, 173–4
historical democracy, 105
housing rebuilding beyond Kazan, 77
impaired children, 175
income statistics, 91
inter-ethnic accord and harmony, 138–40
inter-ethnic marriages, 140, 143
Investment Venture Fund, 110, 164
investors self-interest, 12, 92
IT development, 164
law-making analogy, 55–6
Leasing Company for Small Businesses, 110
local self-government, 179–80
most dangerous time, 52
multiculturalism, viii, 177
national survival, 31–2
negotiating strategy, 58–60
oil industry, 126–8
parliamentary democracy, 176
petrochemical industry, 127–8, 130
possible treaty 2006, 62, 68–9
power-sharing treaty, 52–3, 58–9
pragmatism, 9
President to be fluent in Russian and Tatar languages, 69
press, 104, 180–1, 181–2
private enterprises, 121
privatization, 119–20, 122
rationing, 118–19
referendum 1992, 51–2

regional elite, 99–100
religious coexistence, 186–7
religious tolerance, 74, 142
responsible ownership, 113–14
Russian banks excluded, 111
schools, 135
self-reliance policy, 167–8
service industries, 110
social justice, 93
sovereign in issues of its own responsibility, 62–3
sovereignty not ethnic in nature, 137–8
sports, 83–4, 88n6, 110
'state within a state', 122
statehood, 18, 30–1, 34, 42, 48
technical education, 123
Treaty of the Mutual Delegation of Powers 1994, 53, 60–1, 62
unity of purpose, 48
'village culture', 101–107
voucher auctions, 120–1, 129
Western writers' views, 96
'Tatarstan for the Tatars', 50
Tatarstan history
7th century, 21–2
10th century, 20, 22–4, 72
11th century, 20, 22–4, 72
12th century, 24–5, 72
13th century, 24–7, 72
14th century, 25–7, 72
15th century, 27–9, 72, 102
16th century, 29–31, 72, 102, 104
17th century, 102, 104, 145
18th century, 72, 106, 144–5, 145
19th century, 32, 72, 106
early 20th century, 32, 72, 114
background, 15–16
educational tradition, 103–104
Tatarstan model, vii–viii, 9, 17, 31, 42, 48, 75, 86, 98–100, 107, 130, 140, 161, 180, 188
Tatarstan New Century party, 180
Tatneft (Tatar Oil Company), 40, 95, 121, 127, 160, 187
Tatneftekhiminvest, 128
Tatnefteproduct trading company, 128
Third World concept, 33
TNK-BP, 96
Tolstoi, Leo, 173
TOTS (Tatar Public Centre), 49–50
trading tax, 27
Trans-Dniestr region, 73
Treaty of Mutual Delegation of State Powers 1994, 53, 60–1
truths, apparent and objective, 6
Tsvetaeva, Marina, 162
Tukai, Gabdulla, 134–5

Udmurtia, 139
Ukraine, 33–4, 47, 119, 128, 182, 183, 187
Ul'ianovsk, 50

UNESCO, 74
Union of Soviet Socialist Republics (USSR)
agriculture, 114
collectivization, 114
referendum 1991, 47
unuttered word [independence], 45–6
Ukrtatnafta, 128
Usmanov, Gumer, 40, 43
Usmanova, Larisa, 178
Uzbek-khan, 27

Vaclav (Winceslas), King, 20
Venice, 27
'village culture', 105–7
Vladimir-Suzdal Russia, 24, 35n7
Volga Bulgaria
good neighbour policy, 24–5
Islam as state religion, 21, 22
Islamic influence, 23
Kazan, 72
national survival, 31–2
open society, 23
practical knowledge, 23–4
religious coexistence, 24
resettlement, 102
Volga, River
bridges, 169
Bulak channel, 90, 91
trade, 22–3
'Volga-Urals Constitution', 50
voucher auctions, 120–1, 129
voucher privatization, 54–5
voucher scheme, 112, 120

Walker, Edward W., 51–2, 58–9
Western writers' views, 41, 49, 96, 182–4
White Army, 32
Wolf, Humbert, 98
World Bank, 155–6
World Congress of Tatars, 66, 86, 145–6
World Trade Organization (WTO), 117, 161
World War II, 6–7, 114, 119, 150–1, 171

yams, 27
yarlyks, 28
Yavlinsky, G., 159
Yeltsin, Boris
Kazan visit, 44
President of Russia, 47
pseudo-democracy, 183–4
'Tatar Republic is free to take as much sovereignty...', 44
Treaty of the Mutual Delegation of Powers 1994, 60–1

Zabirova, F., 94
Zavoysky, E. A., 172